INTERNET RESEARCH METHODS

<HTML>
<BODY>

<H1> INTERNET RESEARCH METHODS </H1>

<P> SECOND EDITION </P>

CLAIRE HEWSON, CARL VOGEL AND DIANNA LAURENT

Los Angeles | London | New Delhi
Singapore | Washington DC

KH

Los Angeles | London | New Delhi
Singapore | Washington DC

SAGE Publications Ltd
1 Oliver's Yard
55 City Road
London EC1Y 1SP

SAGE Publications Inc.
2455 Teller Road
Thousand Oaks, California 91320

SAGE Publications India Pvt Ltd
B 1/I 1 Mohan Cooperative Industrial Area
Mathura Road
New Delhi 110 044

SAGE Publications Asia-Pacific Pte Ltd
3 Church Street
#10-04 Samsung Hub
Singapore 049483

Editor: Mila Steele
Assistant editor: James Piper
Production editor: Ian Antcliff
Copyeditor: Neville Hankins
Proofreader: Christine Bitten
Indexer: Martin Hargreaves
Marketing manager: Sally Ransom
Cover design: Lisa Harper-Wells
Typeset by: C&M Digitals (P) Ltd, Chennai, India
Printed and bound by CPI Group (UK) Ltd,
Croydon, CR0 4YY

Library of Congress Control Number: 2015943076

British Library Cataloguing in Publication data

A catalogue record for this book is available from
the British Library

ISBN 978-1-4462-0855-7
ISBN 978-1-4462-0856-4 (pbk)

MIX
Paper from
responsible sources
FSC® C013604

At SAGE we take sustainability seriously. Most of our products are printed in the UK using FSC papers and boards.
When we print overseas we ensure sustainable papers are used as measured by the PREPS grading system.
We undertake an annual audit to monitor our sustainability.

9/23/16

<> CONTENTS </>

<> ABOUT THE AUTHORS </>

Claire Hewson is Lecturer in Psychology at The Open University. She has a long-standing interest in using the Internet to carry out primary research, and has collected data using a range of IMR methods including surveys, psychometrics and experiments, to investigate issues in common-sense understanding, particularly folk psychology; online assessment methods in an educational context; and the validity of IMR methods. She was commissioned to lead a working party to produce the recent British Psychological Society (BPS) guidelines on ethics in Internet-Mediated Research (2013), has delivered a number of talks and training sessions on this and related topics, and has published more broadly in the area of IMR.

Carl Vogel, a Fellow of Trinity College Dublin, is Senior Lecturer in Computational Linguistics and Director of the Centre for Computing and Language Studies at Trinity College Dublin, the University of Dublin. His work in computational linguistics, from the perspective of cognitive science, frequently draws upon evidence abstracted from Internet accessed data, and accordingly he dwells on the accompanying research methodology issues. Vogel was on the Management Committee of the successful European COST Action IS1004: Web-based data-collection – methodological challenges, solutions and implementations (WEBDATANET).

Dianna Laurent teaches a variety of classes for both the English and the Languages and Communication departments at Southeastern Louisiana University and at St. Joseph's Seminary College. She publishes on a variety of subjects involving the Internet. Dr Laurent is the associate editor of the yearly ATTW bibliography and the business manager of *19th Century Studies* for the Nineteenth Century Studies Association.

<> ONE </>
<> INTRODUCTION </>

INTERNET RESEARCH METHODS: THE SECOND EDITION

It is now just over a decade since the publication of the first edition of *Internet Research Methods* (IRM). There we reflected and speculated on the actual and imagined scope of the Internet for supporting and enhancing social and behavioural research. At that time, several early pioneers had been making headway in devising and testing out what we dubbed *Internet-Mediated Research* (IMR) methods; that is, procedures for collecting primary research data which made use of the Internet. We distinguished between *primary* and *secondary* research online. The former involves the acquisition and analysis of data to produce novel evidence and research findings;[1] the latter involves research which utilises secondary information sources (such as books and journal articles) to summarise existing findings and conclusions. We presented some early examples of IMR, as well as selected case studies from our own research, to illustrate some of the techniques, procedures and opportunities available. We outlined some of the caveats that can emerge, drawing upon our own experiences as researchers, and highlighted and offered our own perspective on issues and debates that were prevalent at the time (such as the biased nature of Internet-accessed samples).

Over the last 10 years IMR has expanded massively, increasing in both reach, across disciplinary boundaries, methodological orientations and research domains,

---

[1]Our definition at the time was rather narrow in focus, referring to primary research as that which gathers data from participants. The vast array of existing traces of activity online which may now form data for primary research, and the emergence of methods which make use of these traces, require us to revise this emphasis. Unobtrusive approaches which do not directly recruit participants, but gather non-reactive data, form a key strategy in present-day IMR.

and volume. There now exists a large, diverse body of evidence from IMR studies upon which to draw in assessing its impact to date, and its scope and future potential. New methods, data sources and strategies have emerged. A major and significant revision to the present volume is a consideration of this new evidence, which has now informed many of the issues and debates we outlined in the first edition. We now find it necessary to expand the methodological scope of our discussion in order to reflect properly the present-day nature of IMR. Thus in this second edition we include a more extensive discussion of unobtrusive approaches in IMR; for example, those which take advantage of the wealth of potential data sources created by the emergence of social networking sites (SNSs). We also consider unobtrusive approaches which use advanced 'data mining' techniques to obtain and process very large volumes of information about the structures and processes of people's online activities and interactions ('big data').

Ethical issues in IMR are also given more attention in this second edition. Given the extensive discussions on a range of ethical issues that have occurred over the last decade, it now seems fitting to devote an entire chapter to this topic. Rapid technological developments have also occurred, some of which have confirmed the predictions we made previously. We highlight these developments. A major development has been the emergence of dedicated software tools for implementing IMR study designs. These tools have made the need for presentation of detailed programming techniques, such as those we offered in the first edition, no longer necessary, although we mention some of the main current technologies available for implementing more complex, bespoke designs. Another important development involves the shifting patterns of access to and usage of the Internet, creating changes in the way Internet users can be recruited to participate in IMR studies, as well as who is available. The range of recruitment procedures possible, and the research on the effectiveness of these, are now considered in a dedicated chapter on sampling in IMR. All the above developments, as well as the emergence of Web 2.0 (see below) which has arguably created a qualitative shift in the nature and societal impact of the Internet, have led to what may be called a 'new era' of IMR. It is the purpose of this second edition to provide an updated review and evaluation of IMR methods in this new era. As before, the text is a handbook which outlines and discusses key theoretical issues and debates, methodological principles, and detailed implementation procedures which will assist the readers in creating and launching their own IMR study.

As in the first edition, we draw extensively on our own experience in using the Internet as a research tool. We have gathered primary data to address questions on human reasoning (e.g. Hewson & Vogel, 1994), common-sense beliefs and understandings (e.g. Hewson, 1994), use of social signals, such as emoticons, in online communication (e.g. Janssen & Vogel, 2008; Vogel & Janssen, 2009; Vogel & Mamani Sanchez, 2012) and online assessment methods in an educational context (e.g. Hewson, 2012a; Hewson, Charlton, & Brosnan, 2007). We have also implemented studies to validate IMR instruments and procedures (e.g. Hewson & Charlton, 2005), and been engaged in the development of software procedures and implementation of IMR systems (Buckley, 2004; Buckley & Vogel, 2003; Graham, 2006), and ethics guidelines (BPS, 2013). We offer showcase examples from research studies, including our own, throughout the book (replacing the previous edition's 'case studies' chapter).

Who the Book is Aimed at

Active researchers and students alike may find the Internet useful for both primary and secondary research. Thus we have aimed to make the book accessible and of interest to both. Using the Internet to locate secondary resources can have great pedagogical value and, we argue, enhance (but not necessarily replace) more traditional library-based methods. For those involved in research and teaching, the wealth of information available online – from databases of journal articles to copies of lecture notes – is invaluable. These resources can help locate information quickly and cost-effectively. The important issue to bear in mind is establishing the quality and accuracy of the resources found, and in Chapter 2 the book provides guidelines for ensuring this. Primary research using the Internet may benefit students who are undertaking an undergraduate project, or conducting postgraduate research, due to the scope for obtaining large volumes of data in a short time and with minimal costs. Researchers at smaller institutions, where the resources available (time and funding) for supporting research may be more limited, may similarly benefit. However, the value of IMR is not limited to these contexts, and as we shall see the last decade has seen a dramatic increase in the volume and range of IMR methods being implemented.

While our own disciplinary commitments will inevitably lead to some degree of bias towards examples of IMR from psychology and cognitive science, we have taken care in this second edition to include a broad range of illustrations from other disciplines and areas which fall within the general category of the social and behavioural sciences.[2] The methodologies we discuss (which include surveys and questionnaires, interviews and focus groups, observational studies, document analysis and experiments) are certainly widely used across disciplines. Certain disciplines, or sub-areas within those disciplines, may of course be associated with particular methods (e.g. cognitive psychology draws heavily on experiments), but the information presented here should be broad enough in scope for researchers from different disciplines to pick out what is relevant to their own particular research domain. Our aim has been to select a good range of illustrations to demonstrate the diversity and scope of IMR methods. Earlier chapters explore the theoretical, methodological and ethical issues which IMR raises, and these are then taken up

---

[2]Which we consider to include (among others) psychology, linguistics, sociology, economics, political science, cognitive science, anthropology.

in more detail in later chapters, which outline how the issues interact with specific procedures and implementations. The scope of IMR is discussed early on, through consideration of the range of methodologies that can be and have been adapted, looking at the successes to date, and considering the advantages and disadvantages of using IMR as opposed to more traditional approaches. Thus the readers can get an impression at this point of the extent to which their own research might be supported by IMR methods, before reading more about implementation details and resources in later chapters. Potential problems are also highlighted so that the researcher may be forewarned of these, and take steps to avoid them. In the unfortunate event that problems do occur (even in a carefully designed study unforeseen problems can nevertheless arise), recovery strategies are suggested.

A further important aspect of the book is that it does not assume the reader has any prior computing expertise, at least not beyond some basic skills such as sending and receiving emails, reading and posting to discussion boards, and searching the World Wide Web.[3] Thus the book is aimed at providing the practising researcher, or student, who has some minimal level of computer literacy, with the necessary information, tools and insights to be able to assess the extent to which the Internet can help support their research needs, and to be able to carry out Internet-based research.

We now conclude this introduction by giving a brief outline of the history of the Internet, followed by a description of the content of each chapter.

HISTORY OF THE INTERNET

The Internet grew out of the ARPANET, commissioned in 1969 by the US Department of Defense for research into computer networking (for a more detailed history of the Internet see Zakon, 2015). In 1971 there were 15 nodes on ARPANET connecting 23 host computers. Email was invented in 1972 by Ray Tomlinson of Bolt, Beranek and Newman (BBN). The first international connections did not come until 1973 when England and Norway each added nodes. BBN introduced the first commercial version of ARPANET in 1974. From then on a number of network systems emerged, including Usenet in 1979 and BITNET in 1981. The latter started as a cooperative email-based system between CUNY[4] and Yale. The first MUD[5] was produced in 1979 by Richard Bartle and Rob Trubshaw of the University of Essex.

---

[3]These procedures are very easy to get to grips with, for readers who are not already familiar with them. Any introductory guide to the Internet should provide instructions (e.g. Buckley & Clark, 2009; Kennedy, 2001). See also http://www.archives.gov/research/alic/reference/internet-users-guide.html (accessed April 2015).

[4]The City University of New York.

[5]Multi-User Dungeon (cf. 'MUD, object oriented' or MOO).

Protocols, namely the Transmission Control Protocol (TCP) and Internet Protocol (IP), were introduced in 1982. Effectively, the 'Internet' began with that standardisation and denotes networked TCP/IP systems.

It was not until 1984 that the number of networked host computers exceeded 1,000, and in that same year the Japan Unix Network was put into place, as was the Joint Academic Network (JANET) in the United Kingdom. In 1986 the NSFNET was established by NASA and the US Department of Energy as a way to facilitate connections outside the ARPANET security and bureaucracy. By 1987 the number of Internet hosts exceeded 10,000, and BITNET hit the 1,000 point. Just a year later there were 60,000 Internet hosts, this number increasing to over 100,000 within the next year. By 1992 the number of Internet hosts stood at over 1 million, increasing to 3.2 million by July 1994 and reaching a figure of 56,218 million networked hosts by July 1999, five years later. In July 2014, the Internet Systems Consortium (ISC) counted over 1 billion IP addresses that have been claimed with domain names, which can be taken as a reasonable estimate of the number of Internet hosts (http://ftp.isc.org/www/survey/reports/current/ [accessed October 2014]). A plot of the expansion in use of available domain names (roughly corresponding to the number of Internet hosts) is given in Figure 1.1; measurements were made in January and July in each year except 2003. Growth between the January and July measurements appears to have slowed. The Oxford Internet Survey report (Dutton, Blank, & Groselj, 2013), published every two years since 2003, indicates that 78% of the UK population over the age of 14 has Internet access. This growth in number of hosts is mindboggling, particularly when considering that the individual hosts can serve many more individual users. While writing the first edition of *IRM*, we noted that the terms 'World Wide Web (WWW)' and 'Internet' had become household words, and that every day more and more people were accessing the Internet through academic, private, military, government and commercial interests, primarily through networked computer systems. Now, a decade on, some significant developments in Internet technologies and patterns of usage have taken place.

At a most basic level, the sheer estimated size of the Internet-user population (IUP) has grown from around several hundred million in 2003 (Hewson, Yule, Laurent, & Vogel, 2003) to over 2 billion in 2013 (see Chapter 4 for further details and sources), dramatically expanding IMR sampling possibilities. A particularly noteworthy development has been the emergence of social networking technologies and services (e.g. Facebook[6] and Twitter[7]). Another has been the

---

[6]Facebook (2011) reports more than 800 million active users, 50% of whom log on to Facebook in any given day (http://www.facebook.com/press/info.php?statistic; accessed November 2015). Recent estimates put the number of active users at close to 1.5 billion (see Chapter 4). However, this figure can only be an upper bound, since it is not difficult to find people who profess to have more than one Facebook account and access the system from more than one IP address.

[7]For a (journalistic) comparison of Facebook and Twitter usage, see http://www.guardian.co.uk/media/2011/nov/07/twitter-facebook (accessed April 2015).

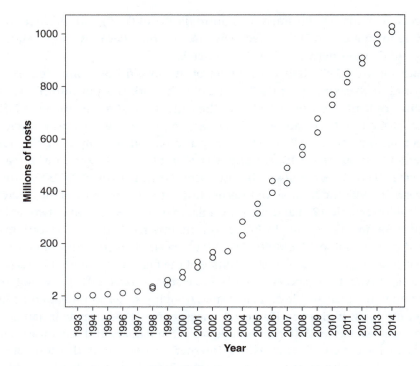

Figure 1.1   Yearly growth in Internet domain name use

Note: Measurements taken in January and July of each year surveyed.

Data Source: Internet Domain Survey of the Internet Systems Consortium.

emergence and proliferation of mobile technologies (e.g. smart phones, tablets) and 'apps' (short for 'applications') that reside on them. These technologies and services are described and discussed in more detail in later chapters, where their relevance to particular IMR methods is considered. Hand in hand with these developments, the penetration of the Internet and its services into daily lives has expanded on a vast scale; we discuss these developments and their impact upon IMR methods in later chapters (particularly Chapters 3 and 4). *Web 2.0* is a term (O'Reilly, 2005)[8] which has emerged to describe some of these developments, particularly the shift from the Internet as a relatively static space for the dissemination of published final documents to a massively connected, fluid, interactive, participatory, collaborative space where content is constantly

---

[8]Though the term was first coined by Darcy DiNucci back in January 1999 (DiNucci, 1999). She describes the notion as follows: 'The Web we know now, which loads into a browser window in essentially static screenfuls, is only an embryo of the Web to come. The first glimmerings of Web 2.0 are beginning to appear, and we are just starting to see how that embryo might develop. The Web will be understood not as screenfuls of text and graphics but as a transport mechanism, the ether through which interactivity happens.'

in flux and under revision. Wikipedia – itself an example of a Web 2.0 service[9] – offered the following description in December 2011:

> The term Web 2.0 is associated with web applications that facilitate participatory information sharing, interoperability, user-centred design, and collaboration on the World Wide Web. A Web 2.0 site allows users to interact and collaborate with each other in a social media dialogue as creators (prosumers) of user-generated content in a virtual community, in contrast to websites where users (consumers) are limited to the passive viewing of content that was created for them. Examples of Web 2.0 include social networking sites, blogs, wikis, video sharing sites, hosted services, web applications, mashups and folksonomies. (http://en.wikipedia.org/wiki/Web_2.0 [accessed December 2011])

In March 2015, this Wikipedia entry started as follows:

> Web 2.0 describes World Wide Web sites that emphasize user-generated content, usability, and interoperability. The term was popularized by Tim O'Reilly and Dale Dougherty at the O'Reilly Media Web 2.0 Conference in late 2004, though it was first coined by Darcy DiNucci in 1999. Although Web 2.0 suggests a new version of the World Wide Web, it does not refer to an update to any technical specification, but rather to cumulative changes in the way Web pages are made and used. (http://en.wikipedia.org/wiki/Web_2.0 [accessed March 2015])

These two descriptions demonstrate the way Wikipedia entries evolve and change as various users edit, update and add to them (which anyone can do, having first created an account; clicking on the 'View history' tab offers a detailed record of the edits that have been made to an entry, searchable by year and month). There has been some debate about whether the emergence of 'Web 2.0' represents a *qualitative* shift in the nature, form and use of the Internet, as opposed to merely an expansion in size and diversity.[10] Either way, the technological developments we have seen in more recent years, as embodied in concepts such as Web 2.0, have no doubt been a significant instrumental factor in the expansion and increasingly widespread use of the Internet for conducting primary research across a very large number of disciplines and research perspectives. As noted by Lee, Fielding, and Blank (2008, p. 4) the terrain occupied by IMR methods is by now large and variegated, as well as complex and rapidly changing, with arguably particular importance to the social sciences. Coverage of some of these newly emerging approaches and

---

[9]As opposed to, for example, 'Encyclopaedia Britannica Online' which is a Web 1.0 model of knowledge management (Wakeford & Cohen, 2008).

[10]For a challenge to the idea that Web 2.0 is something fundamentally distinct from earlier notions and structures of the WWW, see the developerWorks interview with Tim Berners-Lee, on 22 August 2006, available from http://www.ibm.com/developerworks/podcast/dwi/cm-int082206txt.html (accessed April 2015).

methods since we wrote the first edition of *IRM* (and particularly in unobtrusive observational research) is a major addition to this second edition.

The aforementioned historical developments have cultivated new attitudes to the Internet, including conflicting attitudes towards privacy (see also the further discussion in Chapter 5). Jenson, Potts and Jensen (2005) report that despite increased self reporting of privacy concerns, users tend not to examine published privacy and data protection statements on e-commerce websites, and Acquisti and Gross (2006) report that privacy-concerned individuals nonetheless voluntarily expose a great deal of personal information about themselves and friends in social networking facilities. National governments have undertaken to investigate and potentially regulate privacy provisions in social networking sites (Cullen, 2011), balanced by increased use of social networking data in even criminal cases (O'Floinn & Ormerod, 2011). While in 1996 we referred to exponential growth in Internet use, and this appears to persist (see Figure 1.1), recent news articles have indicated, for example, that growth in UK Facebook usage has ceased (Rushton, 2012). More anecdotally, we note among our colleagues and among members of the general public a different understanding of the Internet: it is no longer a novelty, but an assumption. People do not approach the Internet in the same way when it is a novelty as when it is the only mode of access afforded to community or commercial services. Such changing understandings of, and ways of engaging with, the Internet have implications for its use as a tool for gathering primary research data, as discussed in later chapters.

Figure 1.2   A word cloud of the complete text of *IRM*, first edition

One interesting way of representing in graphical form the key topics, themes and concepts in any chunk of text is to produce a 'word cloud'. Word clouds have become very popular and now appear all over the place. Word cloud generators are freely available (e.g. www.wordle.net) and use algorithms to display words from a specified piece of text in different sizes, positions and colours, depending on their frequency of occurrence. In Figure 1.2 we have created a word cloud of the full final manuscript for the first edition of *IRM*, and in Figure 1.3 we show a word cloud generated by the same algorithm using the full final manuscript of this second edition as input. These graphics are fun and pretty, but also do give some indication of the way in which the landscape of IMR has changed over the last 10 years, at least in terms of the terminology and concepts that emerge and re-emerge when providing a discussion of the area. In fact, these word clouds are very similar. But note, for example, how the term 'HTML' in the first edition appears more prominently, while 'software' appears as more prominent in the second edition.

A further indication of changes since we were writing the first edition of *IRM* can be found in Figures 1.4 and 1.5, which highlight the differences between the first and second editions. In Figure 1.4, the larger the word is, the more it is used in the second than the first edition; for example, 'google' (mid-right in the plot) appears 57 more times in the new volume than in the first edition. Figure 1.5 shows as larger the words which are used more in the first edition; for example, 'mail' appears 115 times more in the first edition, and 'Internet-based' is used 36 times more in the first edition than in the second.

Figure 1.3 A word cloud of the complete text of this second edition

Figure 1.4 A word cloud emphasizing the greater frequency of words and phrases in this second edition than in the first edition

Figure 1.5 A word cloud emphasizing the greater frequency of words and phrases in the first edition than in this second edition

Figures 1.2, 1.3, 1.4 and 1.5 were produced using the following wordcloud package: Fellows, I. (2014) Wordcloud (2.5). https://cran.r-project.org/web/packages/wordcloud/index.html

OVERVIEW OF CHAPTERS

Chapter 2: The Internet

The focus of this chapter is firmly on secondary research, that is the gathering of information that is already constructed, though some of the Internet resources mentioned may also be useful in primary research. This chapter outlines how secondary research can be carried out using the Internet.[11] We present an updated description of the resources available to conduct a literature search of secondary resources for research purposes (e.g. discussion groups, library catalogues, newspapers, indices to periodical literature, art archives, government official databases, electronic texts, online newspapers, Google Scholar, social media and networking sites) and explain how best to locate and use these resources. We emphasise both the time that can be saved, as compared with traditional (library-based) methods, and the additional information that can be accessed. However, the chapter also stresses the importance of assessing the relevance, quality and reliability of these resources. The amount of information available is limitless, and the researcher (and student) should be especially careful in ensuring that sources drawn upon are of high quality. Thus emphasis in this chapter is on providing guidelines for how to use the Internet effectively, and how to recognise bogus or limited sites.

The secondary information sources described provide a wealth of information relevant to many disciplines within the human sciences. The chapter explains how to use these resources, without assuming any prior familiarity. Yet the chapter also provides valuable information for the user who may already have a basic familiarity with these resources, by providing recommendations for good practice, which can enhance efficiency and quality of materials gathered. Many readers will be familiar with using search engines to seek specific information, but will also be aware of the frustrations involved in having to trawl through volumes of useless information to find what is required. There are a number of alternative and extremely useful access points to information available, with which many researchers may be unfamiliar. These are described, with an emphasis on selecting those sites which are unlikely to go out of date soon. In summary, Chapter 2 gives a comprehensive introduction to the range and depth of information available on the Internet (with a focus on that relevant to social and behavioural research), and how to access and test the quality of this information.

Chapter 3: Internet-Mediated Research: State of the Art

This chapter presents a review and evaluation of the range and scope of IMR methods, considering what has been tried and tested, and outlining and assessing the successes as well as less successful applications and techniques to date. From early

---

[11]The reader is referred also to Ó Dochartaigh (2012) which is complementary to the current book, though at a more introductory (undergraduate) level.

pioneering examples, through to recent emerging methods and techniques, illustrations selected to demonstrate the range and penetration of IMR methods are
presented and discussed. Thus the chapter aims to provide an up-to-date account
of the state of the art in IMR, highlighting key issues, debates and theoretical
underpinnings of the various methods and strategies which have emerged. Both
obtrusive and unobtrusive approaches are considered, and a framework for classifying different IMR methods along the *obtrusive–unobtrusive* dimension is offered. The
blurred boundaries which can sometimes emerge between different methodological approaches in IMR, due to the idiosyncratic nature of some of the supporting
technologies and Internet structures, are explained and illustrated. The scope for
adapting traditional offline methods to an IMR medium, as well as the potential
for facilitating new, creative approaches and techniques, are considered.

Throughout Chapter 3, a focus on the extent to which Internet methodologies are
able to produce valid and reliable data is maintained. Advantages and disadvantages
of Internet-based implementations are considered, compared with traditional
methods, as well as with each other. Some of the features of Internet-based primary
research are access to larger and more diverse samples, reduced costs and reduced
timescale. In addition, the Internet allows entirely anonymous communication,
but with higher levels of interactivity than has previously been possible. Further,
IMR opens up new possibilities for unobtrusive observational research. These and
other features of IMR are discussed. Caveats are also addressed. A major concern is
the reduced level of researcher control (over participants, materials and procedures)
which IMR procedures often entail. Issues relating to current technological
limitations, as well as demands for technological expertise of both researcher
and participant, are also discussed. The ways in which all these issues can impact
upon IMR are considered. Solutions are offered, though these await more detailed
elaboration (in terms of the tools and procedures available) in subsequent chapters.
Overall, the chapter provides a basic introduction to Internet-mediated primary
research, outlining the scope, possibilities and issues which arise.

Chapter 4: Sampling in Internet-Mediated Research

In this chapter we consider the range of sampling possibilities in IMR. Sampling
bias is an issue given some consideration in this chapter, though this is less of a
concern than in the early days of IMR, for reasons outlined there. The chapter
spends some time exploring the types of sampling strategies which are available
in IMR, and highlights how these interact with the types of samples which can
be obtained. Research is reviewed which compares Internet-accessed and traditional samples in terms of sample characteristics (e.g. representativeness of a
broader population) and the quality of the data they produce. Recommendations
for procedures which maximise data quality are given. Advice is offered on some
of the tools and resources available, which can help to assist the researcher in
accessing Internet samples. Overall, the chapter concludes that there is scope for
obtaining high-quality data from Internet-accessed samples, including emerging

possibilities for obtaining data which are more broadly generalisable than has pre-viously been considered possible (e.g. using large-scale online probability panels).

Chapter 5: Ethics in Internet-Mediated Research

This chapter considers the key ethical issues and dilemmas which emerge when port-ing research methodologies to an IMR context. The chapter covers guidelines for eth-ical behaviour by researchers from a wide range of disciplines. We draw upon a range of examples to highlight and demonstrate the nature of the ethical dilemmas that the Internet introduces as compared with traditional methods of data gathering. Key issues discussed are: informed consent, withdrawal and debrief; participant confi-dentiality; data anonymity; data security; the distinction between public and private spaces online. A number of caveats are outlined, and solutions offered, in adhering to key ethics principles in IMR. The chapter emphasises that ethics guidelines for IMR need to be flexible, and adaptable, as new technologies and research findings emerge. Ultimately, a researcher will need to make context-specific decisions and choices, taking into account a range of relevant factors in any particular research setting.

Chapter 6: Tools and Design Strategies for Internet-Mediated Research

This chapter outlines some of the key Internet technologies and tools which are avail-able to support implementing IMR studies (some of which have been mentioned in Chapters 2 and 3). The key methodological categories outlined in Chapter 3 are revisited in order to offer a more detailed consideration of implementation details. Discussion of design issues, choices and good-practice principles is incorporated. The aim is to provide the moderately computer-literate researcher with knowledge of the resources and tools available to enable IMR study design and implementation without detailed programming knowledge or expertise; thus emphasis is on review-ing some of the software tools available to assist in this process.

Web-based approaches are particularly important for many IMR methods, and we consider some of the available software packages which can help construct and disseminate web-based experiments and surveys. Web-based surveys in particular are given a more detailed consideration, in the final section, since they are in particular a widely used, attractive option, relevant to many research domains and disciplines. That section outlines software tools and design principles for web-based surveys, with illustrated implementation examples. This shows the reader how to get a web-based survey up and running. Other tools and resources considered include: email and mailing lists; discussion groups; online chat; social networking sites; multimedia sharing sites; online documents. Despite the more recently emerging large range of off-the-shelf software packages to support web-based surveys (and some to support experiments), more complex and bespoke implementations will sometimes be necessary and in this chapter we highlight some of the main current technologies available for implementing more complex, bespoke designs. Such techniques can create very flexible and powerful systems with functionalities which may not be supported by many existing software solutions (though the more advanced and open-source solutions often allow bespoke editing options, also). Various issues are covered which are essential to producing well-controlled and robust designs which can lead to the generation of reliable, valid data (e.g. tracking participants, maintaining consistency over display parameters, and so on).

The chapter emphasises the need for simple, robust designs if an implementation is to be widely accessible. By following the guidelines in this chapter the reader should (presuming access to the necessary tools) be able to produce a well-designed survey which can be placed on the Web, and which incorporates some of the principles of good practice emphasised throughout this book.

Chapter 7: What Can Go Wrong?

This chapter revisits many of the issues from earlier chapters, particularly issues of sampling from Chapter 4, ethics from Chapter 5, and design and implementation from Chapter 6. Ways that things can go wrong in implementing Internet studies, including issues relating to methodology, etiquette and vandalism, are all considered. Hardware requirements and software tools and procedures are considered. One of the main issues at stake involves selecting the right level of technology for the research question at hand. The more technically involved the study, the greater will be the demands on a researcher's level of technological expertise in order to be able actually to implement it in a properly controlled fashion (particularly with more complex experimental designs). Also, as technological demands increase, the population of potential participants equipped to take part in the research may be restricted. We point out some common pitfalls that can occur, and suggest solutions. We consider the issue of hackers, whether random hackers or those moving under the mask of bona fide participants. We discuss issues of data protection, and make some suggestions about file location, password protection and user accounts generally. We stress throughout maximal researcher control over materials and data. We do not suggest that researchers should become competent programmers, however. We rather promote the alternative strategy as discussed in Chapter 6, involving using third-party software and servers provided for non-programmers to construct and conduct studies over the Internet. Nonetheless, some researchers will be sufficiently competent at programming to develop their own systems or adapt existing open-source systems to their purposes, and we hope the guidelines that we suggest will help them avoid risks as well. Even those who do not program their own systems will do well to ask questions about how the third-party software that they contemplate using addresses the issues that we raise.

Afterword

Here we summarise the key points raised throughout the book, and offer a final comment on the current state of the art in IMR, and our projection for likely future developments.

<> TWO </>
<> THE INTERNET </>

We are buried beneath the weight of information, which is being confused with knowledge: quantity is being confused with abundance and wealth with happiness. We are monkeys with money and guns. (Tom Waits, in Maher, 2011: 444)

INTRODUCTION

Research on the Internet begins like any other research. Possible research areas are explored until a final topic is settled; the reliability of sources is judged; solid information is gathered; a working bibliography is framed; and databases at research centres are accessed. Using traditional research methods, it is possible to spend countless hours in the library, interviewing sources, and combing through library catalogues, journals and indices. In fact, most student research starts on the Internet with a Google search, a check of the university library webpage, and in some cases the perusal of a wiki, blog or social network. Using the Internet to access information is by far the easier and more efficient method.

Thousands of library catalogues, including all major university research libraries, are easily accessible online. Searchable online databases of thousands of journals and tables of content are available. Online catalogues allow a search by author, title, subject or keyword to facilitate the compilation of a working bibliography and, indeed, even offer automatically downloadable citations for sources, in much less time than is required for traditional methods.

With all research, it is important to learn how to find information without wasting time. The best way to achieve this goal is to learn how to use the Internet search and discovery tools and learn to evaluate the findings in terms of reliability, quality and relevance.

It is our goal to provide strategies for finding Internet sites that are not likely to be outdated soon because of their reliability, quality and relevance. This chapter describes various sources for secondary information that are available over the Internet. It includes reference to additional new technologies and resources that have emerged since the first edition of this book was written. The focus is secondary research, the gathering of information that is already constructed, though some of the Internet resources mentioned may also be useful in primary research as we shall see in later chapters. (The remainder of the book will shift to a focus on primary research, the gathering of data from which information can be constructed.)

The Internet makes longitudinal study more practically feasible and enables a more comprehensive search than was possible before its widespread use. But there is a two-fold problem: finding the right material in the morass of information available and gaining access to the sites that are closed to general audiences. In the past 10 years, we have seen more primary sources become available. And researchers now have more direct access to many individuals from different locations interested in the same topic and access to information held in common.

Is it Reliable?

It is impossible to work comfortably on the Internet without established guidelines for judging the reliability of webpages. Proficiency in judging the reliability of a site is important because it is a daily and recurrent task since change, manipulation and reconstruction of webpages happen so often.

The first step in establishing reliability of a site is to search the Web for the author's name. If a biographical link is available, follow it. An author's homepage will sometimes contain helpful information, such as education, affiliations and body of work. The goal is to establish the author's qualifications; in other words, is the author an authority in the field?

The next stage in judging reliability is to see if the site represents other sources fairly. Check the resources to see if there is adequate information and if that information gives a fair hearing of the topic. Next, check the accuracy of data at a particular source by following links to cited sources. When researching in the library, a quick check of the source date is required; likewise, a check of the currency of the web source must be made. What is the date on the material? When was the material last updated? When was the webpage last updated? The ability to recognise bogus or limited sites quickly enables the researcher to spend time efficiently.

It is important always to keep in mind that data are not knowledge. The inexhaustible distribution of data on the Internet has proceeded at a greater rate than their rational organisation or coherence. Researchers have to overcome these problems when deciding the usability of a site.

The Web allows for different search objectives. Any topic or subject can be researched. Corporate and commercial information has both inundated and overwhelmed the Internet. Both public domain and shareware programs can be downloaded from the Internet. Directories of individuals can be utilised to contact people, while special interest groups can be contacted through discussion groups. This chapter looks at different resources for social science[1] search areas.

Secondary Sources Available for Researchers

   Subject-based discussion groups

   Library catalogues

   Newspapers

   Indices to periodical literature

   Art archives

   Government official databases

   Electronic texts, including literature

   Social media and networking sites

SUBJECT-BASED DISCUSSION GROUPS

Electronic discussion groups (formerly known as LISTSERVS; also known as 'lists', or 'mailing lists') are effective and widely used platforms for interaction among groups of people. Discussion groups provide opportunities for collaboration, information sharing and forming virtual communities. They operate with or without monitoring by a list owner or moderator. Yahoo maintains the easily accessed 'Yahoo Groups' which enables anyone to search available groups by subject.

Examples of discussion groups include technical support forums, interest groups, fan clubs and professional networks. Members of a discussion group communicate around a common topic or area and form a distribution list of their email addresses. Members of the group can send a message and have it automatically distributed to everyone on the list. Administrative functions such as subscribing and unsubscribing (i.e. joining or leaving) are generally automated. As email is still the lowest common denominator of network access, even if a user

---

[1]We use the term 'social science' for brevity, though as explained in the Introduction, the issues raised in this book are relevant to a range of disciplines in what may broadly be termed the social, behavioural and human sciences.

does not have web access, the user may still have email access. Consequently, email-based electronic discussion groups have been among the most popular and successful of all academically oriented Internet tools. Thousands of different email discussion groups exist on almost every topic imaginable. Messages are typically announcements, questions, statements, or replies to other members. To receive a discussion group's posting, a subscription request must be sent to the group from an email account.

Discussion groups include open lists where anyone may subscribe and post messages, moderated lists where a human moderator reviews messages before they are sent to the group, and closed lists where permission must be requested to join.

> **Helpful Hint**

Consult a mailing list directory such as the one at http://www.h-net.org (accessed April 2015) for a searchable extensive list and description of different discussion groups by topic.

After subscribing, save the emailed confirmation letter because it contains information about sending messages, contacting the list owner, suspending messages for a day or two, and unsubscribing. Some confirmation letters will also give information on where to find the FAQs (Frequently Asked Questions) for the list. Answers to questions about the netiquette (etiquette of the online group) observed by each particular group are usually found in the FAQs.

After joining a group, it is a good idea to monitor the messages for a week or so to get a feel for the community. Topics considered appropriate to each group will become clear, and the group dynamic will become apparent to the newcomer in a short time. Ask for private responses when appropriate, since not all messages need to go to all group members. Do not clutter the group with off-subject messages, and reduce the number of duplicate responses by replying privately. Another important piece of advice is to delete extraneous text when responding to previous postings.

Netiquette

Netiquette – or etiquette on the Internet – prescribes some simple rules. Since tone and attitude are not easily discerned in a written message, it is important that the writer give clues to the reader about the intent of a post. Some important standards apply: for instance, using all caps means that the writer is being emphatic, even yelling; it is considered poor form. End all messages with your name and email address to make it easier for others to respond. Always give a subject heading to a post, unless sending messages to list software for administrative purposes. Cross-posting, that is sending a message to multiple lists (sometimes also used to mean sending a message seen on one group to another group, or groups), should only be attempted if the subject of the post will be of interest to each of the groups. Examples of acceptable messages to cross-post are announcements of conferences, internships or job details. Often an apology for cross-posting precedes the message. Be aware: warnings about viruses usually turn out to be false and should not be cross-posted.

It is good to be concise when using email to post to a group. Messages need not be short, but they should be to the point. People have little time and lots of email to read. Wordiness only muddies the message.

Be tolerant of errors in the messages posted. Absolutely nobody wants grammar or spelling errors pointed out. Unless an error makes the message unintelligible, figure out what the writer meant and move on. If a post seems unintelligible, it is a good idea to reply privately to the writer to ask for clarification, or to wait for the poster to resubmit the message. Only quote the portion of a previous post that is necessary for understanding the message that you write. Long or full quotes waste space and time.

Since the primary goal of the Internet is communication, it is important not to offend inadvertently others who are members of the group. Also, be aware that what seems like a great and clever retort can end up being an embarrassing mistake when posted to thousands of readers on a list and later indexed for millions to read in the archives. Take time to think through how readers may interpret a response to a post.

Finally, do not engage in flaming or flame wars. A flame is a message that is an angry reply to a posted email message. If you feel the need to reply to a flame, do so privately, and keep it out of the group discussion.

LIBRARY CATALOGUES

Academic research used to begin in a library. But it is no longer necessary to go to the brick and mortar building to get information. Online searches of library holdings are possible in a fraction of the time it takes to search using a *library card catalogue* (now largely replaced, library card catalogues involve records of all items in a library printed on cards), reference books and paper indices. Digital library catalogues provide an index to materials owned by a particular institution. A search for information can be easily launched by author, title, subject or keywords. Currently, it is possible to find full-text versions of materials rather than just abstracts of journal articles, and works in the public domain are abundant. Remarkably, it is now even possible to see the Rosetta Stone at the British Museum and illuminated manuscripts at the Vatican Museum online (see http://www.britishmuseum.org/explore/highlights/highlight_objects/aes/t/the_rosetta_stone.aspx, and http://mv.vatican.va/3_EN/pages/MV_Visite.html [accessed October 2014]).

When querying an online library catalogue, the results received are often pieces of information about a physical resource of the library, rather than the resource itself, though many libraries have added full-text indexing features to their catalogues. Library catalogues often provide indices to journal articles themselves; the journal titles will be provided in the search. When these catalogues are available, it is usually only for the students, faculty and staff of the university where the catalogue is located or to participants of partnership networks such as LOUIS (see https://sites01.lsu.edu/wp/louis [accessed October 2014]), not to every Internet user. Therefore, specific journal articles may be easier to find using electronic or paper indices, most of which are not publicly available on the Internet, but are still common in academic libraries. Electronic indices are discussed later.

Searching a library catalogue is done for one of three reasons: to locate a book, journal or other material to check out of the library; to find bibliographic information; and to see what books or journals are available on a particular topic or by a particular author. Searching a library catalogue by Internet, now a very common way of retrieving journal articles, is done to locate library holdings and in most cases retrieve the material electronically, as well as to find out the availability of sources on a particular topic.

Fortunately, library catalogues are designed to make searches easy, to accommodate people with different levels of computer expertise. In the past 10 years, searching library catalogues has become increasingly simple via computer. Usually the first step is to access the homepage of a university, then look for a link to its library catalogue. Each library catalogue looks a little different and many have a unique set of commands, but all operate with the intent to help the patron find resources.

Most university libraries have an extensive collection of secondary sources. Usually, electronic databases are accessible by remote access, as well as within the library. Reference librarians, a valuable and underutilised resource, are available at the library to answer your questions and to provide their expertise.

A library homepage is the gateway to accessing the library collection. You will also find sources in EBSCO, INFOTRAC, JSTOR, LexisNexis, PROQUEST and Wilson among the many databases.

If you are seeking to keep current with events reported by the media, the following are among the many sites available to you through the Internet:

Current Events Sites

 businessweek.com (Business Week)

 cnn.com (CNN)

 pbs.org (PBS)

 LeMonde.fr

 BBC.org

 NPR.org

 Spiegel.de

 Aljazeera.com

If you are seeking results of public opinion research, the following are among the many sites available to you through the Internet:

Public Opinion/Survey Sites

 gallup.com (The Gallup Organisation)

 norc.uchicago.edu (National Opinion Research Center)

 publicagenda.org

 people-press.org (Pew Research Center for People and the Press)

 pollingreport.com

 questia.com

 ropercenter.uconn.edu (Roper Poll)

 https://yougov.co.uk/publicopinion/archive/ukdebate.co.uk

 nationalarchives.gov.uk/webarchive

> **Helpful Hint**

Public opinion research conducted by the Gallup Organisation that is not available to the general public can be accessed through Gallup Brain, brain.gallup.com

NEWSPAPERS

LexisNexis

LexisNexis (lexisnexis.com) contains the full text of thousands of newspapers, reports and journals from Australia, Canada, France, Hong Kong, South Africa, the United Kingdom and the United States. From the library, you would connect to Nexis, while Lexis is a database of legal information, used by law offices and law students for research. Comprehensive information on which publications are indexed and provided by LexisNexis is available from its homepage. LexisNexis works by allowing searches of information, using a search language that provides full Boolean search features (Boolean operators are the words AND, OR and NOT; when these words are placed between keywords, they expand or limit the scope of the search) to refine queries. The News library contains 5 billion documents of source information and manages over 100 terabytes of data storage. Publications range from *The New York Times* to *Western Morning News* to *The Moscow Times*. The focus is business and financial news. On LexisNexis, results can be displayed, saved or printed as full-text articles all the way to the citations of the articles. This database is expensive; however, most libraries have access to it. Searching through use of a library or college is an option in many places. Since LexisNexis is a comprehensive source for current news or business information, it is a valuable resource.

Dow Jones News/Factiva

Like LexisNexis, Dow Jones News/Factiva (dowjones.com/factiva) is another commercial information service available on the Internet; however, it is also expensive.

The Business Journals, a Division of The American City Business Journals

The American City Business Journals (bizjournals.com) searches the archives of specialised business newspapers from 35 US cities. This is also a subscription service.

An increasing number of papers are putting their articles behind pay-walls. *The New York Times* online allows visitors to read 10 articles before prompting them to subscribe. It is likely to see this model used by even small regional dailies as readers continue to unsubscribe from print newspapers. Because of this trend, specific URLs may quickly date through cessation of free access.

News aggregators index the articles (with first lines typically) so that one can get a sense of the headlines. The Google news aggregator (news.google.* *=com;ie;co.uk) and Europe's Joint Research Centre (emm.newsbrief.eu/overview.html) are good places to start.

Some newspapers have apps that are either free or cost a small fee. The *Guardian* charges for its app, while *USA Today* is free. Other UK and US newspapers also have online/mobile access.

Newspapers Online

BBC News	bbc.co.uk/news/
The New York Times	nytimes.com/
The Washington Post	washingtonpost.com
The Irish Times – Ireland	irishtimes.com
Detroit Free Press	freep.com
San Francisco Chronicle	sfgate.com
Guardian	guardian.co.uk

INDICES TO PERIODICAL LITERATURE

Document delivery refers to the electronic transmission of journal articles. Document delivery developed not only for its convenience to the user, but also because libraries cannot afford to subscribe to every journal which students, faculty and staff might need. Most libraries subscribe to many core journals and to a commercial document delivery service that can transmit articles from the journals not in their collection. Most document delivery services send the requested documents electronically by computer. There are many document delivery services available to libraries. Two popular services are JSTOR and EBSCO. All of them operate in the same basic manner.

EBSCO is an online database that delivers documents. To access it, researchers usually enter through their institution's online library site. After logging in via a faculty or student identification number and password, a search page appears where it is possible to conduct a search by subject, author, title or keyword. Searches can be narrowed by publication type, year, whether or not it is peer reviewed, and language. Once the search criteria are decided upon, type them in, and the results come back. At this point, you can further narrow your search by shortening your date range or any other of a number of limiters. You have the option to save a source to a folder, export sources to collaborators, or export to your own email address. Citation services now available allow easy download/email of sources, a particularly handy tool for researchers. EBSCO has a convenient automatic citation service, and you can choose the bibliographic style: Turabian, APA, MLA and Chicago Style.

In the UK, a common way of acquiring items not held in or subscribed to by a local library is via the Inter Library Loans service, which supports document delivery. Items are requested by users, sourced by the library, and delivered often in electronic (otherwise hard copy) format. The British Library supplies many such requests. The local library is charged a fee for each item delivered, and this may be passed on to the user in some circumstances (e.g. if a registered student has already used up his or her yearly quota allowance). The British Library also hosts a direct document supply service (http://www.bldss.bl.uk/BLDSS/) that can be used by anyone, though inevitably this is a more costly option than going via one's local university library.[2]

ART ARCHIVES

Websites from international museums to local galleries designed to educate and entertain both the serious art student and the casual art lover can be found on the Internet. Many art museums offer everything from basic background information on a particular artist to sophisticated virtual technology tours of a museum's entire collection. There are even online art museums that exist only on the Web. Some art museums around the world are open 24 hours a day, seven days a week, to anyone with Internet access. Many art museums are putting collections online that they do not have space to show on site, and Google has an online gallery for emerging artists: https://www.google.com/opengallery/. Using the Web to learn about art allows the researcher to follow more easily an artist, a line of interest, or a school or movement than using the traditional method of art books and classes.

Some museums present their stellar art objects, while others display lesser known works and feature historical information. For information about an artist, it is easy to perform a keyword search on a web browser and download all the information.

Several national museums offer multimedia tours of their collections. The National Gallery of Art site (nga.gov) in the United States offers a comprehensive virtual tour of over 100,000 objects including major artefacts in painting, sculpture and graphic arts from the Middle Ages to the present. The collection can be searched by specific artist or title or by medium and school. Tours are offered in several languages including French, Spanish, German, Italian and English.

---

[2]Most academic journals currently charge an access subscription fee, but do not charge a publishing fee to authors. However, recent UK directives have proposed changing this model to a pay-to-publish, 'gold' open-access model. For further information see www.research infonet.org/wp-content/uploads/2012/06/Finch-Group-report-FINAL-VERSION.pdf (accessed April 2015). Clearly, this would alter the way UK libraries and academics (and indeed members of the public) access journal articles.

> **Try This Exercise**

To learn about Van Gogh at the National Gallery of Art site (nga.gov), begin by clicking on 'Virtual Exhibitions' (http://www.nga.gov/exhibitions/webtours.htm) and then choose between the QuickTime and nonplug-in tour. Technical requirements for both tours are described. The plug-in tour allows a visual walk through the rooms of the gallery, clicking on paintings for larger image views, details and more information. Directions are provided on how to use the keyboard to zoom in and out and find important viewpoints. Details on the artwork and Van Gogh's life can be heard by clicking on the RealAudio file. The QuickTime tour allows the user to select and enlarge paintings and also obtain information.

The National Gallery of Art Homepage also gives the options of Collection Tours, Web Tour of the Week, Online Tours, Paintings, Sculpture, Works on Paper, Photographs, and Decorative Arts. In-Depth Study Tours are broken down by Artist, Specific Work of Art, or Theme. Artists included in tours are such notables as Alexander Calder, Rembrandt and Mark Rothko. Specific artworks include Picasso's 'The Tragedy' and Jackson Pollock's 'Number One – 1950 (Lavender Mist)'. Themes include American Impressionism and Realism, Still Life, Toulouse Lautrec and Montmartre among others. The architecture tours include the West Building, the East Building and the Sculpture Garden.

An important and free resource for the study of art and architecture is the Getty Research Institute (getty.edu/research). Researchers interested in how art masterpieces are cleaned and restored should go to the Getty Conservation Institute. Oxford Art Online (oxfordartonline.com) is the access point of academic libraries to art reference resources.

The Louvre online (louvre.fr) features the history and collection of more than 6,000 European paintings dating from the late thirteenth to the mid-nineteenth century. Three different virtual tours are available: Egyptian Antiquities, Remains of the Louvre's Moat and Galerie d'Apollon (see http://www.louvre.fr/en/visites-en-ligne [accessed October 2014]). At least 44 online videos are available. Currently, two apps are available for the iPhone and iPad. Audio guide apps are available for sale.

Visit these Online Art Museums

The Tate, London	tate.org.uk
The National Gallery, London	nationalgallery.org.uk
National Gallery of Art, Washington, DC	nga.gov

(Continued)

(Continued)

Metropolitan Museum of Art, New York	metmuseum.org
The Museum of Fine Arts, Boston	mfa.org
The Minneapolis Institute of Arts, Minneapolis	artsmia.org
Museum of Contemporary Art, San Diego	mcasd.org
The Louvre, Paris	louvre.fr/
The Smithsonian, Washington, DC	si.edu
The Hermitage, St Petersburg	hermitagemuseum.org
Galleria degli Uffizi, Florence	uffizi.com

An excellent site for information about museums is the World Wide Web Virtual Library Museums page supported by the International Council of Museums (icom. museum). The list is split into sub-lists by country or region. Museums are listed first by country, then alphabetically with links directly to each museum. This site lists all types of museums from planetariums to virtual library zoos.

GOVERNMENT OFFICIAL DATABASES

Thomas

THOMAS (thomas.loc.gov) is one of the most valuable sources on US legislation. Aside from legislation, THOMAS covers congressional records and committee information. This resource provides information about the activities of the US Congress, including the full text of all bills and legislation. The information can be searched by bill number or type of bill, by keyword in the text of the bill, by department, and by representative, senator, committee or process. A feature called 'Weekly Top Ten' directs the user to bills in the media that are most frequently referred to and those most often requested from legislative librarians.

THOMAS contains legislation as far back as 1989 for bill summary and status. Public Laws by number are available from 1973 to the present. The Congressional Record can be accessed from 1989 to the present. Treaties from 1967 to the present are available. The following databases are offered by THOMAS: Bills, Resolutions, Activity in Congress, Congressional Record, Schedules, Calendars, Committee Information, Presidential Nominations, Treaties, Government Resources and THOMAS for Teachers.

A convenient feature of THOMAS is that it contains the text of new bills within 48 hours.

In addition to THOMAS databases, the THOMAS homepage provides links to The Legislative Process, Historical Documents, US Congressional Documents and Debates: 1774–1873, House and Senate Directories, Library of Congress Web Links.

Library of Congress Online Catalog

LOCIS (loc.gov), the US Library of Congress Information System, is a database of about 12 million records representing books, serials, computer files, manuscripts, cartographic materials, music, sound recordings and visual materials in the Library of Congress's collection. It provides information about books and non-print materials catalogued by the Library of Congress, federal legislation, copyrighted materials registered with the Library of Congress, braille and audio materials, bibliographies for people doing basic research, and foreign law material. The Library of Congress also provides high-resolution scans of many items.

National Technical Information Service

The National Technical Information Service (https://www.ntis.gov/) is a website maintained by the National Technical Information Service of the US government. It offers multiple distribution channels to provide information links to reports from all agencies of the US government. NTIS is the largest central resource for government-funded scientific, technical, engineering and business-related information. This site offers a comprehensive central access point to search, locate, order and acquire government and business information. It has full text of many databases including the NTIS Database, the National Technical Reports Library, The Davis–Bacon Wage Discrimination Database, Service Contract Wage Determination Database, the Federal Research in Progress Database, and World News Connection.

Gov.uk

GOV.UK (gov.uk) is the homepage of the UK government. This site provides links to information on UK ministerial departments, agencies and public bodies. The various links provide access to public information on employment, benefits, pensions, citizenship, and so on, as well as live information on 24 ministerial departments (including the Department for Education, Department of Health, HM Treasury). Links to information on governments in 227 other countries worldwide are also available. Links to pages on consultations, policies, publications and statistics are all also available; each page is searchable by keyword, and searches can be filtered by specifying other parameters (e.g. topic, department, publication date). For example, searching for consultations after January 2013 with the topic 'borders and immigration' returned no results. Changing the topic to 'equality, rights and citizenship' returned several results, the first of which linked to a consultation on equal marriage (https://www.gov.uk/government/uploads/system/uploads/attachment_data/file/133262/consultation-response_1_.pdf [accessed May 2014]).

The National Archives

The National Archives website (nationalarchives.gov.uk) is the UK government's national archive for England, Wales and the United Kingdom, holding over 1,000 years of the nation's records. The website provides public access to millions of documents, files and images, and also offers a selection of freely available online teaching materials via a virtual classroom (as well as face-to-face workshop and videoconferencing options).

> ### ❯ Helpful Hint
>
> http://www.nationalarchives.gov.uk/education/great-fire.htm (accessed May 2014) provides a teaching resource pack on The Great Fire of London. Searches by keyword can be conducted of all records, or online records only.

Legislation.gov.uk

The online official home of UK legislation can be found at legislation.gov.uk. The website is managed by The National Archives on behalf of HM Government. Here, UK government legislation documents can be browsed by category (e.g. UK Public General Acts), or using an advanced search by keyword, title, date, etc. The 'New Legislation' link provides up-to-date information on all Acts passed (listed by publication date), aiming to publish these online simultaneously with, or within 24 hours of, publication in printed form. Free-of-charge subscription feeds are also available. All current bills are listed on the UK Parliament website http://services.parliament.uk/bills/. This site shows the progress and current stage of each bill. At the time of writing, the most recently updated bill was the Marriage (Same Sex Couples) Bill, with the latest event listed as '2nd reading: House of Lords 3 June, 2013'.

Visit these Government Resources

GOV.UK	gov.uk
www.parliament.uk	parliament.uk
The Library of Congress	loc.gov
The US Department of Education	ed.gov
The White House	whitehouse.gov

ELECTRONIC TEXTS, INCLUDING LITERATURE

Although every researcher has respect for books, the weight of the volume, the feel of the page, the smell of the leather binding on an older edition, researchers appreciate the shift from print to digital format that greatly expedites research. Nothing can replace the satisfaction of a fine edition, but there is also a need for quick and easy access to a growing mass of print material.

Google Scholar

Google Scholar (scholar.google.com) provides an easy way to search for digital or physical copies of scholarly articles. It covers many disciplines and includes articles, theses and books. Searches can be made by author, title or date, and an email alert system is provided. Email alerts are provided to track articles by the researcher or when the researcher is cited in another article. It is also possible to date-restrict searches and download hits to citation index software.

Project Gutenberg

Many electronic text archives, such as those maintained by Project Gutenberg (gutenberg.org), are composed of works in the public domain. Project Gutenberg began in 1971 when Michael Hart was given free computer time, which he decided to use by creating a file of online electronic texts. The project offers 42,000 free e-books, either to download or read online. The philosophy of the project directors is to make information, books and other materials available to the general public in forms that can be easily read, used, quoted and searched.

Project Gutenberg was divided into three portions: light literature, heavy literature and references. It is easy to look up quotations heard in movies, music or other books because of the easy to find e-text format. From the homepage, it is a simple task to browse the Index/Catalogue by title and author or to use the search engine to find and download books. Also the whole list of Project Gutenberg books is available as a plain text file or a zip file. Step-by-step directions are given on how to get books.

Online Books Page

The Online Books Page (digital.library.upenn.edu/books/) is another helpful site. Its homepage offers a search engine of over 1 million free books.

Searches are conducted by author or title. Search results provide links to the texts.

SOCIAL MEDIA AND NETWORKING SITES

Entire books can be written on the emergence of individual social media applications and all of the networking sites which are available to researchers. We list here the most widely used. Social media are the wide variety of online technologies and practices that people use to share opinions, insights, experiences and perspectives. Social media take different forms, including text, images, audio and video.

Popular Social Media Applications

Wikipedia (reference)

Facebook (social networking)

LinkedIn (business networking)

YouTube (video sharing)

Second Life (virtual reality)

Tumblr and Instagram (photo sharing)

Twitter (presence app)

Reddit (news aggregation)

Academia.edu (academic networking)

Pinterest (photo and video sharing)

Vine (video sharing)

Vimeo (video sharing)

Social media equalise content and the role of people in the process of reading and relaying information, sharing and creating content.

The study of social networks has grown and with it analytics peculiar to the particular sites. The analytics connect the social media to business results to discover a user's influence. For example, tweet.grader.com offers an account summary of a user's power, reach and authority. This informs the user of the impact that a particular account may have, based on the number of followers, power of followers, updates, update recency, follower/following ratio and engagement.

In conclusion, it is easy to become familiar with a full range of secondary sources available on the Internet. We have only showcased a small but representative selection of those available. The learning curve for becoming proficient in any one area is certainly worth the time saved when looking at long-term study in a particular field. As in any research, countless hours can be spent, but by fine-tuning the focus of the investigation, becoming efficient in online computer skills, and making an effort not to get lost in the innumerable links to fascinating, but useless information, research can be accurate, appropriate and efficient. A caution, parallel to the one stated at the onset of this chapter about verifying the reliability of an Internet resource, is to avoid the assumption that if information is not easily found on the Internet then it does not exist.

<> THREE </>

<> INTERNET-MEDIATED RESEARCH: STATE OF THE ART </>

INTRODUCTION

The previous chapter's focus was on how the Internet can be used as a secondary research tool in the social and behavioural sciences. A range of resources were outlined along with instructions on how to use them. The present chapter is concerned with the scope of the Internet for supporting *primary* social and behavioural research. Here we review the current state of the art in IMR, outlining the range of methods that have been tried and tested, as well as the results that have been obtained. We consider some of the most recent developments and speculate on future possibilities. Subsequent chapters follow up on this broad overview, considering in more detail how particular methods can be implemented, including how potential participants can be located and recruited, and outlining caveats regarding the kinds of things that might go wrong, and how researchers may strive to guard against them. Chapter 5 offers a detailed discussion of ethical issues in IMR. First we provide a short history of IMR, followed by a classification scheme for types of IMR study to help frame the ensuing discussion. We include a brief summary of the main advantages and disadvantages of IMR. The methods we discuss are: surveys and questionnaires; interviews and focus groups; observational approaches; experiments; document analysis.

A SHORT HISTORY OF IMR

From around the early to mid-1990s pioneers started considering and implementing IMR methods (e.g. Bordia, 1996; Dillman, 1991; Hewson & Vogel, 1994; Krantz, Ballard, & Sher, 1997; Mehta & Sivadas, 1995; Szabo, Frenkl, & Caputo, 1996). Twenty or so years later, though the field is still relatively young and evolving, an impressive range of approaches have been conceived and tested. Surveys and questionnaires remain the most widely implemented IMR method, being prevalent in the early days (e.g. Buchanan & Smith, 1999a; Joinson, 1999; Mehta & Svidas, 1995; Stones & Perry, 1997), as well as more recently (e.g. Bigelsen & Schupak, 2011; Gosling, Vazire, Srivastava, & John, 2004; Hewson & Charlton, 2005; Malhotra & Krosnick, 2007; Temple & Brown, 2011). Early pioneers also implemented Internet experiments (e.g. Hewson, 1994; Krantz et al., 1997; McGraw, Tew, & Williams, 2000), interviews (e.g. Chen & Hinton, 1999; Gaiser, 1997; Murray & Sixsmith, 1998) and observational studies (e.g. Bordia, 1996; Herring, Johnson, & DiBenedetto, 1998). While a starting point was often considering how existing offline methods could be adapted to an IMR context, to provide comparable, reliable, valid data, early researchers also considered the ways in which the Internet might enhance and expand methodological opportunities beyond what is possible or practicable offline (e.g. Bordia, 1996; Givaty, van Vaan, Christou, & Bulthoff, 1998; Hewson, Laurent, & Vogel, 1996). Both online IMR methods which strive to mimic closely established offline approaches and novel IMR methods which have attempted to move beyond what has been possible in offline research have flourished since the early days, and technological developments have played an important role in facilitating both types of approach.

For evidence of this growth, consult some of the recent texts on IMR (e.g. Batinic, Reips, & Bosnjak, 2002; Fielding, Lee, & Blank, 2008; Gosling & Johnson, 2010; Joinson, McKenna, Postmes, & Reips, 2007; Salmons, 2011) and the increasing number of reports of IMR studies published in journals such as *Behavior, Research Methods*; *Computers in Human Behavior*; *Social Science Computer Review*. The emergence of dedicated topic-relevant conferences such as General Online Research (GoR), ACM Web Science Conference, and Internet Research also attests to the popularity of IMR methods. Organisations dedicated to discussing issues in IMR, such as the Association of Internet Researchers (AoIR), WebSurveyMethodology (WebSM) and WebDataNet, have also emerged. Finally, the expanse in websites dedicated to hosting collections of IMR studies (e.g. The Web Experiment List, The Web Survey List, Online Social Psychology Studies, Online Psychology Research UK) and other webpage resources which provide specialist information, tuition and advice on IMR methodologies (e.g. Exploring Online Research Methods: ORM) are further indicators. For more information on the aforementioned events and resources see Box 3.1.

BOX 3.1   Resources for IMR-Related Events, Organisations and Repositories of Active Studies

Events

GOR: Annual conference organised by the German Society for Online Research; see http://www.gor.de (accessed May 2014).

ACM Web Science Conference: The 2013 conference website is available at http://www.websci13.org/ (accessed May 2014).

Internet Research: Annual Conference of the Association of Internet Researchers (AoIR); see aoir.org (accessed May 2014).

Organisations and information websites

Association of Internet Researchers (AoIR: aoir.org).

WebSurveyMethodology (WebSM: http://www.websm.org).

WebDataNet (http://www.cost.eu/domains_actions/isch/Actions/IS1004).

ORM (http://www.restore.ac.uk/orm).

Online study clearing houses

The Web Experiment List (http://www.wexlist.net), previously the 'Web Experimental Psychology Lab' founded in 1995 at the University of Tübingen by Ulf-Dietrich Reips, now as named here and housed at the University of Zürich.

Web Survey List (available from the above Web Experiment homepage link).

Online Social Psychology Studies (http://www.socialpsychology.org/expts.htm).

Psychological Research on the Net (psych.hanover.edu/research/exponent.html).

Scouring the IMR literature to date, quantitative approaches seem to have dominated (and particularly, as noted, the online survey), though numerous examples of qualitative approaches (especially interviews and ethnographic studies) also exist, in what has now become a diverse, broad and interdisciplinary methodological strategy. As noted in Chapter 1, observational approaches, particularly those involving unobtrusive 'data mining' techniques, have enjoyed particular growth since we were writing the first edition of this book. This growth has been facilitated by the expanding integration of the Internet into people's everyday lives, and the traces this has created of various aspects of intra- and interpersonal online behaviours and activities. The emergence of Web 2.0 (as discussed in Chapter 1) has played a pivotal role in supporting many of these developments.

One point worth highlighting is the way expansions in the range and scope of IMR methods, and their supporting Internet technologies, has led to blurred boundaries emerging between different methods (see examples offered later in the chapter). Another is the vast reach of IMR methods, across disciplines, research domains and methodological traditions. It would be practically impossible for any individual researcher to keep up with all the ongoing developments. Here we aim to offer a good selection of examples from the key methods that have been used to date, drawing upon both qualitative and quantitative approaches, across different disciplines in the social and behavioural sciences. The next section maps out the present landscape of IMR by identifying the key methods used to date, and offering a way of classifying these.

A FRAMEWORK FOR CLASSIFYING TYPES OF IMR STUDY

There are now enough examples of IMR studies to start to think about a classification scheme to represent the range and nature of approaches which have emerged. Figure 3.1 presents a framework for classifying key types of IMR study design along the *obtrusive–unobtrusive* dimension, since this dimension becomes relevant to many issues in IMR (e.g. in ethics, sampling, and so on; see below and later chapters). Other ways of classifying IMR methods, such as quantitative or qualitative, can also be useful, but the obtrusive–unobtrusive dimension seems useful for framing the present discussion. As already noted, blurred boundaries between different IMR methods emerge, particularly as new technologies and practices enable innovative approaches which may not have offline equivalents. For example, the distinction between observational approaches and document analysis is not always clear due to new ways of interacting and publishing online (e.g. blogs may be seen as interactively produced, organic documents with multiple authors, individual diaries with regular updates, or something in between; see further discussion below). The distinction between survey and interview methods can become blurred (the distinction is blurry even in face-to-face situations, and on-line administration of surveys and interviews gives surveys and interviews more common properties) when considering strategies which may make use of an *online virtual interviewer*. Also, many approaches may be seen as *more* or *less* obtrusive or unobtrusive, rather than falling into clearly defined discrete categories.

Figure 3.1 shows the key IMR methods we discuss in this chapter placed along the obtrusive–unobtrusive dimension, based largely on the ways these methods have commonly been implemented to date. Broadly speaking, surveys, questionnaires, interviews and experiments are primarily obtrusive approaches, where the norm is to obtain valid consent from participants before they knowingly participate in a process of actively contributing research data. Different design choices may influence the positioning of any particular study, as indicated. For example, a synchronous interview is likely to be more obtrusive than an asynchronous interview, since in the latter participants can respond as and when they choose. Emailed surveys could be seen as more obtrusive (and perhaps 'intrusive') than web surveys, since they arrive in a person's own personal email inbox, and generally require more effort to complete and return. Although it is possible to conceive of experimental designs where participants contribute unwittingly, IMR experiments have generally been carried out obtrusively (though see Chapter 5 for some counterexamples). At the unobtrusive end of the dimension lies document analysis, which is almost always unobtrusive, whether disclosed or undisclosed. Observational methods in IMR span the dimension most broadly, and key design choices will

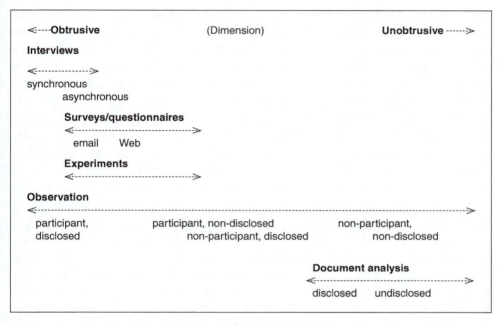

Figure 3.1 Mapping IMR methods along the *obtrusive–unobtrusive* dimension

determine where a particular study falls. For example, participant approaches will typically be more obtrusive than non-participant approaches. Disclosed observations will normally be more obtrusive than non-disclosed approaches. In Figure 3.1 disclosed, participant observation (e.g. immersive ethnographic research) is indicated as the most obtrusive, and non-disclosed, non-participant approaches (such as analysis of stored discussion archives) as the least. Other combinations will fall somewhere in between.

Figure 3.1 provides a rough sketch of how different IMR methods may be classified as obtrusive or unobtrusive, and how different design choices can affect this. Of course, other factors will also be important in determining the level of obtrusiveness in any study (e.g. whether multimedia technologies are used, such as in an online interview, levels of actual and perceived anonymity, and so on). These factors will be discussed throughout the present chapter. Before turning to look at each of the key methods outlined in the figure, we briefly summarise some general advantages and disadvantages of IMR methods, compared with offline methods.

ADVANTAGES AND DISADVANTAGES OF IMR

The general advantages and disadvantages of conducting a study via the Internet have by now been well rehearsed (e.g. see the reviews in Birnbaum, 2004; Hewson & Laurent, 2008). The examples offered throughout this book serve to illustrate the potential and demonstrated benefits of IMR approaches, as well as highlight caveats. Established advantages include: broad reach leading to potentially very large, diverse samples (e.g. Birnbaum, 2001; Musch & Reips, 2000); the collapsing of geographical boundaries (e.g. facilitating cross-cultural research; see Pohl, Bender, & Lachmann, 2002) and facilitated access to specialist and traditionally hard-to-reach populations (e.g. Bigelsen & Schupak, 2011); cost and time efficiency compared with many traditional offline methods (e.g. Grandcolas, Rettie, & Marusenko, 2003; Hessler, Downing, Beltz, Pelliccio, Powell, & Vale, 2003); potential enhanced reliability due to automated procedures which can help reduce problems associated with human error (e.g. Hewson & Laurent, 2008); heightened levels and perceptions of anonymity, which may lead to enhanced candour and levels of disclosure (Hessler et al., 2003; Hewson et al., 1996); convenience to participants of being able to participate remotely, which may lead to empowerment and possibly elicit richer data (e.g. Madge & O'Connor, 2002). As we noted in the first edition, some of these features could be particularly important for smaller institutions which may have limited time and funding available for supporting research projects. Potential disadvantages of IMR include: limited scope for obtaining probability samples (discussed further in Chapter 4); reduced levels of researcher control over and knowledge of procedural aspects (e.g. Couper, 2000; Hewson & Laurent, 2008) and participant characteristics (e.g. BPS, 2007); technology-related issues and constraints, such as the need for expertise and/or training in computing techniques, and potential unreliabilities in hardware systems and software (e.g. Jowett, Peel, & Shaw, 2011). We highlight below, and further in Chapter 6, where these advantages and disadvantages become particularly relevant to the various methods, techniques and procedures discussed. A key focus throughout the book is the ways in which different methods, design choices and characteristics of the online environment might impact upon the validity, quality and integrity of the data obtained, and conclusions reached.

SURVEYS AND QUESTIONNAIRES

Proliferation of Web-Based Surveys

The proliferation of survey and questionnaire methods in IMR more recently has been assisted by the widespread availability of cost-effective software solutions (these solutions are discussed further in Chapter 6). These have made programming implementation guides (such as those offered by Batinic, 1997; Birnbaum, 2001; Goritz & Birnbaum, 2005; our own in the first edition of IRM) less necessary and enhanced the accessibility of IMR survey methods (particularly web-based survey methods). There are now a number of texts wholly dedicated to the approach (e.g. Balch, 2010; Couper, 2008; Sue & Ritter, 2012). The 'quick evolution of web surveys from novel idea to routine use' (Dillman, 2007, p. 447) over the last

10 years or so is reflected in the increasing number of studies reported in peer-reviewed journals (e.g. Bigelsen & Schupak, 2011; Göritz & Schumacher, 2000; Gosling et al., 2004; Hewson & Charlton, 2005) and the examples available via IMR study clearing houses (see Box 3.1). Many of the latter involve psychological research (such as the examples available at www.onlinepsychologyresearch.co.uk). However, survey and questionnaire approaches in IMR have extended well beyond the discipline of psychology, and examples also appear in marketing research, political science, sociology, geography, economics, and medical, health and nursing research (e.g. Im & Chee, 2004; Mehta & Sivadas, 1995). Researchers have used IMR approaches to implement very large-scale surveys (e.g. Reece, Rosenberger, Schick, Herbenick, Dodge, & Novak, 2010), psychometric test instruments (e.g. Anderson, Kaldo-Sandstrom, Strom, & Stromgren, 2003; Hewson & Charlton, 2005; see also the myPersonality Project, information available at myPersonality.org [accessed October 2014]), and market research (Pincott & Branthwaite, 2000) and consumer attitudes surveys (Grandcolas et al., 2003). Resources such as the WebSM site (see Box 3.1), which have been set up to provide guidance and advice on web-based survey methodology, further reflect the recent interest in this method. Email-based methods are also an option for delivering surveys via the Internet (for examples see Dommeyer & Moriarty, 1999; Welker, 2001), but by far the most widely used approach these days is the *web-based survey*.

The enhanced accessibility and growth of IMR survey methods have led to talk of the 'democratisation of the survey' (e.g. Couper, 2000). It is now relatively easy to construct and disseminate a web-based survey at low cost. While this may facilitate high-quality social and behavioural research projects by helping researchers with fewer resources or tighter budgets to gather data (Carter-Pokras, McClellan, & Zambrana, 2006), some authors have also noted caveats. The ease with which it is now possible to create and publish a survey on the Web opens up possibilities for an influx of badly constructed and/or intrusive examples (Lee et al., 2008). This could lead to negative public perceptions of survey-based research, just as telemarketing has arguably negatively impacted on telephone survey methodologies (Couper, 2000; Tourangeau, 2004). Anyone who regularly uses the Internet for activities such as shopping, banking, social networking, and so on will be familiar with the proliferation of the Internet 'pop-up survey', used by many corporations wishing to gain customer feedback and satisfaction data quickly, cheaply and in large volumes (in Chapter 6 we outline strategies to help maximise perceptions of credibility, value and integrity of a piece of research).

Advantages and Disadvantages of Web-Based Surveys

Web-based surveys may have a number of advantages over traditional methods (for a comparison of different offline modes – postal, telephone, face to face – see Bowling, 2005). Some of the earliest examples of IMR surveys used email (e.g. Dillman, 1991; Mehta & Sivadas, 1995; Tse et al., 1995), which at the time had the advantage over web-based methods of ease of implementation. Sending survey questions in the body of an email was technologically straightforward compared with writing programming code and setting up server configurations to enable web-based survey presentation and data collection. Email methods[1] continue to be used (e.g. Bigelsun & Schupak, 2011), but as well as the enhanced accessibility of web-based methods due to the emergence of affordable dedicated software packages, they also offer greater functionality, flexibility and reliability over email approaches. The generation of reliable, high-quality data from very large sample sizes using web-based survey methods has been demonstrated by a number of researchers (e.g. Chang & Krosnick, 2009; Gosling et al., 2004; Meyerson & Tryon, 2003; Pettit, 1999). Others have successfully obtained high-quality data from smaller, specialist samples (e.g. Bigelsen & Schupak, 2011; Coomber, 1997a; Stones & Perry, 1997). Some researchers also report obtaining very large sample sizes from specialist populations; for example, Hirshfield et al. (2010) obtained a sample of 7,000 men who have sex with men. Web-based approaches are often reported as being able to recruit large and/ or specialist samples far more cost- and time-effectively than is possible using offline methods (e.g. Meyerson & Tryon, 2003; Pettit, 1999). Box 3.2 offers an illustration of a web-based survey which generated responses from a very large sample. Box 3.3 presents an example of an email-based survey which acquired data from a specialist sample.

BOX 3.2   Featured Research: Reece et al. (2010)

Method

In all, 25,294 gay and bisexual men were recruited to complete a survey on sexual behaviours, by sending email messages directly to registered users of a popular Internet site for men seeking social and sexual interactions with other men who resided in the United States. A $10 voucher for merchandise reward was offered in return for participation. The email contained a description of the study and a link to the web survey, which took around 20 minutes to complete. A total of 127,489 individuals opened the email invitation; 34% of these clicked on the study website link, and 60% of those went on to complete the study.

---

[1]In which the survey itself is sent in the body of an email (including as an attachment) for completion and return via email, as opposed to emailing potential participants and asking them to follow a link to access a *web-based* survey.

Results

Demographics as well as survey data on sexual behaviours were collected. Participants were well represented across age group categories (18-23 to 60+) and educational levels. The majority of participants were white (82%).

Conclusions

The data provided useful insights into the use of vibrators by gay and bisexual men, allowing relationships between demographic factors and behaviours and experiences to be explored. However, although a very large sample of men from the United States was obtained, it was a convenience sample of men from a single Internet social and sexual networking site, thus limiting the extent to which the findings can be generalised to the entire population of gay and bisexually identified men in the United States. Challenges remain for establishing true nationally representative samples of gay and bisexual men for research.

Comment

This study is a good example of how it is possible to obtain very large sample sizes using the Internet, in ways that would often be difficult (and more costly and time consuming) offline. However, it also highlights concerns regarding the representativeness of Internet-accessed samples, even though in this case obtaining representative samples of the population of interest is also difficult using offline methods. The sample obtained here did support the diversity of Internet samples, at least in relation to the variables of age and educational level. It is worth noting that while IMR methods are generally *more* cost effective than traditional offline methods, the costs in participant fees for this study were significant (over $250,000 worth of merchandise vouchers).

BOX 3.3 Featured Research: Bigelsen and Schupak (2011)

Method

A volunteer sample of 75 female and 15 male participants who self-identified as excessive or maladaptive fantasisers was recruited via posts to a health-related website. Interested individuals were asked to make contact via an email address, and were then emailed a questionnaire on excessive daydreaming, which they were asked to complete and return by email.

(Continued)

(Continued)

Results

Participants were of diverse nationalities (including from the United Kingdom, United States, Canada, India, South Africa, and other countries). Age ranged from 18 to 63, though 90% of participants fell in the 18–39 years age group.

Conclusions

The IMR design enabled access to a very specialist and widely geographically dispersed population which could not otherwise have been obtained. The study allowed further insights into the perceptions and behaviours of people who identified as excessive fantasisers, and was the first to study a large, non-exclusively traumatised sample. The bias towards respondents under 40 could be due to their over-representation in the online medium used for recruitment, or their greater willingness for disclosure. The higher proportion of females remains unexplained. Recruitment from websites which discuss fantasy distress is likely to have generated a biased sub-population of excessive fantasisers.

Comment

This study demonstrates how the Internet, via its online communities and information-sharing potential, can allow minority (and possibly stigmatised) groups to become more vocal, visible and accessible as participants for research. Interestingly, the researchers report that after a paper they had published on compulsive fantasising became available online, they were contacted by a number of individuals seeking advice and help on their own related experiences. This led to the present study. The researchers note: 'members of our study sample are representative of a self-concealed population that has only recently revealed itself via the anonymity of the Internet; and thus has not been previously recognized by the research and mental health communities' (p. 1635). This demonstrates how the Internet can facilitate research with specialist, hidden populations.

Web-based survey approaches may also offer enhanced data quality over offline approaches, particularly postal surveys, due to their being able to implement reliability checks, such as response completeness and format prompting. However, they also have potential disadvantages. Concerns over the representativeness of Internet-accessed samples have been voiced. While the IUP has clearly expanded and diversified a great deal over the last 10 years, reliable sampling methods which can allow generalisation to a national (or similarly broad) population have not yet been well established (though some encouraging results have been achieved;

see Chapter 4). A further potential issue for web-based surveys (though some similar concerns arise in relation to offline postal surveys) is the lower levels of researcher control compared with offline methods. Possible procedural variations due to technological (hardware and software) issues is one potential source of reduced control, although recent technological developments, and present-day software solutions, have helped address this issue. Not being able to monitor survey respondents' behaviours, due to the lack of physical proximity (Are they intoxicated? Multi-tasking? Who they say they are? and so on), creates another source of reduced control. On this point, it has been noted that in IMR a level of trust of participants will always be needed (Hewson, 2003). Situations where richer cues are available (e.g. a structured survey interview using Skype) may alleviate these concerns somewhat.

IMR Validation Studies

Reassuringly, despite the above caveats, there is now a substantial body of research indicating that IMR studies can generate data of comparable quality to that generated by offline methods. A common approach in survey and questionnaire research has been to compare equivalent implementations in both offline and online modes. For example, studies have tested the validity of web-administered psychometric scales by comparing their psychometric properties and norms with those when the same scales are administered offline, the typical finding being equivalence (e.g. Brock, Barry, Lawrence, Dey, & Rolffs, 2012; Hewson & Charlton, 2005; Kosinski et al., 2003; Riva, Teruzzi, & Anolli, 2003; Weigold, Weigold, & Russell, 2013). Similar approaches in non-psychometric contexts have compared response patterns, relationships between variables, effects of demographic factors (e.g. gender), and so on, also often finding equivalence (e.g. Best, Krueger, Hubbard, & Smith, 2001; Birnbaum, 1999; Epstein, Klinkenberg, Wiley, & McKinley, 2001; Stephenson & Crete, 2010). Though far fewer, there have also been some reports of non-equivalence between online and offline administrations (e.g. Barbeite & Weiss, 2004; Davis, 1999; Fouladi, McCarthy, & Moller, 2002). However, it is not always clear that these findings lead to the conclusion that the online data are inferior. Further research will help clarify the nature of such observed differences. Hewson and Charlton (2005) note that studies finding a lack of equivalence have tended to use multidimensional rather than unidimensional psychometric scales, but in their own validation of the Multidimensional Health Locus of Control Scale (Wallston & Wallston, 1981) they found equivalence of online and offline administrations. Box 3.4 describes this example, taken from our own research, as an illustration of an IMR validation study.

BOX 3.4   Featured Research: Hewson and Charlton (2005)

Method

A comparison of offline (pen and paper) and online (web-based survey) administrations of the Multidimensional Health Locus of Control (MHLC) Scale (Wallston & Wallston, 1981) was carried out in order to assess the robustness of the MHLC Scale when delivered online. Offline participants consisted of 200 respondents recruited from undergraduate students at the start of lectures and members of the general public (convenience sample). The Internet sample ($n = 167$) was recruited by posting invitations to a selection of newsgroups, asking interested parties to visit a webpage link in order to view and complete the questionnaire.

Results

The Internet sample was found to be more balanced in terms of sex and age than the offline sample and displayed higher representation in the high-earning, highly educated, and professional and IT-related occupation categories. The Internet sample was more diverse in nationality. Scale reliabilities (Chronbach's alpha) and factor structures were found to be at least as good for the Internet as for the offline data. MHLC scores were comparable for paper and Internet administrations, although the Internet sample scored significantly lower on the Powerful Others subscale (indicating a lower tendency to attribute one's state of health to 'powerful others'). Comparing this result with existing norms, the most parsimonious explanation is that the higher socioeconomic status of the Internet sample could account for this finding (this factor having been found to produce similar results in previous studies). Overall, MHLC scores observed in the present study were comparable with previously established norms.

Conclusions

The authors conclude that, overall, the results show administration of the MHLC Scale via the Internet can produce data comparable with those obtained by pen and paper methods. However, it is also concluded that generalisation of these findings beyond the psychometric test instrument and sampling procedures used here is not warranted. Further such studies are needed to determine whether IMR methods can produce results comparable with offline methods in different contexts.

Comment

This study shows how comparing offline and online administrations of a psychometric scale can help determine whether IMR methods are able to produce results equivalent to those obtained offline. Both scale properties and scale norms can be compared in this way. Such validation studies are important in determining whether different IMR methods and instruments can produce valid, reliable data, comparable with data obtained using offline methods.

Some studies which have found a lack of mode (online versus offline) effect have used equivalent samples, such as undergraduate students randomly assigned to either online or offline administration modes (e.g. Epstein et al., 2001; Herrero & Meneses, 2006), rather than use Internet-based sampling methods (for the online mode) as was done by Hewson and Charlton (2005). However, we would question how useful such designs are in assessing the validity of IMR methods, which would seem most beneficial when participants are recruited via the Internet. It cannot be assumed that mode equivalences demonstrated using random assignment from the same sample to each mode will generalise to these more naturalistic IMR contexts where both mode and sampling method vary. Given the mostly positive results to date, in terms of comparability of IMR and traditional methods, we would argue that the most fruitful direction for validation studies (and the most efficient use of research resources) is to use Internet-accessed samples in such comparisons. Most validation studies have adopted this approach.

Enhanced Anonymity of Web-Based Surveys

A noteworthy feature of the Internet is the scope it offers for maintaining high levels of anonymity (e.g. for participants and/or researchers) while also enabling high degrees of interactivity. Modern web-based survey methods can support degrees of flexibility and functionality (e.g. question-tailoring based on previous responses; answer-format checking; incorporation of video and audio; etc.) while also ensuring complete anonymity for participants. Offline methods cannot achieve this, since postal methods, which can allow for high degrees of anonymity, lack the same flexibility and functionality. Face-to-face (FTF) survey methods, on the other hand, support flexibility but reduce levels of anonymity. As we have previously speculated (e.g. Hewson et al., 1996) this might make web-based survey methods unique in some respects, such as their potential for reducing biases due to perceptions of biosocial attributes, or researcher demand characteristics, while maintaining desired levels of interactivity and flexibility. This could enhance opportunities for gathering data with high levels of candour, and perhaps facilitate disclosure of sensitive, personal information. There is some evidence that computer-mediated communication (CMC) contexts can lead to higher levels of self-disclosure than FTF contexts (e.g. Bargh, McKenna, & Fitzsimons, 2002; Joinson, 2001; Joinson & Payne, 2007). Also, there is evidence that such effects may be constrained to *visually anonymous* CMC settings (Joinson, 2001). Further investigations on this topic would be informative, and potentially relevant to IMR survey methods.

Future Directions

So far, we have considered some existing examples of survey and questionnaire methods in IMR, and highlighted some of the benefits, and caveats, which emerge.

Validation studies have demonstrated that high-quality data can be obtained using a range of IMR survey designs, across a variety of disciplines and research domains. Considering future possibilities, a number of promising avenues seem noteworthy. The emergence and increasingly widespread ownership of smart phones and other mobile Internet-connected devices create opportunities for contacting participants on the move, which can support mobile surveys and approaches using ongoing continuous or time-sampled measurement (Vehovar & Manfreda, 2008). The latter, for example, might involve prompting participants when a response is required by sending an audio alert to their smart phone, and providing either a link to survey questions or some other means of responding. The 'Mappiness' project (see http://www.mappiness.org.uk/ [accessed August 2014]) is an example of this approach, in which participants (anyone with an iPhone can take part by visiting the above link, at the time of writing) download a smart phone app which bleeps daily to prompt them to report on their current level of happiness, and answer some additional questions (where they are, who they are with, etc.). Taking advantage of such possibilities (which some researchers have already started to do) may lead to innovations in survey research, which were not previously easily achievable using offline methods. These may include immersion in real-life contexts and physical locations as an integral feature of survey design, allowing participants to provide responses when situated in a particular specified setting. Additional contextual information (e.g. geolocation data, multimedia data) may also be collected (the aforementioned Mappiness project allows participants to upload pictures of their current location). Benefits arising from such approaches might include less reliance on recalled information, scope for collecting richer response data (pictures, videos, spoken word, etc.), enhanced possibilities for examining context effects, and so on.

Innovations in survey research arising from Internet technologies may lead to blurred boundaries between surveys and other methods (additional to those that occur for offline methods). The possibility of a 'virtual survey interviewer' has been mentioned (e.g. Vehovar & Manfreda, 2008). This could potentially incorporate multimedia features, using graphics, video, audio and perhaps language and speech recognition software (e.g. Couper, 2005). Fuchs (2009) has piloted the use of video recordings of interviewers to administer survey questions (about relationships and sexual behaviours) to participants, noting that gender-of-interviewer effects occurred, similar to those found in proximal FTF contexts. The use of audio and video technologies could also enable real-time survey interviews with a live human researcher to be carried out. Such approaches might blur the boundaries between survey and interview approaches. The distinction between survey and observation methods might also become blurred, in approaches incorporating multimedia and on-the-move response features (geolocation information, audio and video recordings, and so on). This could potentially lead to new ways of conceptualising and categorising social and behavioural research methods. Perhaps these types of innovations will enhance and facilitate mixed methods research. It is certainly conceivable that IMR approaches may facilitate the simultaneous collection of both quantitative and qualitative data within a single research study (for discussions of mixed methods research in IMR, and some examples, see Hesse-Biber & Griffin, 2013; Hewson, 2008). As researchers continue to try out these various possibilities in survey-based IMR, their scope and benefits will become clearer.

INTERVIEWS AND FOCUS GROUPS

One of the intriguing features of the Internet, as already noted, is its ability to facilitate fairly sophisticated levels of interaction while enabling high levels of anonymity (due to reduced visual and extralinguistic cues). This feature becomes particularly relevant and interesting in relation to online interview approaches, since in traditional offline interviews the interviewee and interviewer are typically physically present in an FTF setting. In an IMR interview, even when using real-time synchronous contexts (e.g. online chat software), the whole process can be conducted with each conversational partner knowing little or nothing about the other's physical and biosocial attributes. While early accounts (including our own in the first edition of this book) speculated on what this might mean for online interview approaches, a body of evidence is now available from researchers who have used this method. Qualitative researchers conducting online interviews have generally strived to overcome the more detached, anonymous nature of online interactions, for example by devising carefully constructed techniques for establishing rapport (such as the use of personal disclosure; Madge & O'Connor, 2002). Such strategies contrast with our own early speculations that highly anonymous, richly interactive settings might be beneficial in helping reduce biases normally present in offline FTF interactions. Here, we draw upon the experiences of online interview researchers to consider how the online medium might impact upon levels of candour, establishing rapport, depth and reflexivity, and data integrity and quality in IMR interviews.

Levels of Candour

The idea that online forms of communication might encourage more candid responses and greater disclosure is of interest in the context of online interview methods. Joinson (2005) suggests that visual anonymity enhances identification with a group by increasing the perceived homogeneity of the group, and that this can reduce inhibitions and increase levels of candour due to a reduction in the social cost of disclosure. Reports from online interviewers have supported the idea that candour can be enhanced, and inhibitions reduced, in this medium (e.g. Madge & O'Connor, 2002; Murray & Sixsmith, 1998). For example, Madge and O'Connor report that their online synchronous discussion group interviewees (mothers with young children) displayed a lack of inhibition that the researchers felt would not have been shown in an FTF context. The suggestion that enhanced candour and self-disclosure effects may be constrained to visually anonymous CMC contexts (Joinson, 2001) has implications for the use of video in online interviews. Video interview approaches have not been well used to date, and are currently hindered by issues of low reliability and poor image quality. Whether such approaches might lead to lower levels of candour and disclosure remains largely to be explored. For the time being, issues related to choppy video and low-quality audio are likely to impede the flow and quality of an online interview using this approach.

Establishing Rapport

While there is some evidence that heightened levels of anonymity associated with many online communication contexts (i.e. text-based) can enhance disclosures of personal and sensitive information, establishing good rapport with participants has also traditionally been considered important for obtaining rich, candid qualitative interview data (e.g. Barratt, 2012). However, high levels of anonymity seem unlikely to be very helpful for establishing good rapport. Indeed, the types of techniques that have been adopted in attempting to establish good rapport with participants have used strategies aimed at reducing anonymity and enhancing levels of personal disclosure and engagement (e.g. Madge & O'Connor, 2002). Thus, trade-offs seem to emerge here. Barriers to rapport have been identified as a lack of proximal contact, and reduced extralinguistic cues, in online interview settings (e.g. Jowett et al., 2011; O'Connor, Madge, Shaw, & Wellens, 2008; Orgad, 2006). Strategies to overcome these barriers have thus been considered an important part of IMR interview design (Barratt, 2012; Bowker & Tuffin, 2004; Gaiser, 1997; Madge & O'Connor, 2002). In general, rapport-building strategies have worked well and led to acquiring rich, elaborate, high-quality data. Researchers reporting poor levels of rapport have generally not taken steps to implement clear, explicit, rapport-building strategies (e.g. Strickland, Moloney, Dietrich, Myerburg, Cotsonis, & Johnson, 2003). Thus it would seem that careful planning of rapport-building strategies is important in IMR interview methods. Jowett and colleagues (2011) also point out that, in IMR, rapport building should be treated as an ongoing process which requires attention throughout the interview. One caveat, however, emerges from a comment made by Madge and O'Connor (2002) who explain that their strategy of posting up photographs of themselves as part of the rapport-building process might have influenced the interview process by encouraging 'white 30-something women' to feel more comfortable talking to them than other groups. This is a consideration worth bearing in mind, depending on the study context and target sample.

Depth and Reflexivity

The extent to which depth and reflexivity can be achieved in an IMR interview (a common goal in qualitative interview research) has emerged as a question due to the 'impoverished' communication medium. That is, text-based exchanges lack extralinguistic information present in FTF interactions (tone of voice, body language, etc.). Asynchronous IMR approaches, such as using email, may better facilitate reflexive, detailed responses due to their extended, more relaxed time-scale, compared with synchronous approaches (e.g. using online chat). Thus in an email interview participants can respond as and when they please, enabling time for reflection. Asynchronous approaches alleviate the immediate pressure of needing to provide a quick response, which is present in traditional FTF settings and synchronous IMR approaches (O'Connor et al., 2008). Researchers using asynchronous IMR approaches often report obtaining rich, reflective qualitative data (e.g. Bowker & Tuffin, 2004; Kenny, 2005; McDermott & Roen, 2012; Murray & Sixsmith, 1998). Less successful reports tend to have used synchronous approaches (e.g. Bowker & Tuffin, 2004; Davis, Bolding, Hart, Sherr, & Elford, 2004). It has been noted that 'online chat' has a reputation for being rather playful, flippant and less serious than other online conversational contexts (e.g. Davis et al., 2004; Gaiser, 1997). However, some researchers have nevertheless reported obtaining rich, detailed data using synchronous approaches – for example, Barratt (2012), who conducted one-to-one synchronous interviews with young drug users, and O'Connor and Madge (2001), who carried out synchronous online focus groups with new parents (primarily mothers). Thus, it does seem possible to achieve rich, high-quality data using synchronous technologies. Both Barratt (2012) and O'Connor and Madge (2001) devised careful rapport-building strategies, in which they engaged in personal disclosure to try and establish good levels of interpersonal connection with their participants, prior to commencing the interviews. Thus, as noted earlier, this seems to be an important factor for success. Experience in using online synchronous communication technologies (for both participants and researchers) may also be a relevant factor (Barratt, 2012). Bowker and Tuffin (2004) compared both synchronous and asynchronous IMR interview approaches, and report that the latter was better able to generate rich, elaborate data.

One important beneficial feature of asynchronous approaches may be the ability to look back over the discussion, which might help encourage reflexivity, compared with either synchronous online, or offline FTF, approaches (e.g. Hewson, 2007). However, the greater opportunity for reflection in asynchronous interview approaches has also been noted as a possible disadvantage, since a response that has been so well considered might produce a 'socially desirable' answer, rather than a more genuine, spontaneous one (Gaiser, 2008; O'Connor et al., 2008). However, an alternative point of view is that 'gut' responses may be likely to conform to accepted, socially desirable norms, while more reflective, considered responses might be more truthful and honest. We are not aware of research findings which directly explore this issue. A further possible disadvantage of asynchronous approaches is that they may hinder conversational 'flow', and reduce the coherence and continuity of an interview conversation. This might particularly affect focus group approaches, where participants will come in to comment on particular themes, topics and threads at different times (Gaiser, 2008). However, synchronous approaches may also be subject to issues related to reduced flow, due to the need for proficiency with this relatively new communication medium, including familiarity with relevant technologies, typing dexterity, and so on. Gaiser (2008) has also pointed out that a researcher may be faced with additional challenges when attempting to moderate an online asynchronous focus group discussion, compared with a synchronous discussion, since it will not be practicable to be present the whole time. This issue may be further compounded when a focus group contains participants from geographically diverse locations.

Data Integrity and Quality

As well as the levels of depth, reflexivity, candour and rapport that can be achieved in IMR interviews, other factors may affect the integrity and quality of data obtained. One issue concerns how to avoid misunderstandings, and detect disingenuous or deceptive responses, given the lack of extralinguistic cues available which are present, and informative, in FTF contexts. The enhanced scope for deception online has been a popular theme (e.g. see Epstein, 2007: http://www.scientificamerican.com/article.cfm?id=the-truth-about-online-da [accessed October 2014]). Deliberate intentions to deceive may be unlikely to occur in an online interview context, participants having volunteered their time and commitment, and likely being keen to offer their own genuine insights and experiences on the topic at hand. The experiences of IMR interview researchers to date indicate this to be the case (e.g. Barratt, 2012; Madge & O'Connor, 2002). It should also not be forgotten that determining the authenticity of interview data is an ongoing challenge in offline research. Genuine misunderstandings and conversational ambiguities might be more likely to occur in an IMR context, however, and researchers have sometimes reported this to be the case (e.g. Davis et al., 2004, who conducted synchronous interviews using online chat).

Multimedia approaches which use audio and video might help to reduce the chance of such misunderstandings, at least when the relevant technologies have evolved to allow better quality output and levels of reliability. Hanna (2012) reports using Skype to conduct interviews, and concludes that despite some 'technical hitches' the approach has potential where a closer approximation to FTF interviews is desired, and may be beneficial in offering a greater level of control to participants than offline FTF contexts since the intrusiveness of the researcher into the interviewee's personal space is reduced. This could potentially lead to a more equal relationship between 'researcher' and 'researched' (Hanna, 2012), with possible implications for data quality. The use of emoticons (e.g. :-)) and acronyms (e.g. ROTFL: Rolling On The Floor Laughing) might help to disambiguate what might otherwise be ambiguous written text, in non-multimedia contexts. These extralinguistic devices tend to be more often used in synchronous than asynchronous communications.

Overall, while there have been a number of successful examples of online interview approaches, this IMR method has not taken off in quite the same way as survey and questionnaire methods. Researchers have been particularly reluctant to follow up on the early pioneering examples of *synchronous* online interview approaches (O'Connor et al., 2008). This may in part be due to reports of limited success, and perhaps also because of the additional time and effort required in setting up the technical aspects for a synchronous interview, compared with using email, for example (O'Connor et al., 2008). Given the goals of qualitative researchers, and particularly the emphasis on obtaining rich, reflective personal narratives, it is perhaps not surprising that there has been a reluctance to engage with IMR interview methods, which may seem impersonal and detached compared with traditional FTF contexts. However, considering the experiences of researchers who *have* engaged with IMR interview approaches, it is clear that rich, intimate, personal exchanges can occur online. Some of the benefits that an IMR approach can offer are also appealing. These include access to participants who may otherwise be excluded, such as those not living within a reasonable travelling distance of the research site, or participants with time and/or mobility constraints (such as the new mothers interviewed by Madge & O'Connor, 2002). IMR approaches can also facilitate access to other hard-to-reach groups, such as the young drug users interviewed by Barratt (2012). When considering sampling and accessibility issues, the synchronous–asynchronous distinction becomes relevant. Asynchronous approaches are generally better able to facilitate participation by widely geographically dispersed participants, especially in focus group research. They may also be most suitable when participants with limited typing dexterity are involved, as well as those who cannot dedicate a block of time to attend a 'live' synchronous session (see Chapter 6 for further discussion of design considerations and strategies). Research on sensitive topics might also benefit from IMR interview approaches, due to the possible effects of enhanced candour in online communication contexts.

Future Directions

Looking to the future of IMR interview methods, video-based approaches are bound to become more feasible as the associated technologies become more reliable (Fielding & Macintyre, 2006; Gaiser, 2008; O'Connor et al., 2008). These may offer the closest approximation to traditional offline FTF methods. As the user base of these technologies expands (which it no doubt will due to the benefits offered; for example, Skype allows users with a good Internet bandwidth to enjoy free calls to any country in the world), so does the pool of potential participants for video-based interview research in IMR. The expansion in the availability and use of mobile technologies (smart phones, tablets, etc.) also has potential for impacting upon the direction of IMR interview methods. As discussed in relation to survey-based approaches, enhanced opportunities for creating *in situ*, immersive settings, using real-time geolocation information, incorporating multimedia technologies to gather richer data, and so on, emerge. Such possibilities may support innovative techniques such as 'walking interviews' (e.g. Jones, Bunce, Evans, Gibbs, & Hein, 2008) and 'visual methods' (e.g. Bagnoli, 2009), for example.

Other possibilities include using online virtual reality environments (VREs) such as Second Life (see Chapter 6) as a platform for conducting 'virtual face to face' interviews and/or focus groups (Gaiser, 2008). Such developments could imaginably start to resolve issues related to the reduced flow and/or greater difficulty in establishing rapport in current IMR approaches. Stewart and Williams (2005) (citing Williams, 2003) discuss an attempt at implementing an online focus group in a virtual graphical environment, using avatars. Discussions took place in an open field, which was set up as a virtual private space for research purposes. Finally, while some researchers have strived to create online interview contexts which mimic as closely as possible the processes of offline FTF settings (e.g. James & Busher, 2006),[2] for which approaches using video or VREs might hold most promise, others have questioned whether this is the most effective strategy for IMR methods (O'Connor et al., 2008). Rather, it may be more useful for researchers to think about alternative, creative and novel ways in which IMR approaches might best support and enhance interview research. The value of combining both online and offline interview methods should also not be overlooked. This may allow researchers to reap the benefits of each approach. Indeed, comparison of data obtained from offline and online modes is a research topic in its own right. However, some researchers have expressed concerns about the use of both online and offline interview methods (as done by James & Busher, 2006; Orgad, 2006; Sanders, 2005), arguing that this strategy perpetuates the unhelpful view that online interviews are not credible as stand-alone methods (O'Connor et al., 2008). Such comparisons are nevertheless of value if framed within a context of exploring commonalities and differences between online and offline methods.

OBSERVATION STUDIES

The distinction between observation and document analysis methods can some-times become blurred in IMR, as noted earlier, but a useful working definition is that observation involves looking at *behaviours* and *interactions* (whether these be

---

[2]Though, interestingly, James and Busher (2006) used asynchronous email interviews in striving to achieve this goal.

traces of these, such as discussion group archives, or live in real time), and document analysis involves looking at static, published documents and media placed on the Internet as an authored, final product (e.g. a published article, webpage, song, photo album, a virtual exhibition of an artist's works, or the virtual tours of museum collections as discussed in Chapter 2). Another way to think about the distinction is that observation approaches consider the *processes* of online interaction that individuals engage in, while document analysis considers the final products they generate. Previous working definitions seem too narrow in today's IMR context; for example, Hewson (2007) suggests that online observational research 'uses logs of interactions (typically verbal exchanges) between participants, as opposed to document analysis which makes use of static records constructed specifically for the purpose of dissemination via the Internet, and whose primary purpose is not to facilitate an ongoing dialogue-type communication between individuals' (p. 416). However, not all online observational research uses logs, since it can also be conducted in real time. Also, online observational research may now draw upon a wealth of data sources and materials which extend beyond 'verbal' exchanges. Our working definition proposed here is quite broad, but serves to focus the present discussion without excluding any of the observational approaches we wish to cover.

Referring back to Figure 3.1, observational approaches span the obtrusive–unobtrusive dimension most broadly. Here, we discuss a range of approaches, including those which make use of primarily linguistic data and those that move beyond linguistic data.

Linguistic Observation

Discussion Group Archives. Observation of text-based sources using unobtrusive, non-participant approaches (a least obtrusive design) can proceed by accessing online linguistic discussion group *archives* (discussed further in Chapter 6). This approach opens up opportunities for searching and locating topic-specific content quickly and cheaply. Bordia (1996) used this approach to locate instances of rumour transmission using Usenet, Internet and Bitnet far more easily than is possible using offline methods. Brady and Guerin (2010) collected discussion board posts, covering a two-week period, from archives of a parenting support group website, and subjected these to qualitative analysis. In many respects such unobtrusive linguistic observation techniques in IMR are unique, and do not have offline equivalents, since offline conversations are not so readily recorded, stored and easily searched for topic-specific content. The closest offline equivalent may be to use corpora, such as the British National Corpus (BNC; see www.natcorp. ox.ac.uk [accessed October 2014]) – a large, searchable database of written documents and spoken language sources, including both formal (e.g. radio shows) and informal (unscripted dialogues recorded by volunteers) conversations. Traditional corpora derived from offline sources are unlikely to offer the breadth, diversity and scope of online traces of human conversational interactions, however. For the most part, readily accessible online archives involve asynchronous communications, synchronous conversations being less likely to be automatically recorded.

Asynchronous 'Live' Discussion Groups. An alternative to accessing stored archives is to follow asynchronous discussions in 'real time', by logging on regularly and collecting posts as they appear. Since online asynchronous communications occur over an extended time period, and it is not practicable for a researcher to be constantly online monitoring a discussion, date and time stamps are useful to show the time any individual post was made. Such information is also available in stored archives, of course, but one advantage of following an asynchronous discussion as it unfolds in real time is the scope for participant observation. Further, it is more likely to be possible to gain consent from participants of a live, active forum (archived discussions might involve participants who have since left, even if the forum itself is still active). Fox, Ward, and O'Rourke (2005) conducted a participant observation on a pro-anorexia website, participating in discussions on message boards (posting up questions) and engaging in personal exchanges with individuals who contacted them directly. They fully disclosed their role as researchers. Brotsky and Giles (2007) carried out a similar participant observation, but without disclosure. One researcher joined a selection of pro-anorexia websites, posing as a plausible persona and taking part in discussions, in an attempt to gain insights into the beliefs, perceptions and behaviours of group members. Aho, Paavilainen, and Kaunonen (2012) adopted a non-participant observation approach. After disclosing their intentions as researchers, and obtaining consent from group members, they carried out a longitudinal qualitative study (over five years) of mothers' experiences after the death of a child, by collecting messages unobtrusively from a private Internet support group website.

Participant observation approaches, such as those just mentioned, can support ethnographic IMR, or 'virtual ethnography' (Hine, 2000; see also Markham, 1998). Here the researcher aims to become 'immersed' in a target community. See Hine (2008) for a more up-to-date overview of virtual ethnography methods.[3] Examples of the approach include Ward (1999), who carried out interviews and observations within two feminist online communities, and Baym (2000), who used participant observation, online surveys and interviews, and systematic message content analysis. A more recent example is presented by Tackett-Gibson (2008) who studied online communities engaged in exchanging drug use information. Interestingly, Tackett-Gibson reports that intentions to disclose the research fully were blocked by moderators, who gave permission only to lurk and carry out observations unobtrusively, and access stored archives. One argument for non-disclosure is to avoid disrupting existing online social structures. As these examples

---

[3]Recent accounts have emphasised the importance of also considering participants' offline lives in 'virtual ethnography' approaches, as well as questioning whether virtual ethnography actually brings any 'radical methodological innovation' to the ethnographic methods (e.g. Hine, 2008).

demonstrate, online ethnographers have drawn on a range of methods, including online surveys, interviews, observation techniques, and use of existing documents, to gather data within a single research study. For further discussion of such mixed and multi-methods approaches in IMR, and their potential benefits, see Hewson (2008) and Hesse-Biber and Griffin (2013). For a discussion of 'Netnography' – originally conceived of as online ethnographic research in a consumer and marketing context[4] – see Kozinets (2002); for some recent examples, see Björk and Kauppinen-Räisänen (2012) and Rageh, Melewar, and Woodside (2013).

Web 2.0 and Social Media Technologies. Web 2.0 technologies open up possibilities for unobtrusive linguistic observation approaches which go beyond using the rather earlier (but still enduring) Internet newsgroup and discussion forum technologies discussed above. For example, Tonkin, Pfeiffer, and Tourte (2012) analysed 600,000 tweets on the August 2012 riots in the United Kingdom, looking for evidence that Twitter served as a central organisational tool to promote illegal group action (which the authors report finding not to be the case). Moreno et al. (2011) carried out an observational study on Facebook by analysing the status updates of 200 undergraduate students who had public profiles, in order to look for evidence of depressive symptoms. These examples demonstrate the blurred boundaries that can emerge between observation and document analysis methods in IMR. What constitutes an interaction or a document online can be ambiguous, as can what is labelled an 'archive' or 'live', real-time interaction. It is the ongoing logging of traces of online interactions and activities on a massive scale that creates these ambiguities, which does not occur in the same way in offline contexts. Blogs[5] present a good illustration; starting off primarily as frequently updated, text-based, personal diaries published online (typically in the public domain), they later came to include more interactive, multimedia elements, including commentaries and contributions by various people other than the author. Nowadays, blogs are often viewed as more dynamic and interactive multimedia social spaces (e.g. Wakeford & Cohen, 2008). Herring, Scheidt, Bonus, and Wright (2005) point out, however, that blogs now appear in many diverse forms, existing on a continuum between standard HTML documents and asynchronous CMCs (such as newsgroups). They argue that the recent characterisation of blogs as interactive, fluid, eclectic and outwardly focused has been exaggerated; in their analysis of around 200 blogs they found less evidence of the blogs being externally focused than intimate, individualistic forms of self-expression (Herring et al., 2005). Halavais (2006) has described blogs as 'thinking-in-progress' (perhaps implying avenues for supporting IMR in some areas of cognitive psychology). Wakeford and Cohen (2008) discuss the use of blogs as

---

[4]Though the term has also been used more broadly (e.g. Janta, Lugosi, & Brown, 2012).

[5]Note that the term 'blog' is short for 'web log', but that the latter can also mean a 'log' of server activity (the latter not the intended meaning here).

spaces for placing field notes, during an ongoing study. Existing examples of blog analysis in IMR include Marcus, Westra, Eastwood, & Barnes' (2012) unobtrusive qualitative analysis of blogs of young adults with mental health concerns. In an attempt to gain an unbiased understanding of young adults' experiences, they report acquiring rich, informative data which offered important insights into young peoples' mental health experiences. Clarke and van Ameron (2008) conducted a qualitative analysis of the blogs of 45 men and 45 women who self-identified as depressed, and likewise gained useful data. Fullwood, Sheehan, and Nicholls (2009) conducted a content analysis of MySpace blogs, with the aim of examining the purpose, format and style of these compared with blogs from other blogging-dedicated sites. Again this study was reported to be successful. Blogs, then, provide a valuable potential source of data in IMR.

Synchronous Discussions. Observational IMR approaches, including ethnographic approaches, may also observe *synchronous* live discussions in real time. This approach, on the face of it, seems more likely to require disclosure than accessing asynchronous archives, or even following asynchronous discussions in 'real time'. Particularly in small groups, where lurking is unlikely to go unnoticed, disclosure would seem appropriate. However, some researchers have reported lurking and observing synchronous discussions without implementing any explicit disclosure or consent procedures, but without encountering any reported problems (e.g. Al-Sa'Di and Haman, 2005; Rodino, 1997). On the other hand, other researchers have presented evidence that lurking *can* be problematic, though disclosure has not necessarily proved any more helpful in resolving the difficulties encountered. Thus Hudson and Bruckman (2004) conducted a quantitative study in which they observed responses of chat room participants to disclosures of observation intent (recording the discussion) by researchers, compared with reactions to undisclosed entry and lurking. Hostility was experienced in both cases and these researchers report often being kicked out, though interestingly this happened less often when merely entering and lurking than when explicitly requesting permission. Hudson and Bruckman conclude that disclosure when using such observational methods in IMR may thus be untenable, and detrimental to a research project. However, it should be noted that Hudson and Bruckman made no attempt to engage with participants in any way that resembles the types of good-practice strategies for establishing rapport that were noted earlier as having been successful in online interview and focus group research (such as used by O'Connor & Madge, 2001). A number of researchers to date have reported successfully carrying out observations of online synchronous chat (e.g. Panyametheekul & Herring, 2003; Rollman, Krug, & Parente, 2000; Subrahmanyam, Greenfield, & Tynes, 2004). Both participant and non-participant observation approaches seem viable when following synchronous, live discussions. The choice made will affect the level of obtrusiveness of the study (participant approaches being more obtrusive).

Beyond Linguistic Observation

Social Media Websites. Web 2.0 has enhanced opportunities for observation of interactive behaviours online, including approaches incorporating multimedia. Thus, expanded social networking and sharing opportunities which incorporate audio, images and video have emerged. While these resources (Facebook, Twitter, Blogger, and so on; see also the list in Chapter 2) provide rich opportunities for collecting linguistic data, as discussed above, many also provide rich opportunities for collecting data which go beyond pure text. Several researchers have used multimedia sharing websites, such as YouTube (e.g. Frohlich & Zmyslinski-Seelig, 2012; Thelwall, Sud, & Vis, 2012), with a focus on either analysis of textual data (e.g. comments about shared YouTube videos), or the multimedia content itself. For example, Yoo and Kim (2012) carried out a content analysis of YouTube videos, analysing 417 obesity videos in order to explore how topics of obesity are framed, and how obese people are portrayed. Facebook has been a well-used source of data for observational studies; for example, Zhao, Grasmuck, and Martin (2008) examined identity construction on Facebook by carrying out a content analysis of 63 individual Facebook accounts (though much of their analysis did focus on text-based material as well as pictures that users posted on their profiles). In an analysis of 412 published studies which conducted research on Facebook (from journals and conference proceedings), from a range of disciplines, Wilson, Gosling, and Graham (2012) identify five categories of study type (ordered from most to least frequently occurring): the role of Facebook in social interactions (27%); descriptive analyses of users (24%); privacy and information disclosure (18%); motivations for using Facebook (19%); identity presentation (12%). Other SNSs have also been used to source multimedia, as well as linguistic, data; for example, McCreanor, Lyons, Griffin, Goodwin, Moewaka Barnes, and Hutton (2013) conducted an analysis of the way in which SNSs have been used by alcohol marketing agencies to promote advertising campaigns for their products, considering the role of such networking sites in promoting and supporting youth drinking cultures.

Virtual Reality Environments. Observational IMR researchers have also used VREs (also called MUVEs: Multi-User Virtual Environments) including those that support gaming applications (e.g. Massively Multiplayer Online Games: MMOGs). Such online interactive graphic environments (often 3D) where users (or players) interact with each other in a 'virtual world' hold intriguing possibilities for a variety of IMR methods, including observational and ethnographic research. Schroeder and Bailenson (2008) present a review of IMR approaches using MUVEs (which they describe as 'technologies that allow users to interact via digital representations of themselves in a virtual place or space', p. 227). Most of their examples are from computer science and educational contexts, and tend to use experimental designs. Indeed, one of the advantages of MUVEs is the scope for controlled manipulation of a range of parameters. Bainbridge (2007) also provides a discussion of the scope and opportunities for VRE research, highlighting the potential for supporting ethnographic and interview methods. An early example of VRE research is Givaty et al.'s (1998) study on visual cognition, where participants (recruited via the Internet) were asked to navigate around a 3D virtual environment – which had been set up specifically for the experiment – and then recreate the location of various objects in that environment on a 2D map. Givaty, var Vaan, Chirstou, and Bulthoff (1998) explain how the IMR approach was able to facilitate access to a much larger sample size than is typically possible in this area using offline laboratory methods, leading, they argue, to potentially more valid results. Another early example is reported by Kendall (2002) who carried out an ethnographic study within an MUD (Multi-User Dungeon) environment. More recently, Williams (2007) describes an ethnographic study conducted in the graphical world *Cyberworlds*, where he was able to collect detailed field notes by observing avatars. Williams highlights the advantage (compared with offline methods) of being able readily to record field notes covertly during the observation period. For further discussion of the scope for gathering research data in virtual worlds, see Ross, Castronova, and Wagner (2012). Chapter 6, in this volume, discusses some of the different design choices, and their pros and cons.

Observing Structures and Processes. As well as methods accessing and analysing content found on the Web, or using experimental designs (as discussed above), the observation and analysis of structures and processes in online interaction are noteworthy. Couper (2005) talks about 'paradata' (also referred to as 'metadata') in the context of survey-based approaches; paradata is information about the completion process (e.g. how long was spent on each page or question, which pages were revisited, and so on). Automatic logging of paradata can usefully supplement survey responses. In observational IMR paradata can become primary data. Thus, it is possible to look at webpage navigations, Google searches, social network links (who is friends with who), and so on. For example, online social network analysis (SNA) studies the links which exist between people and groups online (e.g. who has messaged who, and how often, who has befriended who on Facebook, 'liked' or shared another's posts, commented on status updates, etc.). Hogan (2008) discusses SNA approaches in IMR, explaining that essentially these methods adapt principles from offline SNA to an online medium. Thus online SNA is fundamentally concerned with discovering information about the movement, structural properties and relationships of online social groups and communities. Graphical network visualisations are often used to represent the outcomes of SNA (see Hogan, 2008; also the examples available at www. visualcomplexity.com). Now that 'a growing segment of the social world is self-documenting and self-archiving in machine-readable form' (Wesler, Smith, Fisher, & Gleave, 2008, p. 117), online SNA seems a promising area of future development. One drawback of online SNA is that it is less easy to implement than some other IMR methods (e.g. interviews and surveys), requiring more technically advanced data scraping techniques, involving the use of scripting languages, for example. A compelling feature of the approach, however, which may make seeking the required technical support worthwhile, is the ability to capture many weak ties, creating links that a person may otherwise not have remembered in a traditional offline self-reported study (Hogan, 2008). Of course, online social networks are also a legitimate field of enquiry in their own right, so of interest for this reason.

Since data traces obtained using unobtrusive data mining techniques, such as those used in SNA, may potentially include contributions from thousands, millions or billions of individual users, obtaining consent may be practically implausible, or impossible (see Chapter 5 for further discussion of ethical issues in unobtrusive research). One approach to addressing the ethical issues this raises is to collect data while also providing a valuable service to those who contribute the data. Locket and Blackman (2004) present such an example, in a marketing research context. They wanted to collect data on foreign exchange charges made by credit card companies to business travellers. Rather than try and collect the data using survey methods, they developed an online Travel Expenses Calculator (www. xe.com/tec) and Credit Card Charges Calculator (www.xe.com/ccc) which allowed business travellers to calculate the cost of a business trip in their own currency. They made these calculators freely available online. This allowed them to collect successfully the data they required by aggregating the inputted calculations. These authors argue that their data collection procedures were also beneficial to their participants, by offering them a valuable service.

Big Data. Approaches such as those discussed above can lead to extremely large data sets being generated. The notion of 'big data', a term originating in computer science to mean data sets of such magnitude that they are difficult to process computationally, has recently received a good deal of discussion. In an IMR context, big data sets may involve behavioural traces collated across numerous individuals, for example all Google searches over a certain period, which can generate a very large number of data points. Google Analytics (see http://www.google.co.uk/analytics/) is a service, primarily aimed at marketing and business applications, which allows users to generate detailed statistics on a website's traffic, by tracking visitors and their navigation behaviours (including searches initiated, purchases made, etc.). The practicalities of, and possibilities for, obtaining big data sets online for use in social science research is a young, ongoing research area (a detailed review of which is beyond the scope of the present discussion). Investigative projects exploring this topic are already underway, such as the Oxford Internet Institute's 'Accessing and Using Big Data to Advance Social Science Knowledge' (see http://www.oii.ox.ac.uk/research/projects/?id=98; accessed November 2015). At the time of writing, the journal *Social Science Research* was calling for contributions to a planned special issue on 'Big Data' in social science research. The value and role of such data sets in social science IMR remain very much to be explored.

Future Directions

Considering future possibilities in observational IMR, again Web 2.0 technologies and services, and mobile Internet access devices, hold potential for facilitating various imagined avenues. The expansion of Internet access on the move via smart phones, tablets, and so on may open up possibilities similar to those discussed in relation to interview and survey methods, including measurement while participants are immersed in real-life contexts, and the use of geolocation information. Observation of people's movements around a city, or a building, might be one option, for example. Enhanced opportunities for reliably recording video and audio could enrich such approaches. Smart phone and tablet apps offer opportunities for collecting potentially vast volumes of *in situ* data while participants are on the move; indeed, data may be collected as a by-product of personal usage of a service offered, in a similar way to Lockett and Blackman's (2004) collation of data on foreign exchange charges (see above). Some such examples have already emerged (e.g. the 'Mappiness' project, mentioned above). Other imaginable contexts with research potential include fitness, health and dieting apps (and we suspect examples in some of these domains already exist). The 'Internet of things' refers to the integration of everyday objects and online technologies, to create an ever-expanding array of Internet-connected devices. Such devices are already moving well beyond the more common examples of smart phones, tablets and televisions. Already there are prototypes for 'tablets' of the medicinal variety (smart pills) which are Internet connected, so that they can monitor and send data about when medication has been taken, for example. Smart running shoes which monitor performance (distance, speed, route, and so on) and can automatically upload data to an online networking site are currently on sale. Domestic central heating and lighting systems which can be controlled from a smart phone are now readily available. As the Internet becomes more and more integrated into everyday objects, and consequently everyday lives, the scope for collecting all sorts of data in a range of everyday contexts will only expand. The extent to which these data will be of use in social and behavioural research remains largely to be seen. What we have presented here are just a few ideas, some of which have already been piloted. As with the other methods discussed in this chapter, future implementations and innovations will enhance our understanding of what is achievable, and what holds most promise.

EXPERIMENTS

While not usurping the popularity of the web-based survey, web-based experiments have become very much more prevalent over recent years. For examples and discussion of the approach, see Birnbaum (2000) and the special edition of the journal *Experimental Psychology* (Reips & Musch, 2002). Other examples of IMR experiments include Laugwitz (2001), Horton, Rand, and Zeckhause (2011),

Lenzner, Kaczmirek, and Lenzner (2010) and Reips (2001). In the first edition of this book we outlined four key types of IMR experiment: those using only static materials (e.g. text and images); those using video or audio; reaction-time experiments; and experiments involving interpersonal interaction between people. At the time, scope for the first two approaches was promising, but for the latter two less so. Most examples available at the time used text- and graphics-based presentations of stimulus materials. Now there are additional examples using more sophisticated techniques, with success. As well as general improvements in Internet technologies and software (e.g. faster bandwidths), the emergence of a range of packages to assist in developing and disseminating web experiments has helped facilitate the scope and accessibility of the approach. For information on some of the software available, see Rademacher and Lippke (2007), Reips and Neuhaus (2002) and Schulte-Mechlenbeck and Neun (2005), as well as the further discussion in Chapter 6. A large, searchable collection of examples of IMR experiments can be found on The Web Experiment List,[6] and some examples are also available via the other online study clearing houses mentioned in Box 3.1 (see above).

Static Text and Graphics

Approaches which present static text and graphics remain well supported in experimental IMR; these designs tend to place the least demands on the technical skills of the researcher and the technical equipment (hardware and software) required. An early example from our own research which used a very simple, low-tech approach in which experimental materials (vignettes) were emailed to participants is presented in Box 3.5.

BOX 3.5   Case Study: Empirical Evidence Regarding the Folk Psychological Concept of Belief (Hewson, 1994)

Purpose

The study set out to examine the common-sense concept of belief by testing some claims made within the folk psychology debate about the nature of our everyday common-sense (folk psychological) notion of belief (Double, 1985; Stich, 1983).

(Continued)

---

[6]Reips and Lengler (2005) present statistics on the submissions to this list to show that web experiment implementations are on the rise, and that cognitive followed by social psychology experiments are the most common.

(Continued)

Procedure

The study was advertised on a selection of Usenet newsgroups, after recruitment during seminar sessions at a university campus proved time consuming and generated few responses. Within two weeks of posting the advertisement 135 responses had been obtained. Respondents were emailed study materials, with instructions, and asked to return their responses by email. The experimental procedure involved participants reading two short stories, each followed by a question.[7] They emailed their responses back to the researcher's email address. Since materials comprised plain text it was a simple matter to cut and paste the appropriate text into the body of the email message. Participants were assigned to experimental conditions pseudo-randomly, and a record of allocations was kept using email addresses for identification. Each participant's response was saved to a unique file and stored on a secure university account upon receipt. A 'thank you' and debrief message was sent back by email. Data were collated and anonymised, for later analysis using BMDP software.

Discussion

Advantages. The Internet procedure successfully generated a good sample size (compared with the offline approach) cost-effectively and quickly, using only a small number of newsgroups. Photocopying costs were eliminated by sending materials in electronic format, and demands on researcher time were reduced due to the efficiency of email administration (compared with visiting an offline site) and data coming back in electronic format ready for storage and manipulation. The Internet sample was clearly more diverse than what could be achieved using the offline recruitment methods, and the Internet data generated included detailed and elaborate answers compared with what had been achieved in a pilot study offline (which could be due to procedural or sample differences).

Disadvantages. The lack of tight control over procedural factors led to some unanticipated events which could have been problematic. For example, a small number of respondents sent their answers from a different email account to their original response. Thus the tracking procedure which identified participants by email addresses failed in these cases (though all these respondents did in fact alert the researcher to the use of a different email address). More robust procedures for participant tracking are discussed further in Chapter 6 in this volume. Also, a few participants returned their responses without including the original materials sent, which had not been expected, though the tracking procedure employed made this unproblematic in this case. Further discussion of the importance of making participant instructions clear and explicit, and carefully piloting study procedures, is also offered in Chapter 6. Another issue concerned the oversight in contacting moderators prior to advertising the study, which lead to a hostile response from a moderator in one instance, and the removal of the post.

---

[7]See Hewson (1994) for further details of the experimental manipulation and materials.

Limitations and Suggestions for Improvement

The sampling methodology employed here used a convenience sample; newsgroups targeted were selected because they were familiar to the researcher. In the present context this was not considered to be overly problematic, but follow-up studies could usefully consider broader and more carefully selected sampling procedures. The present approach was likely to reach respondents working in academia, and with an interest in psychology. The decision to collect information about educational experience was useful, however, confirming the aforementioned bias, and allowing the conclusion that having training in cognitive science and/or logic influenced answers. Collecting information on a range of further demographic details (not done here) would also have been useful to investigate further sampling bias issues. No expiry date for participation adverts was set here, though this can be useful as it gives the researcher more control over the data collection, and allows monitoring across the exposure period. Creating data backup files would have been a more effective (and cost-effective) method of protecting against data loss than printing out hard copies of individual responses, as was done here. Chapter 7 offers guidance on procedures for the secure, safe storage of data. More rigorous informed consent and debriefing methods could have been implemented to maximise adherence to ethics principles, as discussed further in subsequent chapters.

The example in Box 3.5 demonstrates how experimental designs can be implemented without requiring complex technological solutions, though it also raises issues related to the reliability of such methods and the lack of researcher control (e.g. over response parameters). The scope for implementing experimental manipulations by sending different materials to different participants is, however, straightforward. Quasi-experiments in which differences between groups is of interest also can be done relatively simply in this way. Other manipulations may involve some participants having to take part in a further task or procedure prior to, or in between, measurements. Incorporating graphics into materials should not be too difficult (e.g. as done by Senior, Phillips, Barnes, & David, 1999a), though may present greater scope for reliability issues related to different platforms used by participants, and potential variations on presentation parameters. As well as email, technologies such as ftp, telnet, and so on can also be used to make experimental materials available to participants. Further examples of such relatively technologically simple implementations in experimental IMR exist (e.g. Ahmed & Hammarstedt, 2008; Hewson & Vogel, 1994; Strassberg & Holty, 2003). More advanced implementations using more complex interactive procedures (e.g. see Ruppertsberg, Givaty, Van Veen, & Bulthoff, 2001) will of course be more challenging to develop.

While the above type of approach has been useful, particularly in earlier examples of IMR experimental research, nowadays experiments using technologies such as email, telnet, ftp, etc., are rarely conducted (Reips, 2007). Rather, the Web is typically used as a platform for experiment delivery; participants visit a webpage and interact with experimental materials and processes via their web browser (much in the same way that online surveys are now routinely conducted). There are many examples of this approach available (e.g. Lenzner et al., 2010; Nückles & Bromme, 2002; Pohl et al., 2002; Senior, Barnes, Jenkins, Landau, Phillips, & David, 1999b). The emergence of dedicated web experiment implementation packages, improvements in Internet connection speeds and enhancements in browser capabilities have been important in facilitating this move towards web-based methods for IMR experimental research. Thus the variation in presentation of HTML code across different browsers that we noted in the first edition is less likely to cause problems with implementations developed using software packages which carefully adhere to cross-platform web-based standards. Of course, maintaining levels of control – one of the features which has been raised as potentially problematic in IMR approaches – is particularly crucial in experimental designs. In order to be able to make precise cause–effect inferences (between independent and dependent variables) internal validity must be assumed; keeping tight control over all potentially confounding variables is important in making this assumption. Recent technological developments which have helped to maintain control over presentation parameters in web-based research have thus been important in maximising the validity of web-based experiments.

Audio and Video

Since writing the first edition of *IRM* the scope for using audio and video in IMR has expanded greatly. In that first edition we raised the issue of problems related to download times when using larger files of the type required to support multimedia approaches, including even simple graphics, and concluded that only relatively small, easily downloadable file sizes should be used. Developments in Internet connection speeds have alleviated such problems to a large degree; whereas dial-up used to be a standard way of accessing the Internet, including web-based materials, broadband is now widely available, and widely used. Watching YouTube clips, for example, should not be problematic for many users, and thus taking part in experiments incorporating video clips should also not pose major issues.[8] As new developments such as fibre optic broadband continue to emerge and become more widely available, such issues will become even less problematic. In the first edition, we referred to psycholinguistic studies concerned with speech recognition, and musical perception studies, as domains where manageable-sized sound clips might be used; examples of both types of approach have now been forthcoming (e.g. Knoll, Uther, & Costall, 2011; also see the BBC musicality test at https://ssl.

---

[8]Exceptions may be where very precise timings are required.

bbc.co.uk/labuk/experiments/musicality [accessed October 2014]). We noted that experiments using larger sized video clips may become more plausible in the future; some examples are now also available (e.g. Caro et al., 2012).

Reaction-time Experiments

Experiments involving very precise reaction-time measurements (i.e. to the millisecond) seemed unlikely in the early days of IMR, largely due to inadequate Internet data transfer speeds and low reliability due to network traffic variations, different user platforms, etc. In a traditional setting such approaches are possible by getting the participant to interact with a computer program which can present materials and measure reaction times to the required level of precision, in a very tightly controlled environment. However, more recently examples of successful reaction-time studies in IMR have been presented (e.g. Corley and Scheepers, 2002; Eichstaedt, 2002). These approaches can thus support experiments in cognitive and behavioural science which in the early days seemed implausible. Caveats still emerge; for example, if participants are using older technologies (e.g. dial-up) such implementations may not run without problems, though faster broadband connections now tend to be the norm. Network traffic fluctuations can also lead to issues in reliably sending and receiving data. Still, as technologies and their widespread adoption continue to evolve, these issues can only become less problematic. The impact of Internet traffic, bandwidths, etc., should nevertheless be considered when designing studies which require precise timings, both for presenting stimuli and measuring responses. Solutions which involve downloading a program to a user's own computer to be run offline may still offer a possible solution which can help enhance reliability where it is thought this could be an issue (e.g. as in a user having only a dial-up connection).

Multi-user Experiments

The final type of experiment we outlined in the first edition was where, instead of an individual participant interacting with a computer program, two or more participants are brought together to interact with each other. Experiments on cooperation, for example, have used such an approach in offline contexts (e.g. Locey, Safin, & Rachlin, 2013). Recent technological enhancements have also increased the scope for implementing such designs in IMR. Web-based interactions now abound in many different contexts, such as MUVEs (discussed earlier) and collaborative networking settings where, for example, two or more participants may work together simultaneously on creating a document, graphic, presentation, etc. (e.g. using Google Docs, or one of the many hosted wiki services). Horton et al. (2011) report carrying out online experiments in which participants (recruited via the online labour market Mechanical Turk, see www.mturk.com) interacted in versions of the paradigmatic prisoner's dilemma game. They successfully rep-licated offline lab-based results using this method. However, they point out the present lack of developed, accessible software tools for implementing more sophis-ticated interactive online experiments of this type, noting that bespoke solutions will often be necessary. As noted earlier, virtual environments such as MUVEs hold particular potential for facilitating collaborative, interactive *experimental* designs in IMR. Schroeder and Bailenson (2008) discuss some examples (e.g. Becker & Mark, 2002; Slater, Sadagic, Usoh, & Schroeder, 2000). They mention headcam studies, which take place in a laboratory and a virtual environment at the same time (potentially blurring boundaries between offline and online methods). In such situations participants could potentially be engaging in online virtual inter-actions with other participants, as well as with the experimenter in a non-virtual laboratory.

Future Directions

As indicated above, the scope and possibilities for conducting IMR experiments have expanded substantially over the last 10 years or so, and this trend will likely continue. Enhanced technological developments, and the development and refinement of software packages that make IMR experiments easier to construct and disseminate, should facilitate the approach. Advantages of an IMR approach include many of those outlined earlier (broader geographical reach, time and cost savings, convenience to participants, etc.). Given the popularity of online gaming activities, the novelty value afforded by online experiments which, for example, ask participants to interact and perform tasks in MUVEs could be appealing and enhance recruitment success. Reips (2002b) discusses the various benefits, as well as disadvantages, of IMR experiments, making the noteworthy point that the greater technical variance in IMR contexts may actually be an advantage, since it can enhance the external validity (i.e. generalisability across diverse contexts) of a study compared with very tightly controlled lab-based studies. This challenges the common perception that greater variability in web-based experiments (due to a lack of control over the participation environment, and so on) is a problem to be overcome and minimised (e.g. Horton et al., 2011; Reips & Musch, 2002). Web-based experiments may therefore have a useful role to play in replicating offline findings. Of course, uncontrolled and unknown variability *is* a problem where precise causal relationships between particular variables are being tested for the first time. However, when attempting to replicate established offline findings using online experiments, obtaining equivalent results in an IMR context argu-ably is a test of the external validity of a demonstrated effect, as Reips (2002b) suggests. IMR validation studies were mentioned earlier in the context of online survey methods; similarly encouraging results have been obtained in experimen-tal research (e.g. Horton et al., 2011; Knoll et al., 2011; Pohl et al., 2002). This bodes well for the ongoing prevalence of experimental IMR. Future innovations may make use of the various emerging technologies that have been mentioned in relation to other methods, such as mobile applications, the Internet of things, and enhanced multimedia possibilities. For a useful discussion of some of the current methodological issues to consider in IMR experimental design, see Reips and Krantz (2010), as well as the further discussion in Chapter 6.

DOCUMENT ANALYSIS

There are fewer examples of document analysis in IMR, compared with other methods, but examples of both quantitative and qualitative studies do exist. Analysis of blogs has been a thriving direction in some disciplines, including marketing research and linguistics. Given the volume of published documents available online, the approach has great potential. Thus webpages, blogs (at least those which maintain the traditional role of an individually published personal diary), news articles, scientific articles, online repositories of, for example, photos, musical compositions, artwork, and so on, are all potential sources (see also the online resources outlined in Chapter 2). As already noted, some online resources straddle the boundary between being a static, published final product and an interactive, fluid, regularly updated collaborative 'work-in-progress'. Twitter seems a good example: tweets are short comments, ideas, links to information, and so on, posted by individuals. These elicit comments, and shares (retweets) from other tweeters. Given the size of its user base (at the time of writing, 271 million monthly active users, see https://about.twitter.com/company [accessed August 2014]), Twitter potentially offers access to massively big data sets, of people's passing thoughts, ideas, comments, interjections, observations and information sources (e.g. new articles) that they are interested in. There is really no offline equivalent to tweets as a source of data. The use of Twitter as a source of data for observational research was noted above; the ready access to shared documentary sources via this service also makes it a potential useful site for use in document analysis IMR.

Existing Documents

A number of studies have used existing online sources to carry out document analysis. For example, Thoreau (2006) carried out a qualitative analysis of text and images from *Ouch!*, a magazine website produced largely by and for disabled people, in order to examine representations of disability by disabled people. This approach enabled the gathering of data not easily obtainable via traditional offline media sources (radio, press, television), such as first-hand reports of personal experiences. Another example is Heinz, Gu, Inuzuka, and Zender's (2002) rhetorical–critical examination of texts and images on gay, lesbian, bisexual and transgender (GLBT) websites. These authors conclude that the Web provides a particularly important source of information on transformations in the cultural construction of GLBT identities, noting in particular the transnational nature of many online spaces, which can enable a comparison of 'shifting cultural identities' in a way that would be difficult and time consuming offline. This study illustrates the way IMR methods can collapse geographical boundaries and facilitate cross-cultural research.

As already noted, some authors have undertaken an analysis of blogs, with positive results (e.g. Clarke and van Ameron, 2008); Marcus et al. (2012) emphasise how the use of IMR methods helped them to reach a traditionally under-researched and under-treated population (young adults with mental health concerns). Hou, Chang, and Sung (2010) used content analysis to examine what types of knowledge teachers share on blogs (in this study a blog was set up as part of the research). See also Huffaker and Calvert (2005) who analysed teenagers' blogs to examine issues of identity, gender and language use. A more recent discussion of content analysis methods using data sources from the Web, particularly blogs, can be found in Herring (2010).

Solicited Documents

Another approach is to solicit documents online, rather than access what is already there, as was done in the above-cited studies (except Hou et al., 2010, who set up a dedicated blog space for teachers to use). Hessler et al. (2003) took this approach, asking adolescent participants to submit daily diary entries via email, in a study looking at risky behaviours. This generated rich narratives, and encouraged open, candid responses. In this way, the IMR methodology resolved difficulties in establishing rapport with this target group, which can often be an issue in offline FTF research. These researchers suggest that an IMR approach can be particularly beneficial when conducting sensitive research with young people, as the use of email may offer a 'comforting air of informality'. However, email also has security risks which must be taken into account when using this transmission method. Hessler et al. addressed this issue by setting up email accounts using fake names, to reduce threats to participant anonymity. They also used rigorous informed consent procedures involving gaining signed offline consent from an adult gatekeeper. Possibilities for incorporating multimedia data into document analysis approaches emerge, for example allowing the use of image uploads in elicited diary studies (ethics considerations permitting), or accessing online multimedia sources when using existing documents (e.g. multimedia sharing sites, artists' homepages, etc.).

Of the document analysis approaches reviewed above, document solicitation approaches will be generally less time and cost efficient than searching for and locating existing archives on research-relevant topics. However, as the research of Hessler et al. (2003) has shown, they can still prove to be cost effective when compared with traditional offline methods, and bring particular benefits to a research study. Both approaches seem to hold promise for the future, as the Internet, the documents it hosts and its population of users continue to expand.

In this chapter we have reviewed and illustrated a range of key methods in IMR, considering their strengths, weaknesses and future potential. Integral to any research project is the planning and design of sampling strategies. We now turn to look in detail at sampling issues, opportunities and procedures in IMR, in Chapter 4.

<> FOUR </>

<> SAMPLING IN INTERNET-MEDIATED RESEARCH </>

INTRODUCTION

The previous chapter outlined and discussed some key methods and approaches in IMR. This chapter considers sampling issues and strategies. We revisit the once-prevalent view that Internet recruitment procedures will inevitably generate a biased, select sample, and discuss how, over the last 10 years or so, both the composition of and attitudes towards the Internet-user population (IUP) have changed quite dramatically. Various IMR sampling approaches have now been conceived and tested. As in the first edition, we argue that IMR methods can provide access to potentially vast and diverse sections of the general population, even more so today than when we were writing on the topic around 10 years ago. As previously, we emphasise the point that the types of sampling procedures used will influence the nature of the samples obtained. However, in IMR it is still unclear what types of samples will emerge from the various procedures available. We review existing research which attempts to explicate how such relationships might manifest themselves.

Sampling from the IUP

In the very early days of IMR, when pioneering researchers were just starting to imagine, design and implement Internet-mediated primary research studies, there were widespread concerns about biases inherent in the IUP (the population from which IMR samples were typically drawn). The common concern at the time was that the IUP was composed primarily of white, upper middle-class, well-educated males, largely from North America (e.g. Szabo & Frenkl, 1996). Certain sectors of the 'population at large' were considered to be under-represented, such as poor and minority groups (e.g. Nosek, Banaji, & Greenwald, 2002). This was seen as a seri-ous limitation and shortcoming of IMR methods. However, some authors (ourselves included) remained optimistic about the potential of the Internet for acquiring both large, diverse samples and smaller, specialist and traditionally hard-to-reach samples. Such accounts emphasised the expanding penetration of the Internet into everyday lives of people worldwide, and the implications in terms of creating an increasingly diverse, sizeable pool of potential participants for IMR studies. Over the last 10 years or so this expansion has been seen to be extensive, and attitudes about the value and potential of Internet-accessed samples have become more positive.

One indication of this shift in attitudes is the rapid expansion of IMR methods across a broad range of disciplines and areas of research (as evidenced in the previous chapter). Still, words of caution echo. IMR has been pointed out to remain very 'geographically specific' (O'Connor et al., 2008), mostly centred in Anglo-American cultural contexts (Jankowski & van Selm, 2005) and predominantly embedded within the English language (Thurlow, Lengel, & Tomic, 2004). Such caveats should be borne in mind, and any grand claims about IMR being able to 'internationalise' research methods treated with caution (O'Connor et al., 2008). Gaiser (2008) notes that an online sample will most likely reflect the perspective of a more highly educated and 'higher socially located' population that has resources for access through either work or home environments. While Internet access is clearly ever increasing, these points remain valid.

Nevertheless, the sheer size and diversity of the IUP, and the potential enhanced access to participants from across the globe, is mind-boggling. Offline samples are typically geographically localised, and often Anglo-American-centric (consider the predominance of the English language in published social and behavioural research). The extensive use of undergraduate students in some disciplines (e.g. psychology) in traditional offline research is also noteworthy. Clearly, any critiques of online-accessed samples used in IMR need to be considered in relation to the types of samples that are typically available in offline research. There are two key sources of evidence that can be drawn upon to assess claims about the nature and degree of bias inherent in Internet-accessed samples. One is information about the composition and habits of the IUP: who uses the Internet (and who does not) and for what purposes? The other source involves information about the types of samples (e.g. their demographic composition, personality characteristics, and so on) that are generated by the various IMR sampling strategies available, and the ways in which these compare with samples recruited using offline methods. We now consider evidence from both of these sources.

WHO USES THE INTERNET?

As illustrated in the previous chapter, the number and variety of technologies and services which the Internet supports have expanded dramatically over the last decade. This has created an ongoing expansion and permeation of the Internet into the lives of many people worldwide.[1] Ten years ago we commented that people use the Internet to 'buy, sell, view houses, check the weather forecast, view television schedules, pay bills, manage bank accounts, obtain insurance quotes, book hotel rooms, buy travel tickets, and seek a partner' (Hewson et al., 2003, p. 27). We can now add to this list: tweet (see twitter.com), post Facebook status updates (www.facebook.com), share videos on YouTube (www.youtube.com) and photographs on flickr (www.flickr.com), publish musical compositions on Myspace (www.myspace.com) and SoundCloud (www.soundcloud.com), check road traffic reports and view traffic via webcams, check live transport information (e.g. flight delays and cancellations), plan a customised cycle or walking route, and publish a book[2] (e.g. see the Amazon-owned 'CreateSpace' at https://www.createspace.com [accessed April 2015]).

Many of the aforementioned Internet services are now available via traditional web browser interfaces, and also via apps (applications designed primarily for use with smart phones and tablets, as discussed earlier). There are apps available (some for download as stand-alone software, not requiring a live Internet connection) that allow you to: tune your guitar; monitor your sleep patterns; scan barcodes; test your eyesight; locate a car park or amenities close to your present location; book a restaurant table; track, record and publish online your cycling route (or walking or running) data; access and track university course information updates online (e.g. via a virtual learning environment, VLE); and take part in a cognitive psychology semantic priming experiment (see http://www.sciencexl.org/[3] (accessed April 2015). There are now over 1 million apps available for the iPhone (best-selling smart phone by Apple) alone (see www.apple.com/pr/library/2014/01/07App-Store-Sales-Top-10–Billion-in-2013.html [accessed April 2015]), and these can be browsed here: https://itunes.apple.com/gb/genre/ios/id36?mt=8 (accessed April 2015). Google also houses a large store of apps (play.google.com [accessed April 2015]) for download, which are compatible with its Android smart phones. Apps first became available with smart phones like the (Apple) iPhone, and later were modified for use on tablets like the (Apple) iPad. Apps are a testament to the ubiquity of the Internet. These developments mean that, for a large number of people, interacting with or on

---

[1]Though, of course, there are limitations in terms of who – worldwide – has access to the technologies and services the Internet offers, particularly the division between developed and developing nations.

[2]For a discussion of how this can be done, see www.guardian.co.uk/technology/blog/2010/jan/28/online-publishing-victor-keegan; and for one success story, see www.theguardian.com/books/2012/jan/12/amanda-hocking-self-publishing (sources accessed April 2015).

[3]Also, see the *Wall Street Journal* article 'How Smartphones Could Revolutionize Scientific Experiments': http://blogs.wsj.com/tech-europe/2011/09/30/how-smartphones-could-revolutionize-scientific-experiments/ (accessed April 2015).

the Internet has become a regular part of daily life. While there are inevitably still some restrictions on who has access, clearly there is no longer an overwhelming bias towards 'white, upper middle-class, well-educated males, largely from North America'. In order to gain a better impression of just who does use the Internet, analyses of Internet composition and user characteristics are informative, which we now consider.

Internet-User Surveys

Early respected analyses of IUP characteristics included those offered by the GVU surveys (Graphics Visualization and Usability (GVU) Center, Georgia Institute of Technology), published biannually from 1994 to 1998 (e.g. Pitkow and Recker, 1994; GVU, 1997, 1998). These surveys generally supported common perceptions at the time of the IUP as heavily biased towards young, North American, tech-savvy males of above-average education level and socioeconomic status. However, the surveys utilised non-probability, convenience sampling procedures that the GVU team themselves recognise as biased, and which seem very likely to produce just the type of user profile they report. Thus the GVU survey results cannot be taken as representative of the entire IUP. The findings from such surveys remain problematic: since there is no central register of all Internet users, it is not possible to sample randomly from this population. However, more recent approaches have been able to gain an impression of Internet use and attitudes among specified populations using offline sampling methods. The Oxford Internet Surveys (OxIS, run by the Oxford Internet Institute at the University of Oxford)[4] attempt systematically to investigate Internet use and habits through the use of offline survey methods. OxIS is a part of the World Internet Project,[5] a collaborative venture between 20 universities and research centres worldwide,[6] the aim of which is to study – using detailed panel surveys – the economic, political and social implications of the Internet.

OxIS data have been collected biannually from 2003 to 2013, and findings across all surveys are presented in a series of reports available online at http://oxis. oii.ox.ac.uk/reports (accessed April 2015). These data are relevant to questions about the extent and nature of the penetration of the Internet into people's daily lives, and also about the differences between Internet users and non-users, covering demographics, attitudes and behaviours. The 2011 report (available via the aforementioned link) refers to a 'next generation' of Internet users, who

---

[4]See the OxIS homepage at http://oxis.oii.ox.ac.uk/ (accessed August 2014).

[5]See http://www.worldInternetproject.net/#news (accessed August 2014).

[6]The entire list of participating countries is: Argentina, Australia, Bolivia, Canada, Chile, China, Czech Republic, Estonia, Germany, Great Britain, Hong Kong, Hungary, India, Iran, Italy, Japan, Macao, Portugal, Singapore, South Korea, Spain, Sweden, United States.

access the Internet both from multiple locations and multiple devices (computers, smart phones, tablets, PDAs[7]). These next-generation users are more likely to have a higher income, and less likely to be retired or unemployed (Dutton & Blank, 2011). This report also notes that while the gender divide in access to the Internet has disappeared, the young, wealthy and well educated continue to be the most engaged online. The elderly, retired and poorly educated tend to be the least likely to use the Internet (Dutton & Blank, 2011). The 2011 report notes the largest growing area of use over the previous two years as social networking sites (SNSs), with 60% of respondents saying they used these in 2011, constituting 'one of the most dramatic developments in use of the Internet in recent years' (Dutton & Blank, 2011, p. 33). Other uses such as shopping and bill paying are also reported as on the increase (Dutton & Blank, 2011). The most recent OxIS report at the time of writing (Dutton et al., 2013) notes a growth in 'next-generation' users from 32% to 52% of the British population. It also reports an overall rise in Internet use, with the current figure at 78% of the UK population who are 14 years of age or over, and an increase in Internet access for lower income groups, people with no formal qualifications, the retired and those with a disability. Social networking use is reported as having stabilised at 67% of all users. Since the OxIS surveys used probability sampling methods, they can be trusted to be as representative of the population of residents of Great Britain (with a residential address) as is reasonably possible, and do seem to provide some very useful, informative data, not least showing that the Internet has expanded massively over the last several years in terms of its penetration into the everyday lives of many people living in Great Britain. Of course, the use of survey methods does also raise the usual considerations and concerns over possible response bias; perhaps, for example, those who took up the invitation to take part were particularly avid, enthusiastic Internet users.

Internet Composition

Arguably more objective, reliable measures of who uses the Internet (if less fine-grained) are those which analyse the number and distribution of Internet-accessible hosts. Such data can give a broader indication of the size and diversity of the IUP worldwide, without being affected by response bias issues. Roughly speaking, a host is a 'server' (Internet-connected computer) which acts as a point of access for a number of other computers which are connected to it. The number of recorded hosts has continued to expand since the inception of the Internet. For example, in 2002 the number of hosts was estimated at 147 million (Internet Systems Consortium, www.isc.org/, January, 2002, cited in Hewson et al., 2003). Estimates of the total IUP at that time were around 500 million (e.g. Nva Ltd,

---

[7]'Personal Digital Assistant', also known as a palmtop computer.

www.nva.ie/survey/how-many-online/world.html, cited in Hewson et al., 2003), though when compared with the number of hosts this could be considered a rather conservative estimate (Hewson et al., 2003). Estimates of the total number of hosts since 2003 are shown in Table 4.1 (these figures were represented graphically in Chapter 1). These figures indicate a growth factor of around seven times the number of hosts counted at the time of writing the first edition of this book in 2002.

Table 4.1 Estimated number of internet-accessible hosts since 2003

Year	Estimated hosts (January)
2003	172 million
2004	233 million
2005	318 million
2006	395 million
2007	433 million
2008	542 million
2009	625 million
2010	733 million
2011	818 million
2012	888 million
2013	964 million
2014	1 billion
2015	1 billion

Source: Figures taken from The ISC Domain Survey: http://ftp.isc.org/www/survey/reports/current/ (accessed April 2015).

Concerning the number of actual Internet *users* (supported by these hosts), the Computer Industry Almanac provides detailed IUP data commercially (for a cost; see http://www.marketresearch.com/Computer-Industry-Almanac-Inc-v3269/ [accessed April 2015]), but also has published historical and forecasted growth rates, available at no cost in the executive summaries. Their estimate of the size of the IUP in 2012 was just over 2 billion, projected to be nearly 3 billion in 2015 (based on past growth rates). This would mean the IUP has multiplied by a factor of 6 (at the time of writing) compared with when we were writing the first edition of this book. Internet Live Stats (http://www.internetlivestats.com/internet-users/ [accessed April 2015]) also provides IUP data, currently at no cost, using a range of sources. At the time of writing, the latest figures indicated an IUP of just under 3 billion in July 2014.

Various other pieces of information are available from the Computer Industry Almanac reports. For example, there is an indication that the US Internet share has been going down dramatically, from 90% in 1985 to 12.5% in 2010, projected to be 10% in 2015.[8] Estimates such as these (while perhaps not entirely reliable) can provide useful approximations. Other authors have also drawn upon similar analyses in trying to get a picture of the size and composition of the IUP; for example, Fricker (2008) cites Internet World Stats of 2007 (see Internetworldstats. com [accessed April 2015]) which report that 35 countries worldwide had greater than 50% Internet penetration, the rest of the world having an average estimated 8.7% penetration. The most recent Internet World Stats report at the time of writing (http://www.internetworldstats.com/stats.htm [accessed April 2015]) offers worldwide penetration figures for June 2014, including estimated total number of Internet users and percentage penetration by geographical region and country, as well as region growth estimates between 2000 and 2014. Hewson and Laurent (2008) also refer to estimates of penetration by country, citing the Internet Systems Consortium (www.isc.org.uk; however, this link is no longer active) breakdown of Internet hosts by top-level domain name, which essentially gives an indication of the number of hosts available within a given country: in January 2007, 8.5 million of the 490 million or so hosts were located in Australia (domain name 'au') and 1,034 hosts were located in Uganda ('ug'). What is uncontentious from such data sources is the ongoing increase in penetration worldwide; for example, in January 1997 Samoa ('ws') had no counted hosts, whereas in January 2007, 10 years later, it had 9,191 (Hewson & Laurent, 2008). In terms of saturation levels (the proportion of the population which actually has Internet access), it has been noted that, in some countries, for some socioeconomic groups close to full saturation levels have already been reached (Martin & Robinson, 2007; see also the aforementioned Internet World Stats reports).

We argued in the first edition of this book that the Internet, and the IUP it supports, provide great potential for accessing both large and diverse, as well as small, select samples, which may very likely go beyond what has been traditionally readily available in much offline research. We consider the above statistics – alongside an understanding of the numerous and diverse channels of access to this user population – to strengthen this argument further. As well as evidence regarding the sheer size and expanse of the IUP, developments in the ways in which users access the Internet, as discussed above, provide further support for the increasing diversity and inclusiveness within the IUP and, by extension, potential Internet-accessed samples. Whereas previously we highlighted some key differences in the way UK and US users accessed the Internet – UK users typically being billed for local phone calls by length, while US users typically received free inclusive local calls as part of a phone contract package (dial-up then being the common mode of Internet access) (Hewson et al., 2003) – now, many UK users

---

[8]Again, such figures are difficult to obtain reliably, and issues about methodology emerge. Information about the methodologies used can often be found in published reports and/or on an organisation's website.

also receive free local calls as inclusive. Furthermore, most UK and US users are now likely to have broadband connections which allow continued, unlimited online access for a fixed monthly fee. Thus the types of disparities we reported previously in who might be inclined to log on and spend time completing an online survey, experiment or interview may well now have changed, and in some cases disappeared. According to Vehovar and Manfreda (2008), in 2006 roughly half the households in developed countries had broadband Internet connections. The OxIS 2011 report considers trends in Great Britain, noting that: 'The major change in access since 2003 was the move from narrowband dial-up to broadband always-on Internet connections. By 2009, nearly all Internet users had a broadband connection, increasingly including wireless connections within the household, such as over a WiFi router' (Dutton & Blank, 2011, p. 4).

Technological and commercial developments influencing the way users access the Internet will no doubt continue to affect Internet usage patterns (e.g. high-speed fibre optic connections are now becoming increasingly widely available), prompting changes in the types of samples potentially available to social and behavioural researchers. Ten years ago, Internet access via a mobile phone was a relatively novel idea (Hewson et al., 2003); however, more recent estimates of the number of Internet users accessing the Internet in this way in Great Britain have been placed at 45% (Office for National Statistics, 2011)[9]. OxIS reports that nearly half (49%) of all mobile phone users in Great Britain (all mobile phone users being 97% of the total British population, in 2009) reported accessing the Internet via their phone in 2011 (Dutton & Blank, 2011). The latest OxIS report (Dutton, Blank & Groselj, 2013, at the time of writing) notes that there has been a steady increase in the number of people reporting using mobile phones or tablets (57% in 2013) and wifi (96% in 2013) to access the Internet. The Computer Industry Almanac reports that 47% of the total population of Internet users worldwide access it wirelessly, and predict this figure to rise to 64% by 2015 (https://web.archive.org/web/20131609362600/http://www.c-i-a.com/internetusersexec.htm [accessed October 2014]). This growth in levels of mobile and/or wireless access to the Internet is another example of the way things have changed, quite rapidly, over the last 10 years or so, with implications for expanded sampling possibilities in IMR.

As demonstrated above, Internet composition and user survey statistics can be useful and informative, and offer some insights into the level of penetration of the Internet into people's lives, though careful scrutiny of the methodologies used to obtain these statistics is needed in order properly to assess the conclusions they can support (reports on the methods used can typically be found by visiting the relevant websites). However, these data do not enable clear and detailed insights into how different sampling strategies in IMR might generate different types of

---

[9] See http://www.ons.gov.uk/ons/rel/rdit2/internet-access---households-and-individuals/2011/stb-internet-access-2011.html (accessed October 2014).

samples, or how Internet-accessed samples might compare with samples acquired using traditional methods. For this information, we need to turn to studies which have actually implemented Internet sampling procedures, especially those which systematically compare these with traditional offline methods and samples. We consider such studies to be especially important in helping to gain insights into the effects and outcomes of different sampling procedures and strategies in IMR. It is one thing to know that a massive population of users worldwide accesses the Internet, in a variety of ways and for a variety of purposes, but how might different methods available for recruiting research participants from this population influence the types of samples obtained? This is clearly an empirical question. We now review some work which has addressed this question, including studies comparing Internet-accessed and traditional offline samples.

COMPARING INTERNET AND TRADITIONAL SAMPLES

Some very early studies comparing Internet and non-Internet samples exist. Smith and Leigh (1997) report finding their Internet and non-Internet samples to differ in terms of age and sex, but not sexual orientation, marital status, ethnicity, education and religiosity. However, their sampling procedures – posting to the newsgroup sci. psychology.research to ask for volunteers, and recruiting undergraduate psychology students from a voluntary participant pool (offline) – were likely to generate very similar types of samples. The generalisability of these findings is thus questionable. Other early comparisons have also used methods that would seem likely to gener- ate very similar samples, typically recruiting undergraduate psychology students offline, and volunteers to psychology-related special interest newsgroups online (e.g. Buchanan & Smith, 1999b; Krantz et al., 1997). Several such comparisons have found Internet-accessed samples to be more diverse, on at least some variables (e.g. Krantz et al., 1997; Smith & Leigh, 1997). Others have reported Internet and tradi- tional samples to be very similar (e.g. Browndyke, Santa Maria, Pinkston, & Gouvier, 1998; Stanton, 1998). Yet others have confirmed biases in the directions that have typically been assumed (e.g. Internet samples as more highly educated, and more likely to be male; e.g. Brenner, 2002; Kaye & Johnson, 1999). These inconclusive findings reflect the different types of sampling approaches and techniques that have been employed in such studies, as well, perhaps, as the fluid and evolving nature of the IUP (we present some more recent evidence on relationships between IMR sampling methods and sample type below).

One compelling argument for the value of Internet-accessed samples is that they may offer opportunities for overcoming the heavy reliance on undergraduate students in certain research traditions (e.g. much psychological research: Henrich, Heine & Norenzayan, 2010; McNemar, 1946; Siah, 2005; Smart, 1966). The overwhelming use of psychology undergraduates in certain areas of psychological research is apparent from flicking through the volumes of some key psychology journals (see e.g. Arnett,

2008; Gosling et al., 2004; Hewson et al., 2003). To illustrate, we examined a fairly recent volume of the *Journal of Experimental Psychology: Learning, Memory & Cognition* (vol. 38, no. 1, 2012). Out of a total of 23 reported studies, 18 used student samples only and, of the remaining 5, all but 1 used students as well as other non-student participants. So, the heavy reliance on students in certain areas of psychological research seems still prevalent. Arnett (2008) has carried out a comprehensive review of studies reported in APA journals, and notes that even where non-student samples are used, there is an overwhelming reliance on Americans[10] (who comprise less than 5% of the world's population). It seems reasonable to propose that many IMR sampling techniques will readily produce broader, more diverse samples than these (Hewson et al., 2003; Siah, 2005).

The limitations of IMR methods and samples seem more apparent when compared with traditional approaches that use so-called 'gold standard' *probability* sampling methods, such as random digit dialling (RDD).[11] Unlike non-probability samples, a probability sample is one which employs some form of random selection, using a procedure which aims to ensure that each member of the population has an equal chance of being chosen for inclusion in the sample. There are different processes for obtaining probability samples; for a more detailed explanation of probability sampling techniques the reader is referred to any good social science methods textbook (e.g. Bryman, 2012, provides a lucid and detailed account). Obtaining probability samples can be especially important in disciplines such as economics and political science, where estimates of population parameters are often a key aim (unlike, for example, much work in cognitive psychology[12]). If the aim is, for example, to predict the way a general election result will turn out based on asking a sample of the population about their voting intentions, then the sample must be *representative* of the general national population in order to be able to make inferences from the findings to estimated population parameters. Research in these disciplines is also commonly concerned with uncovering *relationships between variables* which can be generalised to a broader population (e.g. what types of demographic or other factors might predict people's voting behaviour, political affiliations, and so on), and representative samples are equally important in order to be able to make such valid inferences. Probability sampling on the

---

[10]Which we take to mean 'North Americans'.

[11]For more information on random digit dialling methods see Waksberg (1978).

[12]Note, however, that the over-reliance on *WEIRD* research participants, those from 'Western, Educated, Industrialised, Rich, and Democratic societies', has also been argued to be problematic even for domains such as cognitive psychology (and other *behavioural* sciences), where it is generally assumed that the processes under investigation can be assumed to be universal (Henrich et al., 2010). Henrich et al. present a range of examples to demonstrate that WEIRD participants have been shown to differ from participants drawn from small-scale societies, in areas such as folk biological reasoning, spatial cognition and susceptibility to visual illusions (such as the well-known *Müller–Lyer* case). Indeed, it has been suggested that IMR approaches may help overcome such issues (see the *Commentary* by Gosling et al. in Henrich et al., 2010).

Internet remains problematic. Even if the IUP itself provided a suitable sampling frame (the sampling frame is the list of all the sampling units which form a population from which the sample is drawn; see further discussion of sampling frames below) representing the types of populations that researchers interested in making population parameter estimates required (which is often unlikely), there is no central register of the entire, or even a substantial portion, of the IUP which would enable samples representative of this population to be obtained.

Considering findings from recent studies that have obtained samples via the Internet, using a more diverse range of approaches and strategies than the early examples cited above is informative in answering questions about the types of samples that are accessible in this way. Boxes 4.1 and 4.2 feature two such studies which have reached contrasting conclusions about the value of Internet-accessed samples, compared with traditional offline samples. The different conclusions reached can be largely attributed to the different goals and questions being asked. Gosling et al. (2004) were interested in comparing large, volunteer Internet samples with the types of samples traditionally used in much psychological research, while Malhotra and Krosnick (2007) compared a non-probability volunteer Internet sample with an offline probability sample, with the goal of determining whether the Internet sample might be able to provide results representative of the general population. Gosling et al. point out that their sample was *not* representative of the general US population, so their findings are consistent with Malhotra and Krosnick's conclusions that IMR samples (non-probability, volunteer) are not suitable where such broad generalisability is required. Nevertheless, Gosling et al.'s findings support the possible advantages of IMR samples when compared with the traditional samples often used in psychological research. The presence of confounds in Malhotra and Krosnick's study makes it difficult to draw firm conclusions about the reasons for observed differences in response patterns between the two samples; however, their findings do suggest that non-probability volunteer IMR samples may not be as representative of national populations as offline probability samples (the scope for implementing probability sampling methods in IMR, in order to try and obtain more broadly representative samples, is discussed further below).

BOX 4.1   Featured Research: Gosling et al. (2004)

Method

An Internet volunteer sample (who completed The Big Five Personality Test) was obtained by recruiting visitors to a non-commercial website containing personality measures, other information, tests and games for entertainment purposes (outofservice.com). The Internet sample was compared with 510 samples (containing a total of 102,959 participants) taken from all of the 2002 issues of the *Journal of Personality and Social Research.*

(Continued)

(Continued)

Results

In all, 361,703 Internet participants were recruited; 85% of the 510 offline samples consisted of students. The Internet sample was more diverse in many ways than the traditional samples, but was not representative of the 'population at large' (e.g. the Internet sample was less diverse in terms of race than the US population). The data obtained from the Internet sample on The Big Five Personality Scale were comparable with data previously obtained offline (comparing metrics such as scale reliabilities and intercorrelations: Srivastava, John, Gosling, & Potter, 2003).

Conclusions

Internet samples are 'more representative than traditional samples with respect to gender, socioeconomic status, geographic location, and age and are about as representative as traditional samples with respect to race' (Gosling et al., 2004, p. 99). The data obtained support the validity of online methods which sample from Internet users.

Comment

This study illustrates the way that very large sample sizes can be obtained in IMR, which are likely to be more diverse in many ways than the homogeneous, student samples often used in psychological research, but which are also likely not to be fully representative of national (in this case US) populations. The study indicates that sampling from the IUP may help in moving beyond the nationally and geographically restricted samples used in much psychological research. The study also suggests that valid, valuable data can be obtained from Internet samples.

BOX 4.2   Featured Research: Malhotra and Krosnick (2007)

Method

Responses to a survey gathering data on voting behaviour and attitudes were compared for (a) a large-scale FTF probability sample used in the American National Election Study (ANES) for 2000 and 2004, and (b) a US 'non-probability volunteer' Internet sample, selected from a large-scale panel (HPOL)[13] by stratifying to match key population parameters (gender, age, region of residence). Selected online panel members were sent an email invitation; 3,980 responses out of 41,393 invitations were received.

---

[13]Harris Poll Online, which recruited volunteers largely from search engines and websites.

Results

Some differences were found in the distributions of survey responses for the Internet and offline samples, and also in logistic regressions predicting vote choice and turnout for each sample. There was some evidence of accuracy being higher for the FTF sample. In terms of similarity to population parameters on a range of key demographic variables (gender, age, education race, etc.), the offline sample was found to be superior.

Conclusions

Researchers interested in the accuracy of their findings for describing populations should not use Internet volunteer samples for the time being.

Comment

Due to a number of confounds in this study, attributing the reported differences to sample type is not possible (since other factors may have had an impact on participants' answers). The confounds included the surveys administered to each sample not being identical (they used different question wordings, although the authors claimed these measured the same construct in comparable ways), the offline sample receiving an FTF survey interview in contrast to the automated, anonymous Internet survey administration mode, and the data not being collected during the same period for each sample. While differences were observed between the samples on many measures, it was not possible (except in the case of two variables which could be compared with 'the truth', and where the traditional sample was more accurate) to conclude whether the online or offline data were better in reflecting actual population parameters.

Broad generalisability is not always a primary goal in social and behavioural research (e.g. Mook, 1983; Yeager et al., 2011). Experimental approaches rarely use clearly defined probability samples, but here statistical inference is justified since participants are randomly assigned to conditions (Alvarez, Sherman, & VanBeselaere, 2003; Siah, 2005). In experimental designs, compromises in external validity are made in the service of maximising internal validity of causal inference (Malhotra & Krosnick, 2007). Concerns about the use of non-probability, volunteer samples in IMR may thus arguably be least problematic for experimental designs (Alvarez et al., 2003; Edgington, 1966; Reips, 2000; Siah, 2005). Qualitative research designs also traditionally do not strive to make broad generalisations to a well-defined target population by using probability sampling techniques, being more concerned with drawing out rich, meaningful narratives which offer insights into the perspectives and personal understandings of the participants studied. In some domains (particularly in the behavioural sciences, such as cognitive and neuro-psychology), many processes are arguably likely to be relatively universal across humanity, thus rendering stringent probability sampling methods less crucial (though see also

Henrich et al., 2010, for qualifications to this view). However, when broader generalisability is required on more variable (e.g. due to culture, history, individual differences) factors, such as attitudes, Internet samples may not be suitable. It is noteworthy that both the studies in Boxes 4.1 and 4.2 report using convenience 'volunteer' Internet samples. However, as discussed further below, we find it useful to distinguish between methods which place adverts on websites and other public online spaces, as used by Gosling et al. (Box 4.1), and those which send personal requests directly to individuals, such as in email invitations, as used by Malhotra and Krosnick (Box 4.2). Also, Malhotra and Krosnick used stratified sampling in an attempt to match their sample to key population parameters. These different approaches will likely generate different types of samples.

It seems reasonable to conclude from the evidence to date that the typical IMR volunteer or non-probability sample[14] may be useful, or even advantageous, when considering research which traditionally uses relatively small homogeneous samples (e.g. AbuAlRub, 2006; Bowen, Williams, & Horvath, 2004; Gosling et al., 2004), but that caution should be urged, presently, in using such IMR samples as a substitute for traditional, large, representative probability samples (Malhotra & Krosnick, 2007).[15] As Gosling et al. (2004) point out, their favourable conclusions with respect to the value of IMR volunteer samples are not intended to generalise to research contexts where representative samples are required (such as opinion polls and large-scale surveys). Having said this, some researchers have now shown that online volunteer samples can generate comparable data (e.g. in terms of relationships between variables, psychometric test properties, etc.) to offline probability samples (e.g. Alvarez et al., 2003; Miller, Johnston, Dunn, Fry, & Degenhardt, 2010). Furthermore, some researchers have used techniques to obtain probability samples online and shown these can be effective in contexts where broader generalisability is required (e.g. Chang & Krosnick, 2009; Heeren, Edwards, Dennis, Rodkin, Hingson, & Rosenbloom, 2008; Stephenson and Crete, 2010; Yeager et al., 2011). Some such examples are discussed below.

RELATIONSHIPS BETWEEN SAMPLING STRATEGY AND SAMPLE TYPE IN IMR

There is a lack of research on how different IMR sampling strategies may generate different types of samples (Alvarez et al., 2003; Hewson & Laurent, 2008; Temple &

---

[14]While all 'true volunteer' Internet samples will also be non-probability samples, some non-probability samples may not be true volunteers; see further discussion below.

[15]Though see e.g. de Pedraza, Tijdens, de Bustillo, R., and Steinmetz (2010) and Valliant and Dever (2011) for discussions of how 'data weighting' techniques might possibly allow generalisations to be drawn from IMR volunteer samples.

Brown, 2011). However, it seems obvious that posting a participation request to a special interest group on rap music will generate a different type of sample (e.g. in terms of demographics) than posting to a group of gardening enthusiasts. Indeed, strategic targeting of special interest groups has been used to obtain samples with desired characteristics (e.g. Bigelsen & Schupak, 2011; Coomber, 1997a; Madge & O'Connor, 2002; Mathy, Schillace, Coleman, & Berquist, 2002[16]). Gosling et al. (2004) (Box 4.1) report that the participants they recruited from a website with a focus on 'finding out about yourself' were more likely to be female, and older (by two years on average), than participants recruited from a website focused on 'star wars'. The latter were found to score slightly higher on the personality dimension 'openness'. Box 4.3 describes a study from one of the authors' own research[17] which compared different IMR sampling strategies, alongside offline approaches.

BOX 4.3   Featured Research: Hewson and Charlton (2005)

Method

The demographic characteristics of four samples were compared. Two online volunteer samples were recruited by posting participation requests to (a) general and non-psychology-related newsgroups (70 responses obtained) and (b) psychology-related newsgroups (97 responses obtained).[a] Two offline convenience samples were recruited by (c) approaching UK undergraduate psychology students at the start of lectures (100 responses obtained) and (d) approaching members of the 'general public', using methods including asking family and friends, and recruiting from public spaces such as outside shops, in waiting rooms, etc. (100 responses obtained).

Results

The Internet samples did not differ significantly in terms of sex, age, salary, occupation and qualifications. However, they did differ in terms of nationality: the general Internet sample were mostly from the United Kingdom (63%), the remainder mainly from Europe (27%), while the psychology Internet sample was more diverse in nationality

(Continued)

---

[16]These researchers used a 'random' sampling technique which involved obtaining a list of specialist chat rooms via search engines and then asking randomly selected participants in each chat room to participate, as opposed to posting general requests to discussion groups.

[17]This work was published by Hewson and Charlton (2005), but since the focus there was on validation of the Multidimensional Health Locus of Control (MHLC) scale for online administration, details on the relationship between the sampling procedures used and sample composition were not reported. These details are reported here for the first time.

(Continued)

(40% North American, 28% UK, 17% Europe, 15% Other). The combined Internet samples differed from the combined offline samples on all demographic factors, being more balanced in terms of sex and age, more diverse in nationality, higher earning, higher educated, and more likely to be in professional occupations. As may be expected, there were differences in the two offline samples: the student sample scored lower on occupation, age, salary and qualifications and was on the whole more homogeneous. These samples did not differ in nationality (both were recruited in the United Kingdom). Surprisingly, they did not differ in sex, both being predominantly female.

Conclusions and Comment

These findings suggest that Internet samples can be more diverse than traditional convenience samples, particularly where the latter rely on undergraduate psychology students; however, minimal differences were found between the different Internet recruitment methods (posting to psychology-related versus more general interest newsgroups). The observed nationality differences can be attributed to several of the 'general' newsgroups targeted being related to UK-based ISPs.

_____

[a] Online 'general' sample newsgroups: freeserve.chat, freeserve.discuss, ie.general, ntl.talk, alt.sci.sociology; alt.history; alt.politics. Online 'psychology' sample newsgroups: alt.psychology, sci.psychology.misc, sci.psychology.theory, alt.psychology.help, alt.psychology.jung, alt.psychology.nlp, sci.psychology.psychotherapy; sci.psychology.personality.

Hewson and Charlton's (2005) findings, as reported in Box 4.3, show minimal effects of different IMR sampling strategies, though the methods used were not dissimilar (both involving posting requests to online discussion groups). Other studies have compared alternative IMR sampling methods. For example, Alvarez et al. (2003) compared placing banner advertisements on webpages (which when clicked led to a survey website), with 'subscription campaigns' where invitations were presented to individuals during their subscription to online services (on expressing interest, individuals were sent details of the survey website to a provided email address; the surveys were simply described as 'Internet Surveys of American Opinion'). The subscription campaigns were more efficient, in that they obtained participants more quickly, and cost-effectively.[18] The samples generated by each method differed on key demographic variables, including gender, age and education, and both samples differed demographically from the current

_____

[18]Though both methods were expensive, the banner advertising campaign costing $25,000 ($7.29 per participant) and the subscription campaign $10,000 ($1.27 per participant).

'American' Internet population.[19] There was little evidence to suggest that either sampling method led to more reliable survey responses.

Temple and Brown (2011) compared three Internet sampling methods: direct email invitations, invitations placed on websites and forums, and an Internet advertising campaign using Google AdWords.[20] These methods were found to perform differently in attracting potential participants to the study, and gaining participants who continued to complete the questionnaires. The 'high-exposure' Internet advertising campaign attracted the most participants to the study website, the 'low-exposure' email strategy the least, and the 'moderate-exposure' website strategy in between. Conversion rates (the number of visitors who actually stayed and completed the questionnaire) were 11% for the high-exposure advertising campaign, 36% for the moderate-exposure website invitations and 10% for the low-exposure email strategies. All methods were aimed at recruiting cannabis users (e.g. by posting to topic-relevant discussion groups and mailing lists) who were invited to fill in a topic-related questionnaire. The authors comment that their results provide insight into the effectiveness of different IMR recruitment strategies for reaching different demographic groups, reporting that 'for example, females, older, non-cannabis-users, and employed participants were disproportionately more likely to have been recruited through the email recruitment strategy than males, younger participants, and students. In contrast, website recruitment strategies were skewed towards the recruitment of young participants and cannabis-users' (p. 14). They do not report on the comparability of the questionnaire response data obtained for the different sampling methods.

The above examples show that different sampling strategies in IMR can lead to differences on a number of factors, including sample demographics, recruitment efficiency and costs, and completion rates. Not surprisingly, methods with greater exposure seem to lead to more visits to a study website, but not necessarily a greater conversion rate. Further such studies will help to enhance knowledge of the relationships between sampling methods in IMR and sample composition, response and completion rates, and response behaviours.

Now that we have considered evidence on who uses the Internet, and how some of the different sampling approaches available might impact upon sample types obtained, and their behaviours, we turn to outline in more detail the various sampling options that are possible in IMR. We consider three main approaches: posting participation requests to websites, newsgroups and other publicly accessible online spaces, to generate volunteer samples; sending requests

---

[19]Data from the August (2000) Current Population Survey (CPS) were used to obtain information about the American Internet population. The CPS is a panel survey of around 60,000 households conducted by the Bureau of the Census.

[20]Google AdWords is a service which allows the placement of advertising links on Google search pages, for a variable fee. For information, see http://www.google.co.uk/ads/adwords/ (accessed April 2015).

directly to individuals (e.g. by email), to generate non-volunteer samples; and using methods which can generate probability samples.

Internet Sampling Methodologies

The important distinction between *probability* and *non-probability* samples was noted above. Another important distinction, particularly when considering sampling from the IUP, is between *volunteer* and *non-volunteer* samples. While all participants who have willingly agreed to take part in a study have in a sense 'volunteered', it seems important in an IMR context to distinguish between the type of volunteering that involves saying yes to a direct participation request (e.g. sent to one's own personal email inbox) and that which involves actively seeking out and responding to a public announcement (e.g. posted on an online study clearing house page, like those discussed in Chapter 3). For purposes of the present discussion, we call the latter type of respondent a 'true volunteer': in other words, someone who has made an active effort to 'bring themselves to the research'. In IMR, unlike offline research,[21] the use of true volunteers who have responded to public adverts (e.g. on online noticeboards, webpages, study clearing houses, etc.) has been prevalent (e.g. Bigelsen & Schupak, 2011; Buchanan & Smith, 1999b; Hewson, 1994; Hewson & Charlton, 2005; Hirshfield et al., 2010; Smith & Leigh, 1997). Online study clearing houses, in particular, offer access to numerous active IMR studies for volunteers to locate and take part in. For example, on 2 February 2012, *Online Psychology Research* (www.onlinepsychresearch.co.uk; accessed April 2014) listed 267 studies currently available for participation, including studies in social psychology (59), health psychology (31), cognitive psychology (27), forensic psychology (25) and personality psychology (25). Participants who have taken part in an IMR study after receiving a personal invitation, we refer to as 'non-volunteers'. These are comparable with convenience samples, as used in offline research. True volunteers (henceforth 'volunteers') necessarily generate *non-probability* samples, since they bring themselves to the research and this precludes prior specification of a known sampling frame (a list of all units from which the sample is to be selected) from which a final sample can be drawn. Non-volunteer sampling methods can give rise to either *non-probability* or *probability* samples (we use these terms as they are traditionally used in sampling theory, e.g. Davidson, 2006, and as explained earlier).

In the first edition of this book, we pointed out that the scope for obtaining probability samples on the Internet was severely restricted (Hewson et al., 2003), and this point has since been reiterated (e.g. Fricker, 2008; Hewson & Laurent, 2008).

---

[21]Which tends to use 'convenience' sampling when using non-probability methods, whereby individuals are typically approached directly and asked if they will be willing to participate (e.g. as in obtaining an opportunity, or 'convenience', sample of psychology undergraduates).

Below we revisit this issue, 10 years on, after first considering IMR methods for obtaining non-probability samples. While our focus here is primarily on sampling *individuals* (as occurs in obtrusive research), we also mention approaches which use other sampling units, such as webpages, discussion posts, tweets, Google searches, and so on, which have proliferated with the emergence of unobtrusive IMR methods (as discussed in Chapter 3).

Volunteer Samples in IMR

Volunteer samples are probably the most commonly used in IMR. The ease of posting adverts to newsgroups, webpages, blogs, SNSs, and so on to obtain large, diverse samples, or smaller specialist samples, has made this cost-effective option attractive. Offline equivalents, such as placing adverts on noticeboards, in news-papers, or distributing leaflets in public locations, are less widely used. Indeed, it is unlikely that any equivalent offline method could obtain a volunteer sample of 361,703 participants, situated in locations worldwide, in the time that Gosling et al. (2004) were able to do so by posting participation requests on websites. This makes IMR unique in its potential for obtaining (true) volunteer participants. Posting requests to websites (e.g. Bigelsen & Schupak, 2011; Hirshfield et al., 2010; Krantz et al., 1997; Senior & Smith, 1999) and news and discussion groups (e.g. Browndyke et al., 1998; Buchanan & Smith, 1999b; Hewson & Charlton, 2005; Riva et al., 2003) are popular approaches. Once an advert has been spotted, par-ticipation may occur via a number of routes, depending on the way the study has been set up. Perhaps most simple, from a participant's perspective, is to click on a link to access the study website (e.g. Hewson & Charlton, 2005). Alternatively, contacting the researcher by email to receive further materials and/or instructions for participation may be required (e.g. Alvarez et al., 2003; Hewson, 1994). While all such approaches will generate a non-probability, volunteer sample, some con-trol over who takes part is possible by carefully selecting the sites where adverts are posted. For example, Madge and O'Connor (2002) were able to recruit new moth-ers by posting to the website babyworld.co.uk. Anderson et al. (2003) recruited participants with tinnitus by posting on the webpages of the Swedish Hard of Hearing Association (as well as placing adverts in newspapers). Several researchers have noted the advantages of this approach in being able to recruit participants who are traditionally hard to access offline (e.g. Baltar & Brunet, 2012; Bigelsen & Schupak, 2011; Coomber, 1997b; Mathy et al., 2002). Facilitating access to spe-cialist, hard-to-access populations seems to be a clear benefit of IMR volunteer sampling strategies, particularly when broad generalisability is not a primary goal.

Potential disadvantages of volunteer sampling approaches in IMR include *volunteer bias effects* and *(non-)representativeness*. The latter has been discussed above, and arguments made that there are many situations in which non-representative samples can be useful (e.g. in qualitative research, or cognitive and experimental psychology). Nevertheless, researchers should carefully consider the extent to which the types of biases which may be inherent (and often unmeasurable) in volunteer sampling approaches may impact negatively on any particular research project. For example, in the first edition of *IRM* we advised against posting study adverts on the types of online study clearing houses mentioned in Chapter 3, since this would likely attract respondents with a particular professional and/or personal interest in IMR methods. This might lead to increased risks of invalid responses, if, for example, the motivation for participation is to examine the way the study has been designed, rather than a genuine interest in the topic at hand (one useful strategy which can help here is to include an explicit question at the end of the study asking participants if their responses were genuine). Other potential recruitment sites might similarly lead to certain biases in the types of participants likely to respond; these biases and their possible impact on a study should be carefully considered. Of course, where broader generalisability is important, volunteer non-probability samples are unlikely to be suitable (Malhotra & Krosnick, 2007).

Volunteer bias occurs when those who have volunteered to participate in a study differ in some way from non-volunteers who have not participated. For example, there is some evidence that volunteers may differ from non-volunteers on personality variables (Bogaert, 1996; Coye, 1985; Dollinger & Frederick, 1993; Marcus & Schütz, 2005) and sexual behaviour and attitudes (Morokoff, 1986; Strassberg & Kristi, 1995). Of course, such effects may vary depending on the study topic and context (volunteers to a study on sexual behaviours may be different from volunteers to a study on music perception). Careful consideration should be given to the way in which volunteer bias influences may impact upon any particular IMR study and the conclusions that can be drawn. Such biases may not necessarily be problematic; for example, it is likely that volunteers will have a particular interest in the research study topic, but this may not be an issue if it is the responses of members of such special interest groups that are desired. The use of (true) volunteer participants in IMR has, to date, been shown to lead invariably to valid, reliable data, at least in terms of being comparable with that which can be obtained offline (as discussed in Chapter 3). However, it should be borne in mind that the use of true volunteer sampling methods in IMR precludes knowledge of who saw the advert and thus had the opportunity to participate. This means measures of response rate, and non-response bias[22] will not be possible (though it may be possible to get a rough idea of how many participants viewed an advert by monitoring website traffic, for example, which could allow response rate estimates). Studies which rely on gaining accurate response rate and non-response bias estimates will thus require alternative non-volunteer sampling approaches. We now consider some such options.

---

[22]Non-response bias occurs when the responses of those who chose to participate differ in some way from the potential responses of those who did not participate (and is usually discussed in the context of methods in which participants are contacted directly and invited to take part in a study).

Possibilities for Accessing Non-volunteer Samples in IMR

Non-volunteer samples (as defined for the purposes of the present discussion; see above) are obtained by contacting individuals directly, via a personal invitation. In IMR this can be done using email (e.g. Jowett et al., 2011; Reece et al., 2010; Strickland et al., 2003), or any other channel which enables such direct contact (e.g. a personal message sent via an SNS, or a chat room as was done by Mathy et al., 2002). In theory this approach enables full knowledge of who had an opportunity to take part (the target sample) by keeping a record of who participation requests were sent to. However, in practice barriers can emerge, including dormant (unused or unchecked) email addresses and multiple accounts (users often maintain various accounts, e.g. with service providers such as Hotmail, Google and others). Personal messages on SNSs may also remain unchecked for long periods of time. This makes estimates of the target sample in non-volunteer (direct contact) approaches unreliable, to an unknown degree. Certain procedures may help, such as using only addresses that are known to have been recently accessed, or arranging for a notification receipt to be returned to the sender when an email is opened.[23] Ethical issues must be considered when deciding how and where to send such requests. Unsolicited participation requests sent to personal email accounts could be seen as 'spamming', or an invasion of privacy, if the individual user has not opted in to receive such requests. We suggest that this approach should not be ruled out, but certain standards should be adhered to; these include maintaining a professional and polite tone, and respecting anti-spamming legislation and policies (e.g. online survey software providers may outline an anti-spamming policy).

It is possible for researchers to assemble their own email lists for use in contacting potential participants (e.g. see Fricker, 2008), for example using employee, student or other similar databases[24] with information (e.g. demographics) on user accounts. Alternatively, they may make use of any of the lists available commercially. However, several issues emerge with the latter approach. First, lists which have been 'harvested' (i.e. collected from the Web) may not offer a clearly specified sampling frame which can be generalised to a known broader population (from which the list was drawn). This means that generalisability beyond the sample is problematic. Secondly, the addresses contained in the list may not be credible. Bradley (1999) discusses this issue, pointing out the popularity of programs like 'Spam Bait Creator'

---

[23]For example, HTML code can be embedded in the body of an email message, which causes a notification to be sent via a server when the email is opened. To check if an email address is still valid and active this free online tool is available from http://tools.email-checker.com/. Checking last date of access is more involved, but can be done by ISPs and list managers.

[24]Sometimes organisations will have their own mailing software systems, linked to a database of user IDs. For example, the first author has been able to contact all students registered on a particular course at The Open University by using the dedicated software CAMEL (Centrally Administered MEssaging Launcher).

which automatically create webpages with bogus email addresses, the intention being that these will be harvested by email address list sellers and thus reduce the quality of their databases. Thirdly, ethical issues can emerge with the use of such lists (as noted in relation to spamming above), since participants often will not have agreed to be included in the database (Fricker, 2008). Even in cases where agreement is 'officially' obtained, the procedures used may be underhand or misleading. For example, individuals who give their email address during a purchase or product registration may fail to notice that they are required to untick a box if they do *not* wish their email address to be used by other parties. Given these issues, we recommend methods which allow greater control over the generation of email lists for contacting potential participants, or which use existing lists that have used clearly stated rigorous, ethically sound procedures. Lists which include basic demographic information are recommended where measures of non-response bias are important, though email addresses themselves can be used to infer some types of information, such as country of origin or organisation affiliation.

Personal email accounts provide an effective way of contacting potential participants directly, ethical considerations permitting. Recent developments in web technologies and structures have also opened up other possibilities, including the use of online SNSs (e.g. Facebook, Academia.edu, Twitter, Friendster, Google+, SoundCloud).[25] A number of researchers have now reported success in recruiting participants via SNSs (e.g. Baltar & Brunet, 2012). Such approaches offer access to potentially vast numbers of participants; Facebook (see Chapter 3 for research examples), for example, has been reported as having 1.44 billion active users (who have logged on within the past 30 days; figures taken from www.statista.com, on April 2015). The number of active daily Facebook users, at the time of writing, is estimated at 936 million (see http://www.internetworldstats.com/facebook.htm [accessed April 2015]). Possibilities for sampling from this population seem astounding. Most simply a message can be sent, including a file attachment, to any user and users can be searched and located by username, which returns results with some additional basic information such as location. More advanced SNS sampling techniques are possible but beyond the scope of the present discussion (for a discussion of unbiased sampling in Facebook, see Gjoka, Kurant, Butts, & Markopoulou, 2010).

Online 'panels' present another option for accessing non-volunteer Internet samples (e.g. see Göritz, 2007; Göritz, Reinhold & Batinic, 2002), with the range and availability of these having escalated over recent years (for an example, see http://www.harrisinteractive.com/MethodsTools.aspx (accessed September 2014); also SurveyMonkey Audience: https://www.surveymonkey.com/mp/audience/

---

[25]For an idea of the range and scope of such sites, along with number of 'registered users' information, see http://en.wikipedia.org/wiki/List_of_social_networking_websites (accessed April 2015).

international/uk [accessed October 2014]). Unlike some harvested email lists (see above), online panel participants have often been contacted directly and asked if they are willing to sign up to take part in survey research (often with promises of monetary reward). While issues relating to dormant and unchecked email accounts can also emerge with such panels, some panels assure regular reliability checks to help ensure all contact details are active and up to date. Panels can also have an advantage over other email lists since they often include key demographic (and sometimes other) information about each user. This enables contacting only individuals who meet certain desired criteria, as in quota or purposive sampling approaches (e.g. Malhotra & Krosnick, 2007). It also enables measurement of non-response bias. The generalisability of data collected from online panels depends on the sampling strategies used to create the panel. In many cases these may involve non-probability approaches, but some panels claim to provide probability samples of the 'general population'. For example, this may involve using offline RDD methods to make initial contact, and then providing Internet equipment to those that do not already have it (e.g. Knowledge Networks, see Fricker, 2008). For research not requiring broadly representative samples, non-probability panels may suffice. A drawback of online panels is that they tend to be expensive to use. A relatively cheap option which some researchers have taken advantage of (e.g. Paolacci, Chandler, & Ipeirotis, 2010) is Amazon's 'Mechanical Turk' online workforce (www.mturk.com); this service offers access to a panel of participants for a researcher-set fee paid per individual respondent (Amazon takes 10% of this fee in commission).

The approaches discussed above involve obtrusive research, where individuals are contacted and invited to participate in a study. However, sampling units do not have to be individual people. Researchers using unobtrusive approaches have sampled from newsgroup posts (e.g. Bordia, 1996; Herring et al., 1998), webpages (e.g. Horvath, Iantaffi, Grey, & Waiter, 2012), blogs (e.g. Herring et al., 2005) and online behavioural traces (e.g. Papacharissi, 2009) (as discussed in Chapter 3). The present chapter is primarily concerned with *people* as sampling units; however, it is worth noting the potentially vast scope for sampling from other sources, unobtrusively, particularly using data scraping techniques. Wesler et al. (2008) discuss such approaches, noting that: 'With nearly two billion humans now embedded to some degree in inscriptive computational media, rapid population-level analysis becomes a realistic possibility' (p. 117).

So far, we have considered non-probabilistic volunteer and non-volunteer sampling approaches in IMR. In recent years the emergence of SNSs and large-scale online panels has expanded possibilities for accessing non-volunteer participants with ease, and without necessarily incurring great expense (though online panels tend to remain expensive). We now consider developments in the scope for accessing probability samples online, which we noted in the first edition of this book was very limited.

Possibilities for Probabilistic Sampling in IMR

Probability sampling in IMR continues to pose a challenge, particularly since there is no central register of all Internet users (Fricker, 2008; Hewson & Laurent, 2008). Also, individual users may have multiple online identities. This means that reliably obtaining a probability sample of the entire IUP is not plausible. However, obtaining such a sample of an entire similarly large, geographically dispersed offline population is also not plausible. Establishing a sampling frame considered to be a good representation of a target population of interest is necessary,[26] in both offline and online research (e.g. all people registered as living at a UK residential address as representative of the UK national population). In IMR, obtaining a probability sample of a subset of the IUP is possible using a 'list-based sampling frame' to enable simple random sampling (e.g. Fricker, 2008). As noted above, researchers may construct their own list, or may make use of the lists commercially available via online panels. The way in which an online panel list has been constructed must be carefully scrutinised if using this approach, but as noted earlier some lists have been constructed using probability sampling methods (e.g. RDD offline) and thus may be particularly useful for research studies requiring large, representative samples (also, as noted, access to such lists can be expensive). Researcher-constructed lists must also be assessed in terms of how the methods used to generate these lists have implications for the types of generalisations that can be made.

Since we were writing the first edition of *IRM*, there have been some noteworthy developments in the evaluation of IMR probability sampling approaches. Several studies have compared online panel-recruited probability samples with offline probability samples and/or non-probability samples. For example, Yeager et al. (2011) compared a probability Internet sample derived from an RDD-constructed online panel with an Internet sample drawn from a non-probability online panel and an RDD (offline) probability telephone sample. Participants were asked to complete a survey containing demographic and health-related lifestyle questions (e.g. smoking and drinking habits). Yeager et al. found that the two probability samples generated the 'most accurate' data when compared with national benchmarks. Heeren et al. (2008) also obtained an Internet probability sample recruited from a probability online panel, which they supplemented with an RDD telephone sample. They found many similarities between this and a previously recruited FTF probability sample (participants were in each case asked to complete a survey looking at alcohol-related behaviours). These authors conclude that Internet probability samples selected from randomly selected online panels can offer viable alternatives to RDD telephone and in-person samples for measuring some factors related to alcohol-related risk behaviours. Chang and Krosnick (2009)

---

[26]In some cases the population of interest and the accessible sampling frame may be identified as the same (e.g. where smaller, more clearly defined populations are of interest, such as all children who attend a particular school).

compared an RDD telephone sample with Internet probability and non-probability samples, concluding that overall the Internet probability sample produced the most accurate results. They report finding both their probability samples to be more representative of the general population (even after weighting). They also report that the Internet samples displayed lower social desirability levels than the telephone sample, and suggest that Internet probability samples may even be preferable to RDD telephone samples in some cases.

Given that randomly selected online panels (and indeed non-randomly selected panels) are generally very expensive to access, and thus may not be an option for many researchers, assessing the value and role of alternative methods which do not rely on such panels is important. Techniques which can at least approximate list-based probability sampling procedures are possible, and typically much cheaper to implement. One possible strategy is to generate a list of email addresses by first selecting randomly from a freely available list of Usenet groups (or Yahoo or Google groups etc.), and then sampling email addresses randomly from posts to these selected groups, over a certain period of time (assuming that genuine email addresses are readily available to view, which may not always be the case). Other Internet outlets where email addresses or individuals' contact details can be acquired (e.g. webpages, chat forums, blogs, SNSs, etc.) can be used in a similar manner to draw up lists which can then be used as a basis for random selection. Several researchers have used this type of list-based sampling approach, where they have generated a list themselves (e.g. Mathy et al., 2002; Penkoff, Colman, & Katzman, 1996; Swoboda, Muhlberger, Weitkunat, & Schneeweib, 1997; Witmer, Colman, & Katzman, 1999). For example, Mathy et al. (2002) describe their 'Cybersurvey' method which involved first deriving an exhaustive list of specialist chat rooms using search engines, and then randomly sampling chat room participants and sending them a personal participation invitation. Recent Web 2.0 technologies offer a range of resources which may provide potential channels for supporting this type of approach. However, the issue of multiple identities online should not be forgotten when devising such procedures; while the risk may be minimal, the likelihood that separate individual entries in any such list might actually link back to the same person should be assessed. Also, the way in which a list has been generated must be carefully considered in relation to possible biases in the nature of the sample obtained; for example, a list generated from specialist chat rooms will not enable the types of generalisations possible if using a large-scale RDD-constructed online panel. This may or may not be problematic, depending on the particular research goals and context. Finally, it is worth noting that list-based sampling frames may not always be easy to obtain, depending on the type of sample desired. Gaining a comprehensive list of all users of an ISP, or online banking service, or subscribers to a particular newsgroup (for example), may be hampered by security and confidentiality issues. Lists of subscribers to mailing lists may be more readily available, but there remain complications: some apparent subscribers may in fact be aliases of other mailing lists, which would lead to underestimating the actual number of subscribers.

Further possibilities for probabilistic sampling in IMR include devising equivalents to traditional non-list-based random sampling strategies, such as offline RDD methods. While this is less easy to achieve on the Internet, possibilities do emerge. One approach is to use 'intercept surveys' which snag systematically every *k*th visitor to a webpage. Dahlen (1998) piloted this approach by implementing a JavaScript program that was able to track all visitors to a high-traffic website and contact every 200th visitor via a pop-up box which requested participation. A disadvantage of this approach is that it precludes measurement of non-response bias, due to not having an enumerable list of all participants who saw the advert, along with demographic information. As always, the extent to which this is likely to be problematic will depend on the particular research study. A measure of response rates can be obtained using this approach, giving it a potential advantage over the use of true volunteer samples (see above). Approaches which attempt to implement probability sampling (or at least techniques which approximate probability sampling) from webpages in IMR, for example, rather than sampling *people*, have also been implemented, but are beyond the scope of the present discussion (see Schütz & Machilek, 2003, for a discussion).

To conclude, while the ability to obtain probability samples in IMR is still relatively limited, opportunities and scope are expanding. Attempts have been made at least to approximate offline 'gold standard' methods, and these strategies have been shown to prove useful for certain types of research (e.g. Heeren et al., 2008; Yeager et al., 2011). Still, several issues remain. First, the possible biases inherent in the IUP itself (as discussed earlier in this chapter) may limit the extent to which valid broader (e.g. national population-level) generalisations can be made. Secondly, the lack of a central register of the entire IUP precludes drawing a probability sample from this population, or even a substantial proportion of it. Issues relating to access, security and confidentiality are pertinent here. Large-scale online panels recruited using offline RDD methods have been shown to generate data which are broadly generalisable, but these presently remain very expensive. However, where resources allow they may well offer a viable alternative to traditional probability sampling methods, potentially at a lower cost. Indeed, there is even evidence that they may provide more accurate results than traditional offline probability samples (Chang & Krosnick, 2009). The issue of 'time in sample' bias (panel members coming to respond differently, over time, due to regularly taking surveys) should be noted, however (Fricker, 2008). As we noted in the first edition of *IRM*, the limited opportunities for probability sampling online may improve with future technological developments; above we have seen how changing technologies, resources and landscapes of the Internet have already resulted in enhanced possibilities. Future developments may enhance opportunities even further.

This chapter has considered in detail issues related to sampling in IMR. Once a study has been conceived and designed (see Chapters 3 and 6), an appropriate sampling strategy needs to be devised. Table 4.2 summarises some of the key sampling strategies available which have been discussed in this chapter, along with their advantages and disadvantages.

Table 4.2 Sampling approaches in IMR

Sample type	Methods	Advantages	Disadvantages
True volunteers	Posting adverts in public online spaces (e.g. web pages, discussion forums)	Easy to implement, cost and time efficient	Precludes knowledge of who saw the advert, and response rate and non-response bias measures. Limited generalisability
Non-volunteers, non-probability	Direct requests to individuals (e.g. email, SNSs)	Allows estimates of response rate, and possibly non-response bias	Limited generalisability to a broader (e.g. national) population
List-based probability sample	Researcher-constructed list, or use of existing list (e.g. panel)	Allows some generalisability, depending on nature of list used (potentially equivalent to offline probability samples)	Requires greater effort, and/or expense, in generating/accessing a suitable list
Non-list-based probability sample	'Snagging' nth visitor to web pages (intercept surveys)	Allows response rate measures	Requires some effort to implement; non-response bias measures unlikely; limited generalisability

<> FIVE </>

<> ETHICS IN INTERNET-MEDIATED RESEARCH </>

Relativity applies to physics, not ethics. (Albert Einstein)

INTRODUCTION

Researchers need to be aware of the extent and importance of ethical issues and dilemmas that emerge when porting research methodologies to an Internet-mediated context. Issues arise both in properly implementing existing ethics standards and principles (e.g. gaining informed consent from participants) and in negotiating and resolving new ethical dilemmas and challenges that emerge from the novel features of online communication and interaction (e.g. what constitutes public and private spaces and material online). In this chapter we consider ethical issues in IMR in some detail. Extensive ongoing discussions, as well as particular issues and debates, have moved more to the forefront of IMR ethics concerns since publication of the first edition of this book. Emerging methods and techniques such as unobtrusive, data scraping approaches have led to this topic deserving a full chapter. Guidelines for ethical behaviour by researchers from a wide range of disciplines are offered here, drawing upon relevant examples to highlight and demonstrate the nature of the ethical dilemmas the Internet introduces, as compared with traditional methods of data gathering. Key topics discussed are: consent, withdrawal and debrief; confidentiality of research data; ensuring participant anonymity; ensuring data security; navigating the blurred public–private domain distinction online. The challenges of obtaining high-quality data and valid results, protecting research participants from potential harm, and assessing when it might be ethically acceptable to use readily accessible traces of behaviour and communications as research data, are broached.

EXISTING ETHICS GUIDELINES FOR IMR

Because IMR is expanding, guidelines for ethical behaviours for researchers from a wide range of disciplines are necessary to answer the concerns of students, teachers, researchers and Research Ethics Committees (RECs, or IRBs: Institutional Review Boards), as well as the individuals being studied. A number of existing guidelines for ethics in IMR are available, and Table 5.1 lists some of these.

Table 5.1 Existing ethics guidelines for IMR

Frankel, M. S., & Siang, S. (1999). Ethical and legal aspects of human subjects research in cyberspace: A report of a workshop. American Association for the Advancement of Science (AAAS). Available at https://nationalethicscenter.org/resources/187/download/ethical_legal.pdf (accessed April 2015).

Kraut, R., Olson, J., Banaji, M., Bruckman, A., Cohen, J., & Cooper, M. (2004). Psychological research online: Report of Board of Scientific Affairs' Advisory Group on the Conduct of Research on the Internet. *American Psychologist, 59*(4), 1-13.

Markham, A., & Buchanan, E. (2012). Ethical decision-making and internet research. Recommendations from the AoIR Ethics Working Committee (version 2). Available at http://aoir.org/reports/ethics2.pdf (accessed April 2015).

BPS (2013). Report of the working party on conducting research on the Internet: Ethics guidelines for internet-mediated research. Available at http://www.bps.org.uk/system/files/Public%20files/inf206-guidelines-for-internet-mediated-research.pdf (accessed April 2015).

IMR-specific ethics guidelines start with basic ethics codes and principles, and explain how complications, challenges and caveats emerge within an IMR context. The BPS (2013) guidelines, for example, are supplementary to the BPS (2011) *Code of Human Research Ethics* (CHRE), and highlight the specific ethical concerns and challenges that arise when applying those principles (*respect for the autonomy and dignity of persons; scientific value; social responsibility; maximising benefits and minimising harm*) in IMR settings. Similarly, the American Association for the Advancement of Science (AAAS) guidelines (Frankel & Siang, 1999) identify several enhanced risks that emerge when attempting to apply basic research ethics principles (*autonomy; beneficence; justice*) in IMR. It is worth emphasising that guidelines, rather than strict codes, are needed to ensure the flexibility to adapt to evolving technologies and methods, as well as diverse contexts, in IMR. Having guidelines rather than rules allows that there is more than one set of norms, values, principles and usual practices.

Researchers need to make ethical choices by assessing and weighing up a number of key factors (e.g. how sensitive the research is, how vulnerable participants are, etc.) within the context of any particular research study. While researchers are ultimately responsible for their own ethical decisions, they must take into consideration governmental regulations, institutional research policies and the changing guidelines for each particular discipline. Further, ethics standards required of Internet researchers are established at various levels by differing review bodies depending on the context of the study, and funding agencies, which can necessitate multiple reviews to check conflicting requirements (similarly to offline research). Researchers should also remain aware that the issue of ethics must be addressed from planning to publication, perhaps even more so in IMR (e.g. due to enhanced risks of leaking participants' personally identifiable data at the dissemination stage: see further discussion below). Consultation of relevant sources, such as discipline-specific ethics guidelines (e.g. BPS, 2013), throughout the ethical decision-making process is necessary (Markham & Buchanan, 2012).

Some broader points are worth emphasising, before considering more specific ethical issues and principles of good practice in IMR. One point concerns the fundamental need to recognise that there is always a 'person' who may be affected by the research (Markham & Buchanan, 2012). In IMR, this recognition can become potentially more problematic, due to the 'conceptual distance' between researcher and participant which emerges from the lack of direct physical proximity, as well as the types of data and behavioural traces that become readily widely available online as potential data sources. In IMR a researcher may be more likely to see 'data', and less likely to see a humane person, the further the researcher gets from the individual who produced the data. Therefore, in IMR it is important for a researcher to take extra care to remain mindful that behind the data there is a person who should be respected. The notion of 'personhood' also raises additional complexities in IMR, since methods involving documenting individuals using avatars, online pseudonyms, and so on (e.g. in virtual worlds and discussion forums), raise challenging questions about the nature of online identities, and how these relate to real-life persons.

The key ethics principle stating that a researcher should ensure a study has scientific value and credibility (e.g. BPS, 2013) becomes especially pertinent in IMR due to concerns, historically, about the questionable reliability and validity of IMR methods, data and conclusions drawn. However, as discussed in previous chapters (see especially Chapters 3 and 4), there is now a good body of evidence indicating that IMR methods across a broad range of domains can produce valid, reliable, trustworthy data comparable with that which can be achieved using offline methods. Ensuring practices and procedures that serve to maximise data quality and reliability in IMR (as discussed throughout this book) is an important ethics principle to keep in mind; as we have noted elsewhere, the temptation for a researcher to launch a study enthusiastically before it has been fully tested and verified may be an enhanced risk in IMR, which can lead to wasted research participant time and funding resources, and the dissemination of invalid conclusions which may be at best misleading and at worst harmful.

That researchers should strive to maximise benefits while minimising harm is a central tenet of many research ethics guidelines (e.g. Buchanan, 2002; BPS, 2011; Frankel & Siang, 1999). BPS (2013) notes that in IMR (like any other research) safeguards and procedures should be implemented so as to be proportional to the levels of risk of potential harm to participants that the research study entails.

In cases where the risk of potential harm is greater, for example when the research involves a sensitive topic (such as illegal activity) or where intended participants are more vulnerable, the greater is the obligation of the researcher to put additional safeguards in place to ensure robust, reliable procedures which protect research participants. This may involve, for example, using offline methods to add rigour and reliability to the informed consent process, or maximising data security by not using third-party servers for storage (as discussed further below and again in Chapter 7).

Essentially, the unique features of IMR, particularly its potential to facilitate high levels of interaction and interactivity while also maintaining high levels of anonymity, distance between participant and researcher, and a lack of traceability of participants (yet enhanced traceability of data), give rise to the unique ethics challenges that emerge in this context. We now consider in more detail some of the most pressing ethical issues that arise in IMR, before elaborating on these in Chapter 6 (in the context of online surveys) and Chapter 7 (focusing on technological issues related to data security and participant confidentiality), and outline some good-practice principles and effective safeguards that can be put in place. We frame the discussion around the obtrusive–unobtrusive distinction, as highlighted in Chapter 3.

ETHICAL ISSUES IN OBTRUSIVE IMR

Consent, Withdrawal and Debrief

Gaining Informed Consent. In obtrusive research, participants are typically recruited to knowingly take part in a study (but note the exceptions discussed in Chapter 3, such as non-disclosed participant observation), and part of this process involves gaining proper informed consent, also referred to as 'valid consent' (e.g. BPS, 2013). Thus interviews, surveys and experiments all involve participants being recruited in this way, as well as some types of observational research. Gaining informed consent requires ensuring that a participant understands the nature of the research, his or her own rights (e.g. to withdraw, remain anonymous, and so on), and knowledgeably and voluntarily decides to participate. In IMR, additional complications emerge in gaining informed consent beyond what is normally the case in offline research. Particularly relevant is the lack of physical contact with research participants, meaning it can be more difficult to monitor whether a participant has engaged with and understood the consent information, and also to verify participant characteristics (such as age).[1] This problem is greatest when there

---

[1]While some offline methods – notably postal surveys – also involve a lack of direct physical contact with participants, these are not subject to some of the other salient, relevant features of IMR; these include greater scope for engaging with interactive, complex procedures, reduced traceability of and scope for monitoring participants (e.g. due to the sampling methods used, and the fluid, multiple, changing nature of online interactions).

are no visible or verbal cues available to the researcher, as is often the case in 'open' web-based surveys and experiments. A further problem is the reduced ability of a researcher to be immediately present to answer questions and provide clarification during the consent process (as can be done in offline FTF approaches), though in some contexts, such as online synchronous interviews, this problem mostly disappears. Also, documenting informed consent requires different solutions in IMR, since participants are not physically present to sign a consent form (though signing and posting this is an option, as with mailed pen and paper questionnaires).

Suggestions have been put forward on how to tackle the aforementioned issues in IMR. As an alternative to obtaining a consent signature, a common approach in IMR is to ask the participant to click on a button labelled 'I accept', 'I consent', or something similar, after having read a page giving some key information about the study and procedure. While some authors have suggested that this approach to documenting informed consent is not adequate, because a consent button does not have the legal status of a signature (and either a printed, signed, mailed form or a digital signature is needed; see e.g. Barchard & Williams, 2008), it is commonly accepted as a sufficient means of gaining informed consent in many IMR contexts, particularly web-based surveys and experiments (e.g. BPS, 2013). Requiring a participant to print out, sign and mail a consent form, or set up a digital signature (which requires personal verification of identity to the entity that grants the digital signature, and thus can take time and effort), can be both cumbersome and expensive, and is likely to eliminate many participants. It should be noted, however, that some RECs or IRBs may require a request of waiver of documentation of informed consent in order to accept, as an alternative to a signature, asking a participant to choose between an 'I consent' and an 'I do not consent' button.

Using a 'consent' button to verify participant consent can be an effective strategy in many IMR contexts, but as already mentioned, monitoring whether a participant has properly read each element of the informed consent page can be problematic. One solution involves including a list of statements with checkboxes, each requiring a response before it is possible to proceed and take part (BPS, 2013). This can help reduce the likelihood of participants simply skipping the informed consent information, especially where the required responses for these statements are not all uniform, so that simply ticking 'yes' or 'agree' in each case is inappropriate. A further strategy to maximise the likelihood that participants will properly read and digest the informed consent information is to ensure it is clearly written and not excessively lengthy (Barchard & Williams, 2008; Keller & Lee, 2003). Using simple language, avoiding idiom, jargon and technical terms, and conforming to W3C Web Content Accessibility Guidelines (see http://www.w3.org/WAI/GL/ [accessed April 2015]) are all good practice.

Regarding the lack of immediate researcher presence in order to be able to address participants' queries, one possibility is to have the study available only when a researcher is online to answer questions, for example by chat, email or instant messaging, but this seems needlessly restrictive for many research contexts (taking into account different time zones etc.), forgoing many of the benefits of online research. It might, however, be an appropriate strategy for studies which are particularly high risk (Barchard & Williams, 2008). Offering, perhaps via a link to another page, a set of FAQs is another possible strategy. This may also prove cumbersome and off-putting for participants, however, compared with having a researcher present and available to answer direct questions. Of course, providing researcher contact information, both pre- and post-study participation, is important, and if emails (if this is the mode chosen) are replied to in a timely manner, this may be effective in addressing the bulk of participant queries and concerns. For studies involving very wide advertisement to recruit participants, which can lead to extremely large sample sizes (see the examples offered in previous chapters), this strategy could potentially become less effective, or unmanageable, but there is little evidence in reports of such studies to date that this has been an issue. Providing clear and informative material in the consent form, or information sheet, should help limit the number of participant queries that are received. Following the same principles as in offline research, the consent information should include a description of the study process, themes and topics, benefits of the research, and any risks involved. In IMR, additional risks can be present, however, which may not always be obvious to research participants (or, indeed, novice researchers – see the further discussion below and Chapter 7). Where more than minimal risk is involved, this arguably should be disclosed, though it can be difficult to decide what constitutes 'minimal' risk and what types of risks participants should be alerted to in IMR. Any significant threats to confidentiality should probably be disclosed (if, indeed, the research study is still considered ethical to carry out under such circumstances).

The problem of verifying participant characteristics in IMR – particularly their age, since there are both legal and ethical mandates regarding the minimum age at which participants can give consent to participate in research,[2] needs careful consideration. Again, the methods most affected by this issue are those which involve minimal contact between researcher and participant. The risk of harm if a participant who is underage (or unable to give proper consent for other reasons) is able to go ahead and complete a study by giving false information about their age should be carefully assessed. Where risks are higher, such as in sensitive research, then extra stringent safeguards should be put in place. Asking participants to disclose their age is of course good practice, and required as part of the consent process. It can be useful to do this before revealing that there is a minimum required age for participation, to reduce the likelihood of participants being

---

[2]Note that specified minimum age requirements for being able to give consent can vary. For example, BPS (2011) stipulates that a participant must be 16 years or older to give consent, whereas in the United States the minimum required age for consent is typically stated as 18 years or older. Given the international reach of IMR, this can raise issues regarding which standards should be followed – Chapter 7 discusses this issue further.

motivated to lie. Any underage respondents can then be redirected at this point to an exit study page and any attempts to return to complete the study blocked (e.g. using methods such as cookies) (BPS, 2013). A further strategy is to implement sampling procedures which are unlikely to attract those younger than the required age of consent, or who do not meet other requirements needed to be able to give proper informed consent (e.g. Hewson, 2015). This can involve advertising only in adult-oriented venues, and avoiding child-oriented marketing such as the use of animated characters. It could also involve targeting known individuals, or at least individuals of known age, or other relevant characteristics (Chapter 4 has discussed in detail the range of sampling options in IMR). Other safeguards involve implementing more reliable age verification procedures, such as using credit card information, or offline verification methods (e.g. BPS, 2013). In practice, however, the instances of participants trying to enter and fraudulently take part in an IMR study in this way may be rare, so such stringent methods may not often be necessary. As always, the researcher needs to assess the level of risk of harm to potential participants that the online study might pose, and implement procedures commensurate with this level. In some cases, it may even be decided that an IMR approach is unsuitable, and a study should be conducted offline.

Some studies recruit participants who do not themselves have the capacity for consent, and in these cases consent from a parent or guardian is required. In IMR such approaches should be considered with much caution, due to the enhanced vulnerability of these groups exacerbating any risks. Stringent procedures for gaining informed consent will need to be put in place in such contexts, and very careful risk assessments carried out, as well as procedures put in place which allow monitoring of participants and their reactions as fully as possible. However, such studies should not be ruled out (BPS, 2013). Hessler et al. (2003) for example were able, safely and ethically, to implement a study which recruited teenagers, requiring them to submit online daily diary entries, by employing robust, careful offline consent procedures involving securing parent/guardian consent. So, while the ethical challenges can certainly intensify when considering conducting IMR studies using children or other vulnerable groups, these studies should not be precluded.

Withdrawal and Debrief. Consent procedures should involve the assurance to participants that they can withdraw from the study at any time (at least up until a reasonable specified point, such as before data have been aggregated or published). This helps ensure that participation is voluntary. Participants should also be debriefed after completing a study, as well as if they exit prematurely. In IMR, complications can arise in implementing effective withdrawal and debrief procedures. Debriefing procedures can suffer from similar reliability issues to consent, since verifying that a participant has read and understood debrief information can be difficult. Further, making sure debrief information has been presented at all can be challenging in some situations (see below). Withdrawal procedures can be confounded by a participant using unexpected or unintended ways to exit a study, for example by simply closing the web browser in an online survey, or simply disappearing without trace from an online interview or focus group session. In such cases, a researcher is unable to know whether the participant intended any partial data collected to be used, as well as whether the participant left in a state of discomfort or distress. Post-study withdrawal requests can also become problematic with some commonly used IMR methods, such as open, web-based surveys, if the researcher has not collected sufficient information to be able to match individuals with responses.

A number of good-practice strategies, as well as additional safeguards in higher risk situations, can help address the above issues and reduce the likelihood of problems arising. One advisable strategy is to place a clearly visible 'Withdraw' button on each screen of a web-based survey or experiment (BPS, 2013; Hewson, 2015). Also, at the end of a study, a clearly labelled 'Submit Data' button should be provided, so participants can confirm that they want their responses to be used. These practices, in addition to explicit pre-study instructions informing participants that their contribution is entirely voluntary and they may withdraw at any stage (and explaining how to do this), can help reduce the chances of their exiting by closing their web browser, and consequently not seeing the debrief page (which cannot be presented if a participant exits in this way). However, it must be noted that not all third-party software solutions allow easy placement of a 'Withdraw' button on each survey page, which when clicked redirects participants to a debrief statement (e.g. SurveyMonkey does, but Qualtrics does not). Researchers should take this into account when selecting software solutions (see also Chapter 6).

Post-study withdrawal requests require that a researcher has a means of matching individuals with the responses they submitted. In fully anonymous, open web-based surveys and experiments this becomes problematic. One strategy, which can still allow high levels of anonymity, is to ask participants for an identifying password, known only to them, though this may well require bespoke systems, since most commercial software will not allow this option. Another is to ask for an identifying email address, but this inevitably reduces levels of participant anonymity. Appropriate choices need to be made based on the requirements and features of any particular research study; for example, in highly sensitive research anonymity assurances can become more urgent (while so too do reliable debrief procedures, which can cause conflicts and necessary trade-offs to emerge; obtaining a valid email address from participants, for example, can enhance the reliability of debrief procedures since this information can then be sent via email).

Providing researcher contact details, such as an email address, is important at the debrief as well as the consent stage. This provides participants with a means of contacting the researcher, even if they have not noted down these details at the time of consent, and to some extent helps alleviate issues related to the reduced ability of researchers in IMR to monitor participants and detect any signs of discomfort, distress or harm (compared with offline FTF approaches, at least). Researcher availability to answer any queries sent at this point in a timely manner, similarly to at the consent stage, is important.[3] Debrief information should follow the same guidelines for achieving clarity and accessibility as outlined above for consent information, and researchers can also consider providing a set of study FAQs at this point (as well as or instead of at the consent stage), both of which may help prevent too many participant queries being received. In studies involving higher levels of risk, it may be beneficial for a researcher also to be able to contact participants, if for example the researcher is concerned that a participant may have left in a state of distress (e.g. during an interview or group discussion), which may constitute an argument for asking participants to provide a valid email address, or other contact information. Of course, in some IMR approaches, such as email interviews, this contact information will already be available by virtue of the research procedures.

Finally, sometimes it can be necessary (arguably) to deceive participants in the service of science, in cases where fully informing participants about the research prior to participation will impact upon the integrity of the results. In such cases, risks of harm can be elevated, and ensuring that appropriate debrief information is presented becomes even more important. In IMR, a researcher using deception will need to take extra care to ensure that robust, reliable debrief procedures are in place, keeping in mind the caveats outlined above. It will most likely be appropriate in such contexts to require some form of contact information from participants, such as an email or postal address, so that debrief information can be sent directly to them, thus maximising the chance of its being received and read. However, a researcher should carefully consider whether it is ethically appropriate to conduct a study involving deception in an online environment at all, given the range of issues and potential risks involved. The extent and nature of the deception will need to be taken into account, as well as other factors (as discussed throughout this chapter), in making this decision.

Confidentiality

Ensuring the confidentiality of participants' contributed data is an important part of ethical practice in social and behavioural research. Confidentiality is achieved by anonymising data, so that participants are not personally identifiable, and protecting data files so that they are not open to unintended access by a third party. In IMR, a number of challenges arise in ensuring both anonymity and security of data which are not typically present when using offline research methods (Reips & Buffardi, 2012).

Anonymity. If data collected from participants contain no personally identifying information, then risks associated with unintended third-party access are

---

[3]Which effectively means a researcher needs to be available throughout the time a study is 'live', since different participants will be coming and leaving at various different points in time.

minimised. However, IMR methods can make it difficult to collect and store data completely anonymously. Methods which use email, including interviews, surveys and focus groups, are not fully anonymous since email addresses are linked to individuals. However, it is possible to send anonymous emails using one of the various providers that offer this service (a quick Google search will locate any number of these). Alternatively, a dedicated temporary email account could be set up for a participant to use during the study, without any personally identifying information being included in the username. In this way, any responses submitted would not be linked with the individual, except by the researcher's own records of who has been assigned which username. However, a caveat relating to the latter approach is that the IP address through which an email is sent could potentially be linkable to an individual, so this method may not be entirely anonymous (one way round this might be to ask participants to respond from a public computer, but of course this entails its own confidentiality risks).

Web-based data collection methods, particularly surveys and experiments, seem to offer greater scope for fully anonymous responding, but caveats emerge here also. For example, some third-party online survey software solutions automatically store IP addresses along with participants' responses, and, as just noted, this could lead to data becoming personally identifiable. Also, it is often the case that researchers need to collect personal information (such as demographics) as part of the research study design. Depending on the nature and extent of this information, it is possible that it could be amalgamated and used to identify individuals. For this reason, it is established good practice to keep any personally identifying information separate from research study responses, so that the latter remain anonymous (e.g. Barchard & Williams, 2008). This can often be achieved quite easily in offline research, since the researcher typically has full control over data collection, storage and management processes. In IMR, however, difficulties can arise due to reduced levels of researcher control over these processes. Thus, where third-party online survey software is used to collect and store participants' data (using the provider's server), personal data and study response data are stored together in a single file – which, ultimately, the third-party provider has control over. Situations where the system is fully under the control of the researcher (or linked IT team) allow the greatest scope for ensuring that participants' personal data are stored separately from study responses (e.g. in different files, perhaps located on different servers). Chapter 7 discusses researcher control over data collection, storage and management processes in more detail.

Researchers thinking of using existing online discussion and social media sites for collecting data in obtrusive IMR should remain aware that data collected within these spaces will typically be linked with a username or pseudonym linked to an online identity, and this may also be linked to a person's offline identity. As discussed in Chapter 6, there are various reasons why it may often be more appropriate to set up a dedicated research space to carry out, for example, an online focus group, interview or observational study, and this approach also has the advantage of giving a researcher greater control over the levels of anonymity of participants' responses (e.g. by allocating participants a research-specific pseudonym). However, some approaches – such as ethnographic research – are likely to require the use of existing online social spaces, where people interact using established online identities. Keeping personally identifying information, including usernames, separate from other research data gathered in these contexts is thus good ethical practice. However, while this can be done with data files stored locally by the researcher, a researcher does not have control over the storage of the original sources from which these data were drawn (discussion forums, blogs, VREs, etc.). This raises issues about published research findings potentially being traced back to these original sources, and identities being revealed. Some methods are more susceptible to this risk, such as qualitative approaches where verbatim quotes might be used in disseminated research reports. This issue is discussed further under unobtrusive approaches, where it becomes particularly relevant since these approaches often do not involve gaining informed consent from participants (e.g. when using discussion forum archives; see the examples discussed in Chapter 3). In obtrusive research, such as disclosed ethnographic observation, consent is often gained (though see Brotsky & Giles, 2007, mentioned in Chapter 3, who surreptitiously observed a pro-anorexia community by posing as a plausible persona on the community website), which means that at least participants can be informed of any confidentiality risks during the informed consent process, and agree to participate with full knowledge of these risks.

Data Security. Email is a relatively non-secure data transmission mode, since between leaving the sender and reaching the recipient an email can reside on many servers, making it more vulnerable to interception by a third party. Coupled with the personal identifiability of email addresses, this makes it a fairly risky mode of transmission in terms of participant confidentiality, compared with many offline methods (e.g. pen and paper surveys, or experiments conducted on non-networked computers). Also, making a minor typing slip when sending an email could lead to its being sent to the wrong person entirely, which could have non-trivial consequences (e.g. in sensitive research, which should be conducted with care and arguably use encrypted or anonymous email methods, or alternative approaches). Web-based methods are also susceptible to security risks which may potentially breach participant confidentiality assurances. As already noted, if using third-party software (e.g. for web-based surveys, or existing mailing list or discussion group services, as discussed in Chapter 6), storage and management of participants' research data is not fully under the control of the researcher (unless, perhaps, non-hosted options are used). As well as the issue of participants' personal and study response data being stored in the same file at the point of collection, making the participant's study responses not fully anonymous, this also entails a lack of researcher control over protection of these data files from unintended third-party access. Commercial software vendors typically claim to store data with rigorous security safeguards, and information about this can often be found on their webpages. Researchers should check this information carefully to ensure adequate standards are met. One issue which emerges (see Chapter 6) is that if data are stored on a server in another country, then they may not be handled in compliance with a researcher's local data protection legislation. In some cases, it might be decided that using systems over which a researcher has full control is most appropriate.

Another caveat relating to the security of web-based data collection methods is that web browsers are often configured to keep a record of activity, such as pages visited, usernames entered, and so on. This can offer a means of tracing user activity, including participation in a research study, and even the responses given, to a third party who has access to the local computer. Apart from remote hacker access possibilities (discussed further in Chapter 7), someone who has shared access to the local computer (e.g. a partner, or member of the same household) might thus stumble across a participant's study responses, either deliberately or by accident. This poses a potential risk to participant confidentiality which arguably participants should be alerted to, and offered suggested ways of pre-empting, including clearing the browser cache, for example.[4] Potential participants may not be aware of these risks, and thus the onus is on the researcher to provide them with suitable advice and guidance, particularly in contexts where the risk of harm is intensified, such as sensitive research topics. Risks of third-party access to a participant's data in this way might be quite low in some contexts, but higher in others. Employers, for example, are likely to be fully informed about how to trace and track the activity of their employees on workplace computers.[5] Researchers should therefore consider whether they are obliged to advise participants against using workplace or other non-private computers, to reduce the risk of confidentiality breaches. Furthermore, a participant using a workplace computer can introduce risks of confidentiality for the company itself, since the browser on a company-owned computer may well be configured to retain memory of standard form fields, and the general computing configuration will likely include settings that record text that has been recently deleted from other documents. Participants using computers so configured open the workplace to the risk of having data accidentally inserted into open text fields in a survey instrument, potentially infringing on the employer's confidentiality rights.

Other issues that emerge in relation to participant confidentiality in IMR are similar to those that are present in offline research contexts; thus a researcher should take care to protect any local hardware on which participant data are stored against unintended access, by using passwords, antivirus software, minimising

---

[4]Researchers may also want to consider whether they should clear their own browser caches during the implementation and management of a research study.

[5]Data ownership and access issues become relevant here also, since many companies maintain their right to information stored on their own computers.

risks of theft, and so on. The issue of a researcher having an ethical or legal obligation to report certain types of information that might be given to the researcher
in the course of a research study, such as disclosures of harm or risks of harm to
vulnerable individuals, is also relevant. In IMR it is possible that the data collection medium itself might enhance the likelihood of such disclosures, compared for
example with offline FTF methods (see Chapter 3). One way to address this issue
is to warn participants in advance that certain types of information they might
disclose may be vulnerable to confidentiality breaches in this way, and to include
a statement on the consent form such as 'I understand that if my participation
in this research reveals illegal activity, the researcher is obligated to report it to
appropriate authorities.' Finally, the way a researcher stores and processes research
data should take into account data protection laws, which dictate how personally
identifiable data should be handled. Given the international reach of IMR, complications can arise in conforming to data protection laws, which vary from country
to country. Chapters 6 and 7 discuss these issues further.

ETHICAL ISSUES IN UNOBTRUSIVE IMR

Public and Private Spaces Online

One of the main current controversies in IMR, at the time of writing, concerns
when it is ethically acceptable to locate and use as research data existing readily available online sources, including documents, behavioural traces, discussion
forum posts, and so on, without gaining informed consent from those who produced them. According to BPS (2011) the only information that should be used as
potential research data (in observational research) without gaining consent is that
sourced from 'public situations' where those involved would expect to be observed
by strangers. The challenge that arises in IMR is in determining which traces of
individuals' online activities constitute being 'in the public domain', and which
would be expected by the individuals involved to be observed by strangers (and,
indeed, used as research data). While some sources seem clearly private (e.g. private email exchanges) others seem to have ambiguous status (e.g. discussion forum
posts and blog posts). Published documents are perhaps the least contentious in
terms of being clearly in the public domain, and thus arguably available for use
as research data, but researchers should be aware of copyright restrictions, which
might require permission for use to be obtained from authors or other data owners.

To explore the issue of individuals' expectations of privacy online, Hudson
and Bruckman (2004) monitored chat room users' reactions to being observed
under different researcher disclosure conditions (see Chapter 3). They report that
the chat room participants they observed were generally hostile to researcher
attempts to monitor their conversations, but especially so when these intentions
were disclosed, as opposed to when a researcher simply entered a chat room and

lurked. This led them to conclude that non-disclosure is justifiable, and might be the only feasible way to gain valuable research data in some situations. Other researchers have reported success in lurking and unobtrusively obtaining data from synchronous online discussions (e.g. Al-Sa'Di & Haman, 2005; Rodino, 1997), as well as approaching online communities and gaining permission to observe their interactions (e.g. see the examples offered in Chapter 3). A range of different perspectives have been taken on whether it is ethically acceptable to record online discussions unobtrusively, either via live chat rooms or using stored discussion group archives; King (1996), for example, suggests that this practice can be acceptable as long as careful measures are taken to protect the anonymity and confidentiality of the individuals who contributed the data. For further discussion of this issue, see Brownlow and O'Dell (2002) and Hewson (2015).

The perspective taken on the ethics of using readily accessible online traces as research data without gaining informed consent will of course influence research practice. Two contrasting examples were discussed in Chapter 3. Thus, while Fox et al. (2005) observed exchanges on a pro-anorexia website with full disclosure to group members, Brotsky and Giles (2007) carried out a very similar participant observation study without any disclosure, by posing as a genuine member of the online community. The ethical acceptability of adopting the latter approach may seem highly questionable. However, the issues involved are not straightforward or clear cut. Thus, the potential for causing harm by disrupting existing social structures, and possibly fostering mistrust and suspicion within a group, emerges as a possible justification for non-disclosure in such studies, alongside arguments about the social and scientific value of the research. As discussed in Chapter 3, Tackett-Gibson (2008) reports intending to disclose fully to individual online community members the intention to observe their online interactions, but being blocked from doing so by moderators who felt it could be damaging to the community, and therefore granted permission only to access archives and carry out observations by lurking unobtrusively. This raises issues of who has the best authority, expertise and experience to make these decisions. In general, it is good practice for a researcher to consult group moderators if planning to approach a group for research purposes, but it is also worth keeping in mind that in some cases moderators could possibly prohibit a valuable piece of research, or oppose its being conducted in a manner which conforms to research ethics guidelines. Of course, while non-disclosure may be arguably justified for the aforementioned reasons, as well as perhaps for reasons of ecological validity and avoiding contaminating naturalistic data, if a researcher who is surreptitiously monitoring and observing a group does have his or her identity revealed, this could be the most damaging to the group. Thus taking stringent measures to prevent this possibility is crucial.

A further example which involved harvesting accessible online data sources unobtrusively, without permission, is reported by Barak and Miron (2005). They studied the writing characteristics of suicidal people, without obtaining informed consent, in an ethnographic study in which they randomly selected users' messages from a publicly accessible online support group. These authors argue that by deliberately making their communications available in public archives, group members consented to their inspection by others, and thus suspended ethical concerns. They further note that: 'The study of suicidal behaviour is complicated for many reasons. A major reason has to do with suicidal persons' desire to remain unidentifiable, to avoid psychiatric labelling and social stigma, as well as to prevent intervention, in their unusual and commonly unacceptable attitude' (p. 519). This example is noteworthy in that it involves vulnerable individuals and a very sensitive, personal topic. This makes it particularly pertinent, and controversial, in the issues it raises regarding individuals' privacy rights, and what is acceptable ethical research practice in IMR.

The above examples demonstrate the complexity of the issues involved in navigating the public–private domain distinction online, and in making appropriate ethical choices in IMR. Clearly people's privacy perceptions and expectations must be taken into account; however, more research is needed to uncover what these might be, in different contexts (including within different cultural groups; see Hewson, 2015, for further consideration of issues related to user expectations and perceptions of privacy online). What is clear is that a simple rule that, for example, anything which can be accessed without requiring a user account, or password, should be considered available for use as research data without raising any ethical concerns, is inappropriate. Rather, researchers must make informed decisions taking into account a range of relevant factors (as discussed throughout this chapter) in any particular research context. For example, whether a study generates rich, textual data, or quantified aggregate traces, is relevant to issues of risks of potential harm (see Hewson, 2015, for further discussion). Legal considerations also need to be taken into account; for example, strictly speaking, anything which is protected by copyright law is not 'in the public domain', and this would include most archives and traces of online communications (since these are under copyright of the service provider, e.g. Facebook owns all Facebook posts) (BPS, 2013). In practice, precluding any use of such copyrighted material without gaining permission seems overly restrictive, and such sources have been and continue to be used in IMR without disclosure. Legal constraints should of course be taken into account, but may not always dictate what is best ethical research practice.

Confidentiality of Data

Where a researcher has assessed all relevant factors and decided that existing or ongoing traces of online behaviour and/or communication can reasonably be considered 'in the public domain', and so sourcing and using these data for unobtrusive research without gaining informed consent is ethically acceptable, very careful consideration must be given to the way in which this is done so that it does not breach participant confidentiality by allowing research data to be traced back to identifiable individuals who produced them. Such breaches of participant confidentiality can also be a risk in obtrusive approaches, of course, as discussed earlier; however, in obtrusive contexts it is more likely that consent has been obtained, and thus participants have had the opportunity to assess and accept any disclosed risks, including confidentiality breaches. Undisclosed sourcing of traces as research data, as often occurs in unobtrusive research, requires extra stringent measures to ensure participant confidentiality, due to issues related to potential violations of a person's privacy rights. This requires particularly careful attention to the dissemination practices used in unobtrusive IMR, and the risks these may entail, as now discussed.

Harvesting and turning online traces into research data, and engaging in dissemination practices, embody enhanced risks compared with many offline methods due to the enhanced traceability and public accessibility of many online sources, compared with equivalent offline sources. Even if a researcher carefully cleans data of identifying information for publication in a research report, it can be relatively easy to trace quotes back to the individuals' original posts using search engines, particularly if they are obtained from discussion forums, blogs, SNSs and similar online public spaces. Researchers need to be aware of this, particularly where violations of anonymity could lead to negative consequences and potential harm. While publishing verbatim quotes is often practised in offline qualitative research, the enhanced risks involved in doing so in many (particularly unobtrusive) IMR methods needs to be recognised and taken into account. A person's privacy rights could be violated by inadvertently making their original source data identifiable through wider dissemination and publication. These issues are complex, involving both legal and ethical components. The researcher is likely, for example, to have offered insights and interpretations, which go beyond just using what is already in the public domain, and which could be injurious to a participant. In a note of caution, Lipinski (2008) reminds researchers that defamation suits can be brought for dissemination of their own observations of online activity, or by repeating the defamatory comments made by someone else.

One safeguard in IMR is to paraphrase a participant's words, rather than using direct quotes, so they are less likely to be traceable back to source (BPS, 2013). Another is to ensure that the name or address of a website, discussion forum, blog, etc., from which data were gathered is not published (BPS, 2013), since doing so increases the risk of compromising participant confidentiality, and could also have a negative effect on an online community. Some groups and communities (e.g. activist groups), however, may welcome the publishing and dissemination of their discussions, and arguably this may be empowering for these groups. Group moderators should be questioned as they are a valuable source of information and insight when making decisions about which procedures should be implemented to protect the anonymity and confidentiality of online communities and their members (BPS, 2013).

Studies which unobtrusively harvest data about the structures and processes of online behaviours and interactions, such as friendship links in social networks, are likely to be less at risk of confidentiality breaches due to dissemination practices than methods which collect rich, semantic, textual data. Here there is less scope to trace back reports of data analysis and study conclusions to personally identifiable sources (e.g. because data are quantified and reported in aggregate form). However, in all unobtrusive research contexts, it is important for a researcher to remain aware that all the safeguards and good-practice strategies relating to the ethical collection, storage and processing of data – as outlined earlier when discussing obtrusive research methods – apply also in order to maximise protection of research participants' identities.

CONCLUSION

In conclusion, researchers are responsible for ensuring that their study is valid, reliable and ethical by using proper research design, having REC (or IRB) approval, using protocol to secure informed consent where consent is deemed appropriate, monitoring the participants' reactions to a study, balancing risks and benefits appropriately, and ensuring anonymity and confidentiality where these are appropriate to the research design and have been assured to participants. Further, the complexities of navigating the public–private domain distinction online need careful consideration, particularly when undisclosed data collection methods are being considered. In such cases, very careful measures to protect participants' personal identities will need to be put in place. In essence, Internet researchers are accountable and must be respectful of participants, colleagues and the population at large, in the same way as traditional offline researchers. Some of the IMR-specific issues, which may not always be obvious to researchers, and proposed ways to address these effectively, have been outlined in this chapter. Table 5.2 offers some additional sources to consult on ethics in IMR, to supplement the guidelines for consultation listed in Table 5.1 at the start of the chapter. Finally, this chapter concludes by listing some key ongoing debates in ethics in IMR.

Table 5.2 Some resources on ethics in IMR

Journal articles/book chapters

Barchard, K. A., & Williams, J. (2008). Practical advice for conducting ethical online experiments and questionnaires for United States psychologists. *Behavior Research Methods, 40*(4), 1111-1128.

Brownlow, C., & O'Dell, L. (2002). Ethical issues for qualitative research in on-line communities. *Disability & Society, 17*(6), 685-694.

Buchanan, E., & Ess, C. (2009). Internet research ethics and the Institutional Review Board: Current practices and issues. *Computers and Society, 39*(3), 43-49.

(Continued)

Table 5.2 **(Continued)**

Ess, C. (2007). Internet research ethics. In A. Joinson, K. McKenna, U. Reips and T. Postmes (Eds.), *Oxford handbook of internet psychology*. Oxford University Press.

Hewson, C. (2015). Ethics issues in digital methods research. In C. Hine and H. Snee (Eds.), *Digital methods as mainstream methodology: Inspirational digital/social research*. Palgrave.

Rodham, K., & Gavin, J. (2006). The ethics of using the Internet to collect qualitative research data. *Research Ethics Review, 2*(3), 92–97.

Zimmer, M. (2010). But the data is already public: On the ethics of research in Facebook. *Ethics & Information Technology, 12*(4), 313–325.

Journals

International Journal of Internet Research Ethics (IJIRE, http://ijire.net/)

Web resources

Exploring Online Research Methods: http://www.restore.ac.uk/orm/ethics/ethcontents.htm (accessed April 2015)

AoIR Ethics Guide: http://ethics.aoir.org (accessed April 2015)

<> SIX </>

<> TOOLS AND DESIGN STRATEGIES FOR INTERNET- MEDIATED RESEARCH </>

INTRODUCTION

Here we follow on from the discussion in Chapter 3 which outlined a range of approaches, methods and strategies in IMR, and highlighted some of the Internet resources and software tools that can support these. This chapter considers in more detail how some of these tools and techniques can be accessed and used to implement IMR studies. Some of the Internet resources we discuss here overlap with those mentioned in Chapter 2, but here the focus is on using them to conduct primary rather than secondary research. There is now much less need than in 2003 for researchers to engage directly with complex programming languages and techniques in order to create their own systems to locate on their own web server, due to the availability of software packages which can readily handle many of the most common survey designs, as well as simple or in some cases more complex experiments. Here we consider some of the packages available and what they have to offer. For more complex designs, bespoke solutions, which require engaging with programming languages and server configurations, may still be necessary, but these needs are best served by turning to primers on Internet programming and database management. However, for many researchers the current (and expanding) selection of off-the-shelf software packages available for assisting in implementing the various techniques discussed previously, particularly web-based survey methods, may well suffice. Whereas in the first edition of *IRM* we focused largely on tools and design principles for implementing web-based surveys and experiments, the present chapter expands this scope, considering a broader range of methods, particularly now including discussion of unobtrusive methods. We also build on the Chapter 3 discussion of design choices and strategies in IMR, offering here some more detailed principles and guidelines for researchers to work from. In place of the web-based survey programming guide we offered in the first edition of *IRM*, this chapter concludes with a step-by-step guide on using a low-cost, popular online survey software package: SurveyMonkey. For other methods, we outline some of the basic tools and techniques to get started, and provide links to further information and resources for the interested reader.

Emphasis throughout the chapter is on making design and implementation decisions which maximise the validity, reliability and integrity of the data obtained. Key ethical issues and principles, as were covered in Chapter 5, are highlighted and reiterated where applicable. While the pace of development of Internet-related technologies continues to be spectacular by any standard, rendering any summary inevitably quickly dated, this is no reason to despair – one of the reasons why the Internet has become so important is that it is regulated by standards which specify minimal requirements for software compliance. So generally, if something works now, it should work in the future. Future developments will continue, of course, to extend the range of available techniques and technologies for IMR (the shape of some of these developments was speculated on in Chapter 3), yet some of the earliest Internet technologies continue to be widely used, such as email. Others have become largely obsolete, such as telnet, which has been mostly superseded by remote login.

TOOLS AND DESIGN PRINCIPLES FOR IMR

First, it is worth considering some general principles of good practice for IMR. Early published generic IMR guidelines have been offered (e.g. Hewson, 2003; Hewson et al., 1996; Michalek & Szabo, 1998); inevitably such early accounts require revisions and updates to respond to the evolving landscape of IMR methods, and more recent evidence concerning the factors to take into account in IMR research design. Recent guidelines tend to be specific to particular IMR methods, offering more detailed, context-specific recommendations (as discussed further below). Still, a set of more generic IMR principles of good practice can also be useful, as a foundation for more context-specific solutions. Table 6.1 presents what we consider to be some useful broader principles that apply more generally across a range of IMR methods (drawing on those offered by Hewson, 2014a, 2014b). For each principle the type of approach for which it is likely to be most relevant – using the obtrusive–unobtrusive (as outlined in Chapter 3) and qualitative–quantitative dimensions – is indicated. The latter is relevant since qualitative approaches typically generate more elaborate, detailed, rich textual data, often involving individual personal narratives, whereas quantitative approaches tend to generate large, aggregate numerical data sets, where individual contributions are less likely to be easily personally identifiable. Thus different issues tend to emerge as most

Table 6.1 General IMR good-practice principles

Principles	Obtrusive	Unobtrusive	Quantitative	Qualitative
Sampling				
• Carefully consider how different sampling approaches and design procedures may facilitate or restrict access by different groups	√		√	√
• Remain mindful that volunteer samples may not be suitable where broad generalisability is required, and consider alternative offline and online probability methods	√		√	
• If posting participation requests to newsgroups and other social spaces, it is typically good practice to contact moderators or gatekeepers first to request permission	√		√	√
• Make sure participation requests are well constructed, containing information on researcher affiliations, contact details for further information, and value of the research	√		√	√
Implementation				
• Use robust, well-tested procedures which have been well piloted	√		√	√
• Use the simplest low-tech solutions and equipment available that will do the job	√		√	√
• Remain mindful of legal (as well as ethical) issues, including copyright and data protection, especially when harvesting online data sources		√		√
• Aim to use software solutions which have functions to help maximise control, reliability and validity, such as multiple submission checking and prevention, and response format and completeness checking	√		√	
• Aim to use software solutions that conform to established accessibility standards (e.g. compatibility with screen reader software)	√		√	

(Continued)

Table 6.1 (Continued)

Principles	Obtrusive	Unobtrusive	Quantitative	Qualitative
• Remain mindful of the trade-offs involved in ensuring anonymity and gaining participant characteristics information, assessing decisions in the context of study design, context and goals	✓		✓	
• Use appropriate procedures for verifying identity (e.g. offline, audio/video) where this is crucial (e.g. highly sensitive research)	✓		✓	✓
Ethics				
• Remain mindful of the ethical responsibility to inform potential participants of any non-trivial risks they may be unaware of arising from an IMR context (e.g. low security of email)	✓			✓
• Remain mindful of the possible threats to participant confidentiality and anonymity that can emerge from dissemination and publication procedures in IMR (due to the enhanced traceability and searchability of data in online contexts), and take careful measures to minimise these threats	✓			✓
• If considering using deception, or highly sensitive materials, be particularly aware of the extra risks that may arise from lower levels of reliability online in (a) verifying participant characteristics and (b) presenting debrief information	✓		✓	
• If planning to use data without gaining informed consent, carefully consider issues related to the blurred public–private distinction online, and particularly the potential risks of harm due to leakage of personally identifiable data		✓		✓

Source: Adapted from Hewson (2014b).

relevant to quantitative and qualitative research projects, particularly concerning ethical issues (as was also discussed in Chapter 5).

The basic minimal requirements for IMR are much as they have always been – access to a computer (broadly defined to include PCs, laptops, tablets, smart phones, etc.) that is capable of connecting to the Internet. Most modern computers have this functionality. As we predicted in the first edition of this book, the WWW has now become one of the most important delivery systems for research methods in social sciences.[1] Accordingly, participation in many studies will require the ability to access the Web, via a web browser, which is now a normal feature of most modern computing devices, nearly ubiquitously now and in a way that was not foreseeable when we first started exploring these methods in 1993. Here, we discuss the key design choices and supporting tools and technologies for each of the main IMR methods discussed in Chapter 3.

INTERVIEWS AND FOCUS GROUPS

Email and Mailing Lists

A key design choice for IMR interview methods and focus groups is whether to conduct these synchronously or asynchronously. To briefly recap (see Chapter 3), reasons for choosing asynchronous approaches are that they can allow more time for reflection, offer greater control and potentially empower participants, and facilitate participation by geographically dispersed participants. Also, asynchronous approaches tend to have been more successful to date. The key technologies to support asynchronous interview approaches are email, mailing lists and discussion forums. Email is an attractive option, since it is one of the best known, widely used, enduring Internet technologies (according to Zakon, 2015, email actually pre-dates the emergence of the Internet). Most people living in developed nations will now have and use an email account, often on a daily basis. In order to use email, an email client is needed (e.g. Apple's Mail for Macintosh, Microsoft's Outlook for Windows, mutt or pine on Linux). Web-based email client interfaces are also now available, such as Yahoo!, Hotmail and Gmail (all freely available, see mail.yahoo.com, hotmail.com, mail.google.com, respectively). An email interview very simply proceeds by a researcher sending questions to an interviewee, who then sends back email replies to these. The timescale and number and length of emailed questions and responses will vary depending on the particular context and research study design.

---

[1]Since the first edition of this book, a European masters course has emerged in this area: the Master in WebDataMetrics (http://webdatametrics.usal.es [accessed April 2015]).

In order to support focus group approaches, emails can be sent to several individuals at the same time, simply by pasting all the required addresses into the 'To:' field.[2] Of course, this approach relies on all participants remembering also to reply to all these addresses (easily done using 'reply all'). To avoid any issues related to people forgetting to use the 'reply all' option, mailing list software can be used (also called 'subject-based discussion groups', as discussed in Chapter 2 in the context of secondary research). This software circulates any replies to all specified group members, by default, thus guaranteeing that all individuals subscribed to the list will receive any emails sent. There are various mailing list software options that can be used. The first mailing list software provider was LISTSERV, which is still available: see http://www.lsoft.com/products/listserv.asp (accessed April 2015). This service allows mailing lists to be created and maintained, but does require a setup and annual fee, whereas other options are available for free or more cheaply. One such option is PhpList (see http://www.phplist.com [accessed April 2015]) which offers free open-source code for download, or a hosted solution for a very reasonable fee; at the time of writing, the hosted solution was free for up to 300 messages per month, and cost a small monthly fee for message quotas above that, priced on a sliding scale. Another option for creating mailing lists is to use institutional (e.g. university) IT support systems, for example when grant funding is available to support such costs for a research project.

Thus, using mailing lists offers a reliability which simple group emailing does not. In most situations, it will be appropriate to set up dedicated lists for the purposes of the research. An alternative would be to locate and approach an existing mailing list discussion group for participation, but this is unlikely to be well received, and raises ethical concerns (e.g. regarding disrupting existing social structures, and failing to respect the privacy and purpose of existing groups). A possible exception might be when a very small, select group is involved, which the researcher has some kind of existing connection with, and who it is considered may likely be keen to engage in the proposed research; for example, because they would somehow benefit from participating (some activist groups are keen for their 'voice' to be heard). Searchable databases of mailing lists are available (see further discussion under observational approaches below), but, again, 'cold-calling' with participation invitations to groups located via these resources is unlikely to be appropriate or ethical behaviour in many contexts. However, such groups could perhaps be used as a point of contact for sampling purposes (see Chapter 4), after which interested participants are directed to a research-dedicated list. As noted elsewhere, group moderators should be contacted prior to posting any such requests. A study which used a dedicated LISTSERV mailing list to conduct focus groups with pregnant women on home bed rest is

---

[2]For some purposes, it is better to use a 'blind carbon-copy' (Bcc) field in order to maintain the privacy of each of the people to whom a bulk email is sent, although this does not apply in most focus group scenarios.

described by Adler and Zarchin (2002); they recruited participants by conducting a web search to locate a topic-related website and advertising the study on the site's bulletin board. This can be a very useful strategy for locating specialist and/or traditionally hard-to-access populations for recruitment, but, to reiterate, researchers should make sure that moderators are contacted first to gain permission; not doing so is likely to cause offence and may well lead to blocking of the research, and possibly even damage to the reputation of the researchers.

Discussion Forums

One issue that needs consideration when using asynchronous email-based approaches is data security, as well as the related issues of confidentiality and anonymity. Essentially, email is a relatively non-secure transmission mode; emails may reside on many servers between being sent and being received, and thus have potentially multiple opportunities for being intercepted. Also, email addresses identify individuals and thus preclude anonymity. This may be particularly important to consider in research contexts involving sensitive and personal discussion topics (as noted in Chapter 5). Discussion forums offer a further option for conducting focus group interviews (and potentially one-to-one interviews, though email would often seem more appropriate for dyadic contexts). Like mailing lists these support group discussions, but instead of sending messages to individuals' email accounts, users need to log on to a news server to read and reply to the messages which have been posted to the group. This can be done using a 'newsreader' (see the list of options at www.newsreaders.info/recommended-newsreaders.htm [accessed April 2015]). While mailing lists are traditionally often set up for sharing information (e.g. as in technical support forums), discussion groups are traditionally more geared towards supporting conversational, dialogic interactions on special interest topics (making them attractive sources for observational IMR approaches; see below). Web-based interfaces for accessing, creating and managing discussion groups are available (e.g. Google groups: www.groups.google.com; Yahoo groups: http://uk.groups.yahoo.com/ [accessed April 2015]). These services often allow users to locate, join and set up new groups for free.

Web forums are a more recent technological solution for supporting online discussion group interactions. Yuku (www.yuku.com) offers a searchable database of web forums, and also allows users to create their own multimedia, interactive 'message boards', which are in effect small-scale SNSs. This and similar resources could plausibly be used to support online focus group interactions, enabling possibilities for incorporating multimedia content into groups' exchanges. The very well-known, well-used SNS Facebook (which at the time of writing claimed a user base of around 1.5 billion; see Chapter 4) also offers the option for registered users to set up smaller, private 'groups' of invited members. The options for incorporating multimedia content using such resources creates opportunities for supporting some of the innovative IMR interview and focus group techniques which go beyond a purely text-based interactive medium, as touched upon in Chapter 3. The choice of discussion groups, web forums or mailing lists for conducting asynchronous focus group research in IMR should be directed by the particular research context, including the skills and resources available. In general, discussion group software will be less invasive for participants as they need to log on to take part, rather than finding messages arriving in their email boxes.

Virtual Environments

One other option for conducting online focus groups, as discussed in Chapter 3, is the use of online virtual environments. These may be interactive graphic environments, such as MUVEs, VREs, and so on, in which avatars can interact and converse with each other. Second Life is one of the most popular examples, developed by Linden Labs in June 2003 (at the time of writing just having celebrated its 10th anniversary); see www.secondlife.com and www.secondlife.com/whatis for further information (accessed April 2015). This 'virtual life-simulator' is free to play (or has subscription options for non-inclusive extras, e.g. owning your own home), and it takes only a minute or so to sign up for an account and download and install the 'Second Life viewer' software onto a local computer to enable access. Users can choose from a range of self-customisable avatars, including animals, people and robots. Figure 6.1 shows a screenshot of the scene upon entering the social club 'Jadawin', which the first author transported to (using the Second Life search function) after creating a monkey avatar. Using such VRE spaces, or setting up dedicated spaces, for use in a research project is certainly plausible, and in Chapter 3 some examples which have adopted this approach were offered (also see further discussion under observational approaches below). Of course, the virtual location must be chosen carefully; arranging to meet focus group participants in an open public space (such as Jadawin) would – as in offline research – generally be inappropriate. Creating a dedicated research space, such as a private room, is a better option. See the Second Life documentation on how this might be achieved (which is likely to involve a financial cost).

Also, virtual learning environments (VLEs), such as Blackboard (www.blackboard.com) or Moodle (moodle.org), may be used to support focus group interviews. These environments typically incorporate discussion group functions, designed to assist in teaching and learning applications, which allow users to engage in text-based communication exchanges. These may support asynchronous or synchronous contexts (depending on the particular package). Many educational institutions will already use a VLE solution to support teaching and learning, so researchers based at these institutions may have ready access to these resources at no additional cost (assuming institutions are able to authorise usage by research participants, who may not be affiliated with the institution themselves). Such packages may also support one-to-one exchanges, either asynchronously or synchronously.

Figure 6.1   The social club 'Jadawin', a space created for Open University students, tutors and friends

Kenny (2005) has reported successfully using WebCT (now owned by Blackboard) to conduct online focus group interviews in this way.

Chat Software

Most of the technologies discussed so far – email, mailing lists, discussion groups and forums, SNSs and VLEs – may often be most suitable for conducting asynchronous interviews and focus groups, though in some cases they may also incorporate technology for supporting conversations in real time (e.g. as in SNSs such as Facebook which now incorporates chat functions). VREs such as Second Life, on the other hand, are generally designed to support synchronous interactions. Another obvious solution for supporting synchronous communications, which as discussed in Chapter 3 may be useful where immediacy and 'flow' are considered particularly important, is online 'chat' software. Various such options are available. Free solutions include mIRC: http://www.mirc.com/ (Windows only), Colloquy: http://colloquy.info/ (Mac OS X only) and Google Talk: http://www.google.com/talk. These technologies are essentially aimed at supporting ongoing, real-time direct exchange of text-based messages while users are simultaneously present, as opposed to the more disjointed, extended timescales expected in discussion group forum exchanges. More recently, chat software has started also to include options for supporting audio and video (e.g. Google Talk; Skype: www.skype.com) and/or mobile applications (e.g. ICQ: icq.com; Whatsapp: http://www.whatsapp.com/). These developments may thus help facilitate some of the more innovative designs put forward as possibilities in Chapter 3, such as walking interviews and the use of visual methods.

One important consideration in deciding whether synchronous approaches may be appropriate is the extent to which both researchers and participants are readily able to use the proposed communication technologies. For example, users with a physical disability such as a dexterity issue may struggle to use synchronous communication tools effectively. Likewise, those without much typing experience and practice may struggle to keep up with an online chat conversation. In some cases multimedia solutions might help overcome such issues. Of course, some users may find audio and/or video applications problematic (e.g. users with hearing difficulties) and text-based exchanges easier. A further consideration is whether the resources available (e.g. bandwidths, computer power) allow reliable performance of synchronous technologies, which will generally place greater demands on hardware and software resources than asynchronous solutions (e.g. refer back to the Chapter 3 discussion of reliability issues and Skype). Future technological developments will continue to offer improved solutions to address these issues, and thus expand opportunities; at present, however, text-based approaches remain rather more reliable than those incorporating video. Audio-only options (as can be achieved with Skype) can be more reliable than video, and appropriate in some contexts, for example where typing dexterity or literacy is an issue. Such options may have an advantage over traditional telephone interviews in being cheaper to set up and run, and more readily enabling automatic logging of a conversation. When a research context dictates that extralinguistic cues (e.g. intonation, facial expression) are particularly important, and there are good reasons to favour an IMR approach (e.g. geographical dispersion, minimal budget), then multimedia options may be worth considering. Care should be taken, however, to use technologies which have the best chance of facilitating high-quality and reliable exchanges; dial-up connections, or very slow, dated computers, will not be suitable for such applications, wasting the time of both researcher and participant. Referring back to the principles in Table 6.1, careful piloting – particularly of more complex technologies and procedures – should always be carried out to test whether they are suitably robust and reliable for the purposes at hand.

Chat software may support one-to-one and/or group synchronous interactions (e.g. Facebook chat can do both). So both individual and focus group interviews are possible using this range of technologies. For focus group research online conferencing software, which allows several people to communicate synchronously simultaneously, may be useful. Again, many academic (and other) institutions may already have subscriptions to such software; Blackboard Collaborate (http://www.blackboard.com/platforms/collaborate/overview.aspx, previously 'Elluminate') is one such option. Free solutions are also available, but these are generally more limited; for example, they may only support a limited number of users at a time and may be more difficult to set up (e.g. see Php Free Chat: www.phpfreechat.net/). Other options which charge a fee (often a reasonable monthly charge) are generally easier to set up and use, as well as offer more flexibility and functionality; for example, Adobe Connect is a solution which offers yearly, monthly and pay-per-use subscription options (see www.adobe.com/uk/products/adobeconnect. html [accessed April 2015]). As noted in Chapter 3, several researchers have employed chat or conferencing software solutions to implement synchronous individual interviews (e.g. Chen & Hinton, 1999; Davis et al., 2004) or focus groups (e.g. Madge & O'Connor, 2002; Schneider, Kerwin, Frechtling, & Vivari, 2002) in IMR. When focus groups involve participants located in different geographical time zones, however, asynchronous approaches may be most suitable.

The tools and design considerations discussed above (and in Chapter 3) give an indication of some of the technological options available for supporting interview and focus group research studies in IMR. Box 6.1 lists some of the key sources that readers may find particularly useful to consult. For a summary set of good-practice principles more specifically related to interview-based IMR studies, see Table 6.2. The key issues discussed in Chapter 3 – including depth and reflexivity, levels of candour and disclosure, data integrity and quality, and accessibility – should be borne in mind when making choices between the various study design options. Trade-offs are likely to emerge, and decisions should be made within the context, constraints and requirements of any particular research study. Sometimes, multi-method approaches (e.g. using both synchronous and asynchronous interviews) may be appropriate, to benefit from the advantages of each. Reference to the discussion and examples offered in Chapter 3 will help inform researchers in making appropriate design decisions within the context of their own research study.

Table 6.2 Some principles for good practice for Internet-mediated interview and focus group research

- Adopting clear strategies for establishing rapport has been shown to work well and is advisable
- Remain mindful of potential trade-offs when deciding whether to use asynchronous approaches (which may facilitate depth and reflexivity) or synchronous approaches (which may enhance conversational 'flow')
- Related to the above, remain aware of possibilities for combining methods, both asynchronous/ synchronous and online/offline
- Set up dedicated research sites to conduct research interviews/focus groups, as a general rule, to avoid disrupting existing online communities/groups
- Consider carefully how the choice of synchronous or asynchronous communication technologies, as well as text-based or multimedia options, may either facilitate or hinder participation by particular groups

OBSERVATION

Discussion Groups and Mailing Lists

Observational approaches in IMR can draw upon various sources containing traces of and ongoing live interactions between people. Several of the technologies which support such interactions were discussed above. Thus, discussion groups and forums, and mailing lists, offer ready transcripts of (largely) text-based interactional exchanges between individuals. The same resources as cited above may thus be useful in observational IMR. For example, LISTSERV was mentioned and enables the creation and management of mailing lists; a web interface database (CataList), which allows a user to search all existing LISTSERV mailing lists by topic, is available at http://www.lsoft.com/catalist. html (accessed April 2015). This database returns information about the list, including owner and subscription instructions. Thus, in conducting a search (on 29 November 2013) on the keyword 'iguana' no results were returned. Another search using the term 'fish' returned 184 results; rerunning this search restricted to lists with a web interface generated 73 hits. Most of the lists if followed using the active link require subscription by sending an email to the list address, after which users should be able to log on and access and post to the discussion threads. The ethical issues involved in taking such steps as a researcher in order to harvest data from a list have been considered in Chapter 5. For more about LISTSERV and how to search mailing lists, see http://www.lsoft. com/manuals/1.8d/user/user.html (accessed April 2015).

Discussion groups and forums can be similarly accessed via searchable web interfaces (e.g. Yahoo and Google Groups; see above). Searching Usenet archives via the Google Groups web interface is relatively straightforward, as is browsing all groups (see https://groups.google.com/forum/?fromgroups#!browse [accessed April 2015]). Likewise, the Yahoo interface is transparent and easy to use. Some of the Web forum groups are 'open', and archives of discussions are freely accessible, thus creating ready access to topic-relevant material for use as research data (ethical considerations permitting). The well-known and influential (e.g. in political activist campaigns) group 'Mumsnet' is such a resource, accessible at this address: www.mumsnet.com. This website hosts what is by now a very well-established, large online community; the site contains links to news items, blogs, advertisements, reviews and a large selection of searchable discussion threads. Searching on the keyword 'sex' brought up a number of discussions (e.g. on sex after pregnancy, sex in long-term relationships, etc.), as well as a rather intriguingly titled post 'how long should good sex take???' which generated a number of candid replies and subsequent questions to and disclosures by the original poster. It is easy to see how such conversations could be useful as data for a range of research projects, along the lines of the examples using this approach which were offered in Chapter 3. Again, the ethics of accessing and using such posts which are arguably 'in the public domain' (though note the legal aspects related to copyright law on this point, as discussed in Chapter 5) are complex and controversial. While users post under a pseudonym, this is no guarantee that the content of their posts will not be pieced together to uncover their offline identity. Many users will want their identities to remain private; as one Mumsnet user warned in the site's 'tip of the day' section: 'Don't drunkenly tell your in-laws your MN nickname. Even if they never look you up, the fear will take over your life' (accessed February 2014).

Chat Software

While discussion groups and web forums are particularly useful for following asynchronous conversations, either by accessing archives or by following posts as they come in over a period of time, chat room software options (see above) allow real-time, synchronous observations to be carried out. Examples of this approach, and the ethical issues which emerge, were discussed in Chapter 3. To illustrate, the Colloquy chat software client can be downloaded here: http://colloquy.info/downloads.html (accessed April 2015). Opening the client (once installed on a local computer) allows the user to connect to a chat server, which hosts chat rooms. For example, one of the authors connected to the server chat.freenode.net which listed 15,143 indexed rooms (see Figure 6.2). Using the 'filter rooms' box and typing in 'Colloquy' produced two groups, which could be joined. A comparable resource is searchIRC.com (accessed May 2014) which claims 1.7 million users of 165,000 distinct chat rooms. This allows connection via a web browser interface (Java is required, and security settings may need to be configured to enable access to groups).

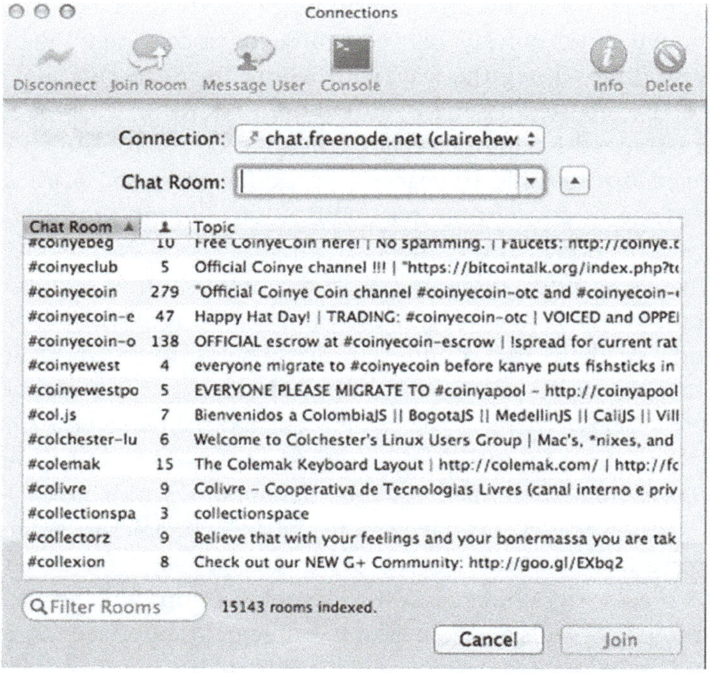

Figure 6.2   Colloquy chat client showing rooms listed while connected to the server chat.freenode.net

Blogs and Social Networking and Media Sites

Other potential observation sites include blogs, SNSs, media sharing sites and any online spaces in which people interact through text-based and/or other media exchanges. YouTube (youtube.com), for example, is focused primarily on sharing video clips, which are typically accompanied by comments on these clips from a variety of people. Various examples of IMR observation studies using such resources were noted in Chapter 3. We have already described how to locate such resources and search these for relevant content (see examples above). A selection of some of the most useful sites which can be used in observation research, and information sources and links explaining how to access and search these, are given in Box 6.1.

VREs

VREs also provide potential platforms for observational research in IMR – in this case, creating opportunities for conducting real-time, multimedia observation within these spaces. While the approach has not been widely used to date, examples were noted in Chapter 3. The well-known VRE 'Second Life' was mentioned above. Once a user has signed up for an account and created an avatar, the user can then navigate around the various 3D graphical spaces in this virtual world, including universities, cafés and bars, parks, museums, dance clubs (e.g. Jadawin, mentioned earlier), and so on. Avatars can port directly to saved favourite places, or 'fly' to move more quickly between different spaces and 'islands'. Avatars will encounter others along the way, with whom they can chat and interact. In 1997 Second Life reported having 7 million users (Hewson, 2008), and in 2013 it reported an estimated 1 million users logging on each month (http://www.linden lab.com/releases/infographic-10-years-of-second-life [accessed April 2015]). This opens up a range of conceivable possibilities for observing interactions within this virtual world (though at the time of writing there was some evidence that the number of active Second Life users was in decline). Another popular VRE is the massively multiplayer online role-playing game 'World of Warcraft' (WoW); recent estimates indicate there are around 7.5 million subscribers (in 2014, see http://www.statista.com/statistics/208146/number-of-subscribers-of-world-of-warcraft/ [accessed April 2015]). Visiting the main webpages of these and similar online environments provides information on how to set up an account, enter and interact within the virtual space. Box 6.1 provides some relevant links. As discussed in Chapter 3, some researchers have created bespoke interactive environments to support observational IMR studies (e.g. Givaty et al., 1998), while others have used existing VRE spaces (e.g. Williams, 2007). Bespoke options will inevitably demand greater technological skills and resources to implement, but have the advantage of being able to create tailored designs and allowing tighter control over predefined variables relevant to the research study at hand (facilitating experimental designs, as discussed in Chapter 3).

Design choices and issues which emerge in the context of observational IMR overlap with those considerations raised in relation to interview approaches. Thus whether to make use of synchronous or asynchronous technologies, or text-only or multimedia contexts, emerge as choices. Many of the same considerations raised earlier (and in Chapter 3) will apply in making these decisions. For example, asynchronous approaches may generate more reflective, detailed, rich communications to draw upon, whereas synchronous approaches may be more superficial and less well considered, but benefit from enhanced topic coherence and flow. Deciding whether to observe discussions 'live' as they unfold (synchronously or asynchronously) or access stored discussion archives should be informed by a number of factors, including the likely impact of intruding into live online spaces (e.g. on ecological validity, harm to existing social structures, etc.), and the need to locate highly topic-specific content (more easily achieved by searching archives). Multimedia observations may require greater resources and levels of technical expertise, but may also offer richer data, incorporating non-verbal information such as the physical location and navigation of avatars, and perhaps other aspects of body language such as facial expressions (where the environments in question support this). Other choices include whether to adopt a participant or non-participant approach, and whether to disclose the research intentions to those being observed. Earlier chapters have offered examples and advice on these points; for example, observation without disclosure may be justified in cases where disclosure risks causing harm to existing online groups. Certain research questions and approaches will make participant observation approaches more appropriate, for example ethnographic research (which will often mix methods, e.g. surveys, interviews, observations).

As discussed in Chapter 3, as well as observational approaches which make use of data involving the content of interactions and their traces, such as text-based discussion group posts, data can be constructed from the processes and structures of online behaviour. Indeed, methods may combine analysis of process and content data. Within such observational approaches, it is possible to deploy sophisticated forms of analysis, relevant to social and behavioural research goals. For example, identifying networks of interaction can be important to some research questions in assessing mutual influence and identifying implicit community leaders (e.g. Healey, Vogel, & Eshghi, 2007). To support such analysis it is possible to 'scrape' data from publicly visible forums analysing message–reply sequences (including within threads) as links in the graphs whose nodes represent the individuals posting, with additional features associated with the nodes and links derived from analysis of the content of the postings. Similarly, much work in sentiment analysis proceeds by either scraping data from popular online forums or using programmers' interfaces to resources like Twitter in order to relate aggregate opinion expressed in texts to independent variables, such as behaviours of stock and commodities markets (Ahmad, Cheng, & Almas, 2006). Large-scale mining of data available from automatically analysing the content of webpages and pages linked to them is the underlying technical process of search engines such as provided by Google or Yahoo, and can be applied by researchers willing to take on these methods (see Liu, 2010). It is noteworthy that where data sets become extremely large, computational complexity measured in the amount of time and space required to achieve desired results becomes important, and special tools attuned to 'big data' processing have emerged (e.g. 'Hadoop' – White, 2010). A detailed consideration of these more technically complex data scraping approaches is beyond the scope of the present text; the interested reader is referred to the aforementioned sources and the relevant resources listed in Box 6.1 below.

Table 6.3 offers a set of guidelines proposed to apply to observational approaches in IMR.

Table 6.3   Some principles for good practice in Internet-mediated observation research

- Keep in mind that different observation sites/sources may restrict or facilitate the design options available (e.g. using archived logs precludes participant approaches and makes disclosure/consent often implausible; observing real-time chat makes undisclosed, non-participant observation often untenable)
- Keep in mind the different types of dialogue and interaction that may be encouraged by synchronous (e.g. playful) and asynchronous (e.g. reflective) technologies when selecting which is most appropriate
- Carefully consider whether undisclosed approaches are appropriate and ethically justifiable, keeping in mind the following key factors: *privacy expectations; sensitivity of data; levels of risk of harm; ecological validity; legal and copyright regulations; scientific value*
- Keep in mind that trade-offs will often emerge and need resolution, especially in relation to ethics procedures; for example, disclosure may respect the privacy and autonomy of participants, but threaten ecological validity and introduce possible risks of harm to a group (e.g. by fostering mistrust)
- Keep in mind the general principle that it is good practice to consult moderators before carrying out research (e.g. using online discussion forums) but that this can be impractical in some contexts (e.g. when accessing archives)
- Related to the above point, remain mindful that moderators may have opinions or agendas which could be prohibitive to a potentially valuable research project; arguably, not making contact may be justified in some contexts

DOCUMENT ANALYSIS

Chapters 2 and 3 outlined some of the online documentary sources which exist and some examples of IMR studies which have used these to derive data. Webpages provide an obvious source of data, for example newspaper homepages which provide access to articles, multimedia features, comments pages, and so on. Personal homepages, blogs, scientific articles and repositories of various types of documentary and multimedia sources (as described in Chapters 2 and 3) all hold potential value for use in IMR. The techniques outlined earlier can be directly applied to support document analysis approaches in IMR, as well as the secondary information gathering and literature searching activities which were the focus of Chapter 2. As with observational research, accessing topic-specific examples of interest is often a simple matter of conducting a search, using the various methods already outlined, with web-based interfaces offering particularly user-friendly, accessible options. Google (google.co.uk; google.com) is a particularly accessible option, and as well as general searches allows more restricted search options, for example to return results within a particular category, such as images, blogs, maps, and so on. Online newspapers can often be searched; for example, the *Guardian* newspaper website (guardian.co.uk) includes a search engine to locate topic-specific content. Box 6.1 includes details of some of the most useful interfaces for accessing and searching online documents which may be of use in IMR.

The extent to which these various described resources may be useful in providing data for primary research will depend upon the particular aims and goals of the research project. Some sources will offer rich, detailed, elaborate data, such as journalistic articles and commentaries, which might be suitable as data for qualitative research, for example using discourse analysis techniques. Other sources may be less rich – Twitter (twitter.com, as mentioned in Chapter 3) is an online space which allows signed-up users to post short bursts of text (including, if they wish, links to other online documents); these 'tweets' are limited to 140 characters in length, so are unlikely to be useful for researchers seeking rich, detailed narratives as data. However, the sheer number of tweets being posted, and 'retweeted', on a daily basis by users worldwide makes it an intriguing source of data for quantitative approaches, such as those looking for patterns in the way information on particular topics and themes is circulated within this vast online network of connected individuals, as well as quantitatively informed analysis of aggregate public sentiment (as mentioned above). Twitter offers a fairly flexible advanced search mechanism (see twitter.com/search-advanced) which enables a search by words, phrases, locations, whether the tweet includes a smiley (':)', taken to indicate a positive comment) and other options.

Ethical considerations must be taken into account when deciding whether readily accessible online documents should be used as research data (see Chapter 5); in many cases published online documents may reasonably be considered to be in the public domain, and authors may be considered to have expectations that these documents will be widely viewed, shared, discussed and cited. Still, as noted in Chapter 5, copyright restrictions should be carefully considered when deciding whether disclosure of intended usage and a request for permission are required. Different contexts will lead to different conclusions. Regarding the possibility of soliciting documents, rather than accessing existing sources (see Chapter 3), this may sometimes be a preferred option; in particular, where a very specific theme or topic is the focus of investigation, and where data may be of a sensitive nature and/or vulnerable groups are of interest. In such cases, gaining informed consent and asking participants to elicit documents using well-controlled, secure methods might be the best approach. Setting security features so that any such blog is private and only accessible to authorised named individuals will be necessary. It is possible to set up blogs in this way, for example using blogger.com. Harvesting very sensitive information from documents (e.g. blogs) readily available online, especially where these involve vulnerable groups (e.g. non-adults), may well raise ethical concerns. Certainly, care should be taken to protect participants' identities (e.g. by not using careless dissemination procedures which might pose a threat to participant anonymity and confidentiality) in such contexts. Document solicitation can be a useful alternative to consider in some cases, when resources allow for the almost inevitable greater time and cost implications involved. Table 6.4 offers a set of good practice design guidelines for document analysis approaches in IMR.

Table 6.4   Some principles for good practice in Internet-mediated document analysis research

---

- Bear in mind that in some contexts soliciting documents might be an appropriate design strategy, but that this requires additional careful consideration of issues related to secure transmission and storage of data (especially where this may be personally identifiable)

- Copyright issues should be carefully considered when using documents that appear to have been placed 'in the public domain', as well as issues related to individuals' likely privacy expectations and informed consent procedures

- Given the often ready searchability and traceability of online documentary sources, extra care needs to be given to appropriate protection of identities in publication and dissemination strategies, when using these sources (particularly where consent/copyright has not been obtained and/or material is of a personal or sensitive nature)

EXPERIMENTS

As noted in Chapter 3, there now exist a number of software packages aimed at making IMR experiments easier to implement without having detailed knowledge of programming languages and server configurations. WEBEXP (http://groups.inf.ed.ac.uk/webexp/intro.shtml; requiring more advanced computing skills, including running a web server) and WEXTOR (http://wextor.org/wextor/en; a relatively user-friendly online web experiment generator which provides a web interface and server hosting) are two such examples. A number of useful guidelines for the design of web experiments also exist (as noted in Chapter 3), including Reips (2000) and Reips and Krantz (2010). These offer general principles, such as using the lowest tech solutions that will achieve what is needed (e.g. Hewson, 2003; Reips & Krantz, 2010) and specifying any necessary hardware or software requirements clearly to participants at the outset (e.g. Hewson et al., 2003). They also incorporate principles derived from empirical research on the various factors involved in IMR experiments; for example, Schwarz and Reips (2001) considered the implications of using JavaScript versus CGI in a web experiment. They found that higher dropout rates occurred in the JavaScript implementation (perhaps due to technical issues which can emerge when using this scripting language for more complex designs). In another early study Buchanan and Reips (2001) found evidence to suggest that users of different Internet technologies may differ on demographics and personality variables (e.g. Mac users scoring higher on 'openness' than PC users). More recent discussions of the way detailed presentation parameters (e.g. stimulus size, luminance, video formats, etc.) might influence the data obtained in experimental and other IMR methods can be found in Reips and Krantz (2010) and Krantz and Williams (2010).

Inevitably, experimental designs are going to demand typically more complex technological solutions than many other IMR approaches. Studies which require only static, text-based materials to be presented and simple response measurements recorded will require the simplest solutions, while those using multimedia (graphics, audio and video) and/or requiring precise reaction time measurements, for example, will demand more complex implementations. As noted in Chapter 3, the latter possibilities are now viable in IMR, and successful examples have been forthcoming. Still, the additional complexities related to threats to reliability, accessibility, and so on which emerge with the more complex implementations (precise stimulus timings, multi-user interactions, etc.) need to be carefully considered. At the simplest level, email-based approaches are possible (see Chapter 3), though there are now very good reasons for preferring web-based methods, including enhanced data security, reliability and a far greater range of functionalities.

Reips and Krantz (2010), as well as providing a very useful overview of some basic considerations in experimental IMR design, outlining a number of principles of good practice, caveats and proposed solutions, also offer a step-by-step guide on how to use WEXTOR. They note that this software incorporates many of the good-practice design principles that have emerged from research and pilot studies within the relevant body of literature on IMR experiments. Use of this software, and other similar packages, can thus arguably help to overcome some of the potential pitfalls that experimental researchers who are new to IMR contexts might otherwise fall into. Of course, a certain level of technical know-how and computer literacy will be required to use these packages, as well as a good knowledge of the principles of experimental design, but the packages which have now become available do alleviate the demands for high-level programming and server management skills which experimental implementations in IMR once demanded. WEXTOR is a particularly user-friendly option as it offers server hosting; this package is available on a free trial basis, after which a subscription needs to be purchased for continued use.

New software emerges unpredictably, and it is therefore advisable to search for new tools, particularly open-source tools, before deciding on any particular package. The needs of the study at hand will determine the particular features required of a software package. For example, only for some questions do precise reaction time records matter, and for any of these it is necessary to review the software specifications for detail of precision in this regard. Some systems enable the recording of 'paradata' information (e.g. response times and patterns), which can be useful, for example in helping evaluate what features of a study may lead to participants dropping out early. In all cases, a main consideration is how data are made accessible to the researcher (whether as a text file with comma-separated values (CSV) that may be imported into a spreadsheet, or some other accessible format, or only through the system-provided data aggregation and analysis facilities). Researchers are advised to prefer systems that let them retain control over the data and provide capacity to monitor the ongoing progress of data accumulation.

Table 6.5 offers some key good-practice principles and tips to keep in mind when planning and designing IMR experiments. Most pertinent to keep in mind is how the use of particular technological solutions may impact upon the research – for example, as noted above, there is some evidence that using JavaScript as opposed to CGI can lead to higher dropout rates (Schwarz & Reips, 2001). Whether this particular finding also applies today would require further empirical investigation. The design of stimulus presentation and response options should also be carefully considered in IMR experiments, as what may seem like relatively trivial factors have been found to influence responses and the nature and quality of the data obtained. For example, Reips (2010) points out that using drop-down menus for answer choices can be problematic (as noted above). Reips (2010) also recommends using a one-item-per-screen design strategy, so as to reduce the impact of interference between items, allow more fine-grained response times and dropout measurements, and reduce interference from 'hidden formatting'. Other specific recommendations have included collecting referring site information in order to help identify self-selection biases (Reips & Krantz, 2010), and placing demographic questions early on in order to reduce dropout and improve data quality (Frick, Bächtiger, & Reips, 2001). The rationale here is to place any features that might lead to dropout early on (e.g. asking for an email address, or reducing anonymity levels in other ways) so that participants who stay in are highly motivated (Frick et al., 2001, provide evidence that early rather than late placement of demographic questions produces lower dropout, as well as fewer missing data, which in turn may lead to higher data quality).

Most importantly, extensive pre-testing of any web-based experiment implementation is crucial (e.g. Reips & Krantz, 2010). As well as referring to the guides mentioned here, it is also useful to follow the conferences of the Association of Internet Researchers (www.aoir.org) and the General Online Research Conference (www.gor.de). A general principle is that the method of experimental design in IMR inherits the underlying logic from experiments that would be conducted without Internet access, but with a need to attend to the potentially confounding variables introduced through IMR (as discussed throughout this book) and the possibility of testing effects enabled only using IMR.

Table 6.5 Some principles for good practice for design and implementation of IMR experiments

- Pay particularly careful attention to the technical complexities of the procedures used and how these might impact upon the reliability of the study (e.g. cross-platform consistency) – the general principle of using the lowest tech solution that does the job will in most contexts be appropriate

- Related to the above, consider how the use of different technologies may interact with and impact upon who takes part (accessibility, response bias) and response parameters and patterns (e.g. dropout rates)

- Where less common software/hardware configurations are required in order to implement a particular study design, alert participants to these requirements in advance

- Keep in mind that what may seem like relatively minor presentation design choices may have an impact upon responses obtained, and take advantage of the available good-practice guidelines which discuss these factors, and software which has been designed with these principles in mind

BOX 6.1   Resources

Communication Technologies and their Archives

Email clients: Microsoft's Outlook; Apple's Mail

Web-based email: Hotmail (hotmail.com); Gmail (mail.google.com)

LISTSERV mailing list software: www.lsoft.com/products/listserv.asp

LISTSERV user manual: http://www.lsoft.com/manuals/1.8d/user/user.html

Searching LISTSERV: CataList (http://www.lsoft.com/catalist.html)

PhpList mailing list manager: http://www.phplist.com/

List of recommended newsreaders: http://www.newsreaders.info/recommended-newsreaders.htm

Newsgroup management/search interfaces: Google groups (www.groups.google.com); Yahoo (groups: http://uk.groups.yahoo.com/)

WWW forums: Yuku (www.yuku.com)

Chat software: mIRC (www.mirc.com); Google Talk (www.google.talk.com)

Multimedia/mobile chat: Skype (skype.com); ICQ (icq.com); Whatsapp (whatsapp.com)

Social Networking/Media Sharing/Blogs

SNSs: Facebook (facebook.com); Myspace (myspace.com/); Google+ (plus.google.com)

Media sharing: YouTube (youtube.com); flickr (flickr.com)

(Continued)

(Continued)

Blogs/microblogs: Twitter (twitter.com); Blogger (blogger.com); BlogsByWomen (http://www.blogsbywomen.org/); Google Blog Search: (http://www.google.co.uk/blogsearch)

VREs and VLEs

VREs: Second Life (secondlife.com; http://secondlife.com/whatis/); 'World of Warcraft' (WoW) (https://eu.battle.net/account/creation/wow/signup/)

VLEs: Blackboard (www.blackboard.com); Moodle (moodle.org)

Conferencing software: Blackboard Collaborate (http://www.blackboard.com/platforms/collaborate/overview.aspx); Php Free Chat (www.phpfreechat.net); Adobe Connect (www.adobe.com/uk/products/adobeconnect.html)

Data Mining Tools and Resources

Google Analytics (www.google.co.uk/analytics)

LogAnalyzer (www.sclog.eu): A tool for analysing server log files, such as those generated by webpages

Web-Harvest (www.web-harvest.sourceforge.net): Open-source web data extraction tool

iScience Maps (http://maps.iscience.deusto.es): Tool for searching Twitter content

Webometrics Analyst (Windows only) (http://lexiurl.wlv.ac.uk/index.html): Free software tool designed to help in producing network diagrams based on web searches of sources including Twitter and YouTube

IMR Experiment Software/Resources

WEBEXP (www.webexp.info)

WEXTOR (http://wextor.org/wextor/en)

Online Documentary Sources

Web searching tools: Google (google.co.uk; google.com); The Internet Archive (https://archive.org/)

Online newspapers: Searchable directory (www.onlinenewspapers.com); the *Guardian* (guardian.co.uk)

Television and news: BBC news (www.bbc.co.uk/news); *Ouch* disability magazine (http://www.bbc.co.uk/news/blogs/ouch/); Channel 4 (www.channel4.com/news)

HOW TO DESIGN AND IMPLEMENT A WEB-BASED SURVEY

This section considers implementation and design considerations for web-based surveys. Many of the techniques we discussed in the first edition of the book, and provided detailed examples of programming code and server scripts for, can now be achieved by using one of a range of available online survey software packages. Email surveys are not considered in any depth here, the web-based survey having now very much superseded them as the most effective, reliable, robust way to deliver surveys in IMR. However, some researchers have found it useful to administer surveys by email, as seen in Chapter 3, and this relatively straightforward method may be an appropriate choice in some contexts. Here we first review design guidelines for web-based surveys and then consider some software solutions.

Design Guidelines for Web-Based Surveys

A number of authors have offered sets of good-practice design principles for web-based surveys (e.g. Andrews, Nonnecke, & Preece, 2003; Dillman & Bowker, 2001; Dillman, Smyth, & Christian, 2009; Fox, Murray, & Warm, 2003; Kaye & Johnson, 1999; Pealer & Weiler, 2003). Perhaps unsurprisingly, given the relative novelty of the approach, the practices and procedures tested and recommended have varied, and the advice offered has sometimes been conflicting. For example, using cookies (small pieces of information stored on a local computer by a web server via a web browser) is a technique used to allow attempted multiple submissions to be detected, which can be important in minimising risks to validity in a study. However, this practice has been identified as problematic when considering privacy issues, and some authors have suggested that it should not be used based on ethical grounds (Cho & LaRose, 1999; Andrews et al., 2003). As this example illustrates, certain conflicts and trade-offs can emerge when considering best-practice design principles for web-based surveys; as we have emphasised throughout this book, the most appropriate choices and solutions in any given situation will depend on the particular research goals and context at hand. Thus, installing cookies may be justified where it is imperative for the validity of a study that multiple submissions are detected and removed.[3] Where this is less crucial, ethical considerations may take precedence and lead to a decision not to use cookies, for

---

[3]There are also legal requirements regarding the use of cookies; for example, EU legislation (introduced in May 2011) requires valid consent to be obtained for cookie use, except in exempt cases. The use of cookies for tracking participants would seem to be one such exception. At the time of writing, EU data protection law is in a state of flux between providing protections of privacy and enabling wide flow of personal data.

privacy reasons. A set of rigid, inflexible rules for good practice in IMR surveys is unlikely to be forthcoming. Context-specific decisions will need to be made, taking into account a range of sometimes competing factors.

Below we outline some key factors to consider, and offer some general guiding principles for thinking about the decisions that need to be made when designing an IMR survey. We consider *sampling strategy*; *response rates and dropout*; *maximising data validity*; *maximising reliability*; and *ethical issues*.

Many established design principles for offline surveys will also apply in an online context, such as keeping questions clear and simple, avoiding double-barrelled questions and statements, and so on. However, there will also be differences to consider, due to the unique features of the online mode. It should not be assumed that all principles established offline will necessarily generalise to an IMR context; new factors to consider will also emerge. We highlight these differences where applicable. For useful general guides on good practice in survey design see Dillman (2007), Groves, Fowler, Couper, Lepkowski, Singer, and Tourangeau (2013), Kalton and Shuman (1982), Kanuk and Berenson (1975) and Sudman (1980). Here we focus on issues and choices which become particularly relevant in an online delivery context.

Sampling Strategy

The sampling approach adopted for any IMR study, including web-based surveys, must be chosen carefully, taking into account the research context and goals, as discussed at length in Chapter 4. Particularly important to reiterate is that where a research context dictates that a broadly generalisable probability sample is required (e.g. as in much national population-level social and political research), the sampling procedures and resources needed will almost inevitably be more time intensive and/or costly. Obtaining probability samples in web-based surveys should not be ruled out – large-scale probability panels are available and can be used when a research budget allows (see Chapter 4). Alternatively, offline sampling methods may be employed and participants directed to an online survey (though note the possible biases related to computer access and skills, with this approach). As seen in Chapter 4, some researchers have successfully used probability sampling approaches in web-based survey research. True volunteer samples are a much cheaper option, accessed by posting advertisements online. As discussed, these have been shown to generate valuable data in many contexts, and can lead to very large sample sizes when advertising sites are chosen carefully. However, there are a number of compelling reasons why sampling methods for online surveys which involve sending direct requests to individuals via their email boxes (or perhaps via known-membership newsgroups) should be preferred over posting general adverts in public locations online. For one thing, it can give the researcher more control over the nature of the sample obtained and – importantly for many studies – it enables a more accurate specification of the sampling frame (especially when using email-based sampling approaches). When tighter control over the nature of the sample obtained is less crucial, such as in a pilot study or exploratory work, posting general adverts may be an attractive time- and cost-effective option. The reader is referred to Table 6.6 below for some sampling principles for web-based surveys, as well as the more detailed discussion in Chapter 4.

Response Rates and Dropout

Responses to Postal Surveys. It is common for survey researchers to want to maximise response rates, both to enhance statistical power and to help minimise the impact of non-response bias (e.g. Tuten, 2010). During the 1950s–1970s a large number of studies emerged looking at the factors which can affect responses to postal surveys; for informative reviews see Kanuk and Berenson (1975) and Sheehan and McMillan (1999) (the latter also covers email approaches). Factors which have been found to increase response rates to postal surveys include preliminary notifications (also found to enhance response speed, e.g. Murphy, Daley, & Dalenberg, 1991; Taylor & Lynn, 1998), follow-ups and reminders, explicit stated affiliation with an official organisation (e.g. a university), including a return envelope, postage by special delivery, and advance money incentives (e.g. see Fox, Crask, & Kim, 1988; Goyder, 1982; Kanuk & Berenson, 1975). Affiliation with a university has been found to result in higher response rates than affiliation with a corporation (Fox et al., 1988; Goyder, 1982), and issue salience (the more engaging, interesting and relevant respondents find the research topic) also has been linked to enhanced response rates (Heberlein & Baumgartner, 1978; Martin, 1994). Regarding factors that have been found to have little impact on response rates to postal surveys, Kanuk and Berenson (1975) include: personalisation, promise of anonymity, and size, colour and reproduction of the questionnaires. In addition, while it is intuitively plausible that questionnaire length will influence participants' willingness to complete a survey, Kanuk and Berenson (1975) conclude overall that there is little evidence that this factor influences response rates to postal surveys. Other researchers, however, have presented evidence that shorter questionnaire lengths can increase response rates (Yammarino, Skinner, & Childers, 1991). Kanuk and Berenson (1975) also report that the only robust finding relating to response bias in postal surveys is that respondents tend to be better educated than non-respondents[4] (studies having considered demographic, socioeconomic and personality variables).

Responses to Web Surveys. So how does the research on postal surveys compare with that for web-based surveys? First, there is some evidence that questionnaire length can affect response rates (e.g. Smith, 1997). However, Smith (1997) also notes that in web-based approaches, compared with email, perceptual aspects of survey

---

[4]Note that (higher) educational level has been one of the factors commonly raised in relation to concerns regarding the potentially biased nature of Internet-accessed samples. Thus it is interesting that there is evidence that this has been a biasing factor affecting long-established postal survey methods.

length can be compensated for by design (e.g. taking care to use layouts which do not require extensive scrolling, or navigating through numerous pages). Other evidence that length can affect response rates comes from IMR experiment studies; for example, Krantz and colleagues (1997) report that of the respondents who started their web study, 17% continued to completion in one condition, whereas 29% continued to completion in another condition which had half the number of trials (their analysis suggests number of trials was a likely cause of the different observed completion rates). It is intuitive to suppose that more lengthy surveys will generally lead to reduced response rates, and potentially higher dropout, due to the additional time commitment required by participants. In an IMR context several features might make such outcomes even more likely – for one thing, Internet use often entails being subjected to various ongoing potential distractions, such as emails to read, instant messages popping up, Facebook notification alerts, webpages to browse, and so on. Indeed, it may well be that survey respondents encountered the participation invitation while engaged in another task online. This might make web-based survey participants more likely to exit before completion (compared with offline modes), with this effect being enhanced as survey length increases since there is then more time for potential distractions to occur. Secondly, unlike with pen and paper surveys, web survey respondents cannot flick through and scan the whole survey at the outset, gauging how long it might take and how interesting it might be. This may potentially lead to higher dropout rates where participants do not have a clear idea of the nature of the survey and time required to complete it at the outset. For this reason, providing a clear indication of survey length on the participant information/consent page, as well as the nature of the topics and themes to be covered in questions, is important. Thirdly, reading text on a computer screen is more demanding than flicking through printed paper pages, and so thresholds for perceived burden and attention span are often reduced (Reips, 2010). Very lengthy web-based surveys may thus prove unmanageable for participants, again leading to potentially higher dropout rates.

All in all, there are compelling reasons why survey length is an important factor to consider when using web-based administration methods. It has been suggested that an upper limit of around 25–30 'medium-complexity' items on a web survey is a good heuristic to work to (Reips, 2010); others have suggested not exceeding around 10 minutes' completion time (Tuten, 2010). Of course, other factors will come into play in deciding on appropriate survey lengths, including issue salience for the target population (when higher, lengthier surveys may be more appropriate). Still, extremely long surveys would seem unwise in most contexts; one example we encountered from a link on an online study clearing house website notified potential respondents that the survey involved six questionnaires and would take up to two hours to complete! We wondered how many completed survey responses these researchers received.

Comparing Online and Offline Surveys. Several studies have compared IMR and postal survey response rates. Sheehan and McMillan (1999) review some of the early findings, and report that email survey response rates have varied widely, ranging from 6% (Tse et al., 1995) to 75% (Kiesler and Sproull, 1986). While a number of factors will likely combine to determine response rates obtained in web-based surveys (as discussed here and in Chapter 4), the evidence to date suggests that response rates to online surveys are generally lower than those to mail surveys (Tuten, 2010). Studies have also considered whether different IMR approaches may lead to differences in response rates. In an early study, Smith (1997) compared email surveys, both with and without an emailed prior notification, with a web-administered survey advertised by posting requests to a range of related-interest newsgroups. The email pre-notification condition produced a response rate of 13.3%, while emailing the survey directly led to an 8% response rate, and one complaint accusing the researcher of spamming. The web survey received 99 responses – while it is not possible to measure how many people saw the request with this methodology, Smith (1997) estimates it was viewed by around 8,000 users, giving a response rate of about 1.25%. These findings suggest prior notifications are a good idea if using email-based approaches. For web-based approaches, we recommend sending a participation invitation with the web survey URL link included. Temple and Brown (2011) also compared different online sampling methods (as reported in Chapter 4), and found that different approaches led to different response outcomes (e.g. conversion rates).

The mixed findings from studies of response rates in IMR (see also Chapter 4) are not surprising, given the range of approaches and strategies which have been employed. Further studies comparing different approaches would be informative. In general, the evidence so far seems to suggest that emailed survey participation requests gain higher response rates than web-posted survey requests. However, given the sheer volume of users who are likely to be exposed to a web-posted survey which is strategically placed/advertised in a high-exposure location, very large sample sizes can be obtained even with low response rates (as discussed in Chapter 4). The main concerns associated with web-advertisement sampling methods, as already noted, are non-response bias and lack of a known sampling frame (the list of all the sampling units from which the sample was drawn). Posting requests to newsgroups may be a convenient option for some projects, which can enable more accurate sampling frame and response rate estimates than simply placing a survey in a high-traffic online location and waiting for people to find it. Controlling access to the survey will be important in maximising knowledge of who had the opportunity to take part, and allowing response rate estimates. Since a newsgroup posting will move down the list of postings fairly quickly, and eventually expire, re-posting the request is strongly advised to maximise response rates. Smith (1997) notes that response rates peaked immediately after each newsgroup posting, suggesting repeat postings are effective. However, care should be taken not to bombard newsgroups with persistent repeated postings and to avoid 'spamming' (posting to a large number of unconnected newsgroups). Coomber (1997a) suggests that reposting to newsgroups once a week is appropriate. Online panels have been shown to offer potentially the highest response rates in IMR, with reports of up to 90% (Tuten, 2010). Of course, panel members have signed up as volunteers to receive research participation requests, often in return for a monetary (or other) reward, and so are already highly motivated to take part. While some authors have suggested using incentives to encourage participation (e.g. Michalek & Szabo, 1998), others have advised against this, noting that it may encourage multiple submissions (to gain further rewards).

As is clear from the above discussion, sampling and recruitment decisions in IMR will influence response rates, as in offline research. Also, design features – the way a survey is presented, which technologies are used, and so on – may affect response and dropout rates. Some evidence on the role of implementation factors in experimental designs was discussed above; many of the same factors and principles will also apply in web-based survey design. Thus the demonstrated beneficial effects of placing demographic questions early on in order to minimise dropout (the so-called 'high-hurdle' technique; Reips, 2010) is relevant. Using lower tech and more widely used software solutions where possible (e.g. not relying on non-standard software) is also a good general strategy for helping to maximise response and completion rates. See Vicente and Reips (2010) for further discussion of how to reduce non-response bias using web-based survey design features.

Maximising Data Validity

Maximising response rates, and taking steps to try and reduce dropout, as discussed above, can serve to help maximise data validity by reducing effects of non-response bias. Data validity can also be impacted by choices regarding the presentation of a survey, since different presentation options may lead respondents to answer questions in different ways. This is related to the issue of *measurement error*. In web-based surveys, a larger array of response option formats is possible compared with pen and paper surveys. For example, multiple choice responses may be presented as radio buttons or pull-down menus. It is not always obvious which format to choose. Some authors have suggested that the use of drop-down menus can be a handy space-saving strategy (e.g. Kaye & Johnson, 1999) while others have advised using them sparingly (e.g. Dillman & Bowker, 2001). As already noted, one caveat is that including an already visible actual valid answer choice will result in that answer being recorded by any respondents who skip the question. Thus, using as the visible choice something like 'please select an answer' is required (Reips, 2010). Skipping questions should generally be enabled by default for ethical reasons (participants should not be forced to respond). In cases where software does not allow a survey to be set so questions can be skipped, including an answer choice of 'prefer not to answer' (or 'none of your business!') is a good workaround. Other presentation design options include whether to construct longer pages (e.g. multi-item) that require scrolling, or whether to avoid scrolling, for example by using a one-question-per-page design. As noted earlier when discussing experimental approaches, use of multiple shorter pages can be useful when measurement of response behaviours is required (e.g. time spent per questionnaire item), as well as when it is desirable to minimise context effects between items (Reips, 2010). On the other hand, scrolling through multiple questions placed on one screen might be appropriate when contextual links between items are deemed important (Tuten, 2010). Reips (2010) argues that a 'linear static format' for web-based surveys will often be most appropriate, and approaches which demand higher levels of user-determined navigation (which will lead to higher cognitive load) – such as following hyperlinks, scrolling through pages, and so on – should be avoided.

Font properties (size, colour, type, etc.), screen background properties, placement of page objects (e.g. left, right or centre aligned), and so on, should also be chosen carefully. A number of useful guides which discuss these choices, and offer some best-practice principles for formatting webpage screens, are available. For example, see Couper (2008), Couper, Tourangeau, Conrad, and Crawford (2004), Reips (2010) and Tuten (2010); also see the regularly updated WebSM (www. websm.org) online resource. Even very small variations, such as the hues used to shade response scale options, have been found to influence responses to web surveys (e.g. Tourangeau, Couper, & Conrad, 2007). More advanced software functions offered by many packages, such as answer piping, skip logic, and so on, can be useful, and may help maximise usability and validity of a survey. However, trade-offs can emerge, and should be carefully considered. For example, such approaches might increase the likelihood of reliability issues arising. Whether to allow survey re-entry, to complete in stages, is another choice, with possible implications for data validity. Individual research contexts will determine whether or not such strategies are likely to be a good idea, and lead to enhanced or reduced data quality. The reader is advised to consider his or her own study designs and goals in consultation with the aforementioned resources and guides. In general, the principle of using simple, clear layouts which closely follow those used in traditional pen and paper format surveys will often be applicable, but researchers should remain mindful that new options, choices and optimal design practices may also arise in a web-based survey context.

One presentation feature commonly used in web-based surveys, which may be useful, is a progress indicator bar. Often this is displayed as a horizontal bar which shows as a percentage, at the top of each survey page, how much of the survey has been completed. The impact of this feature on factors such as response rates, dropout, data quality, and so on, needs further investigation, but there is evidence that various factors will interact to determine the nature of these effects. For example, it has been found that displaying a progress bar can reduce dropout rates in cases where an accurate estimate of the time required to complete the survey has been provided in advance; however, survey length has also been noted as a factor which can moderate this effect (Yan, Conrad, Tourangeau, & Couper, 2011). The possible impact of very lengthy surveys on dropout rates was discussed above. Perhaps even more worrying, participants might become frustrated with very lengthy surveys and simply start picking random answers to rush through to the end, leading to invalid data. The advice offered above – to be clear at the outset about the time commitments involved and avoid subjecting participants to over-lengthy procedures – should help minimise this risk. Also, making sure the survey looks professional, well planned and of clear research value should help discourage disingenuous responses.

Finally, to revisit the issue of whether to collect personal demographic and other potentially identifying information (e.g. IP addresses) from participants, this is relevant to data validity concerns. As noted above when discussing cookies, such information may help in detecting multiple responses. It can also help uncover response biases in a study. However, taking into account ethical considerations, collection of such personal data should be well justified in the research study design (and have received REC approval), clearly showing how it is important for data validity.

Maximising Reliability

The important principle of taking steps to pilot a survey carefully and thoroughly to test for reliability issues, such as consistency between different browsers, should be reiterated. Various technical threats to reliability can emerge (some of which are discussed further in the next chapter). Modern-day dedicated software solutions remove some of the burden of managing reliability from researchers, who previously relied on creating their own bespoke implementations. Currently available dedicated, well-tested, rigorous, reliable online survey systems now greatly reduce the likelihood of some of the earlier problems some researchers encountered – such as server crashes, software crashes, presentation inconsistencies, and so on. These commercial systems undergo extensive testing and development, to make sure they are fit for purpose. Issues relating to slow bandwidths, and Internet traffic, are also less challenging than they have been in the past, due to the ever-increasing enhanced connection speeds which are becoming more and more widely available within the IUP. Nevertheless, despite all these developments, and quality control checks, reliability issues can still occur. For example, in our own recent experience some important functions have been found not to work as intended in certain browsers (the 'exit survey' button is one such example). Hence, thorough pre-study piloting is necessary. Continued technological developments will no doubt help to address some of these issues further.

Keeping implementations as low tech as possible is a principle worth re-emphasising (see also Chapter 7, and Reips & Krantz, 2010, on this point). Where more complex implementations and technologies are needed for a research design, specifying to participants any particular more advanced system or software requirements can be useful, or, where practicable, carrying out automated checks of a client system for any necessary technologies required to participate. The possibility of conducting such checks depends on the level of involvement the researcher has in the development or deployment of IMR tools.

Reliability issues in IMR are related to levels of control, which are often reduced in IMR, compared with traditional methods. Low reliability, of course, poses threats to data validity. Procedures using multimedia (e.g. audio and video streaming) are especially prone to suffering reliability issues (e.g. as discussed in Chapter 3). One of the key ways in which Internet connections vary is in media capacity (Reips & Krantz, 2010). Thus a fibre optic connection will be better able to handle video streaming than a broadband connection, and dial-up will prove particularly poor, or unusable, for this purpose. Surveys using multimedia therefore require especially careful consideration and cross-platform testing for reliability. Also, participant behaviours may vary in unexpected and unwanted ways. Various steps can be taken to try and minimise the chances of such sources of unreliability posing a threat to data validity. Presenting very clear, unambiguous instructions is one important requirement. Taking measures to prevent undesired actions, as far as is possible, using technological solutions (e.g. disabling the ability to revisit previous survey pages in a memory experiment), is another. Specifying the maximum amount of text that can be input to a text box can be a good strategy, to prevent the (admittedly unlikely) possibility of a participant pasting an entire novel into the text box, for example, potentially crashing the server (Reips, 2010).

Ethical Issues

Issues of control also arise in relation to ethics in IMR. Chapter 5 discussed the main ethical issues which emerge. Especially relevant to web-based survey design are the following challenges:

- devising robust, reliable informed consent and debrief procedures;
- storing participants' data in a way that is secure and unlikely to be personally identifiable;
- enabling effective, reliable withdrawal procedures.

So, for example, as noted in Chapter 5 it can be harder in IMR to ensure that participants have digested and understood consent information. Various practical solutions can be (and were) recommended, including keeping the information presented succinct and easy to read, and including checkboxes for participants to indicate they have understood each of the key consent points. Varying whether a 'yes' or 'no' answer is required can be helpful to detect instances where participants might simply go through checking boxes without reading the text properly. Reliably presenting debrief information continues to be problematic if a participant chooses to exit a study prematurely by closing the web browser. Placing a clearly visible 'exit survey' button on each page can help encourage participants to exit by this route, and then makes it possible to link this action to a debrief page. However, some software packages make this easier to implement than others, and those that do will in many cases be preferable. Another possible strategy is to ask participants to provide an email address (best placed early on), to which debrief information can then be sent. Of course, this method is not foolproof, and also will involve trade-offs with ensuring participant anonymity. Tensions between ensuring anonymity (as a vehicle to confidentiality) and allowing identifiability and traceability (e.g. for consent, debrief and withdrawal purposes) will require resolution by carefully balancing the pros and cons of different approaches, within any particular research study context.

   Data security and protection of participants' personal identities are of course important (see full discussion in Chapter 5). In the context of web-based surveys, off-the-shelf software packages often emphasise the measures taken to ensure that data are stored safely and securely on their servers, so that unauthorised access (e.g. due to hacking) and leaking of individuals' personally identifiable data should be unlikely. Issues of data security are returned to in Chapter 7. Legal aspects also need consideration; in particular, data protection laws vary by nation. In the United Kingdom, for example, the Data Protection Act of 1998 regulates the processing of personal data, but issues can emerge when researchers based at UK institutions use services which store data on servers located outside the EU (data stored within the EU are covered by the UK Act). The 'Safe Harbour Agreement' is a scheme which guarantees that signed-up US-based companies are acting in compliance with UK Data Protection laws, and may offer UK-based researchers some reassurance (researchers can check the information pages of online survey software packages to see if they are signed up; many are, for example SurveyMonkey and Qualtrics). Of course, researchers can implement extra safeguards, such as stripping all personal information from individuals' survey responses, or not collecting this information in the first place, as discussed earlier. Survey software packages often store some information by default, such as respondents' IP addresses, and time and date stamps. Where data are particularly sensitive in nature, it might be appropriate to strip away these potentially identifying (though probably low-risk) elements, to leave survey responses entirely anonymous. Any personal information deemed important for being able to link responses with individuals at a later stage (e.g. to be able to process withdrawal requests) can be stored in a separate file, held securely by the researcher.

Respondents' own perceptions of levels of anonymity and confidentiality in web-based surveys are also worth considering. This will be especially important when dealing with very sensitive topics, such as illegal practices. Such perceptions may impact upon both response rates and response validity (Stanton, 1998). Coomber (1997a) has noted potential participants' concerns about the confidentiality of their responses in a web-based study of illicit drug dealing. Web-based surveys can, if constructed carefully, give a high sense of anonymity, compared with other approaches, such as using personal email accounts or public online forums to collect data. In the latter, individual identities are more established, permanent and traceable (via usernames, mail server accounts, etc.). Offering clear information in consent pages on the measures in place to protect individual identities, and keep data confidential, is recommended in such contexts. If respondents remain concerned about confidentiality even in highly anonymised web surveys (e.g. because IP addresses can potentially be traced), they can be encouraged to complete the survey on an anonymous computer, such as in a library or Internet café, or to print the survey off and post it (Coomber, 1997a). Participants may not always be highly protective of their personal identifiability. Kaye and Johnson (1999) report that in a survey on attitudes to political information on the web, 276 out of 306 respondents complied in giving their email address details. It is possible that controlling access to a web-based survey by requiring a password might intensify anonymity concerns (e.g. Stanton, 1998), but as noted earlier may also be a useful strategy in order to control the sample, in contexts where this is important, or to be able to trace participants in case of subsequent withdrawal requests. Yet again, it is clear that tensions and trade-offs will often emerge. Kaye and Johnson (1999) argue that unrestricted access in web surveys should be avoided, and that passwords provide a useful method for restricting access to a select and measurable sample. However, it is worth bearing in mind that more recent studies have demonstrated that useful data can be obtained with more open sampling approaches, such as open web adverts (as discussed in Chapters 3 and 4). Both 'open' and 'controlled' access approaches may have value, depending on the research goals and context.

In Table 6.6, we summarise the preceding discussion by presenting some key design principles for web-based surveys, driven by the central criteria of data validity, reliability and good ethical practice.

Table 6.6 Design guidelines for web-based surveys

Sampling

- Remain mindful that research requiring broadly generalisable probability samples will demand IMR procedures which can be particularly time consuming and/or costly, compared with many other IMR approaches
- Posting to subscription-based newsgroups can be a useful option which allows some level of control over who sees the request (compared with open, web-based methods) and which can enable specification of a sampling frame
- Carefully consider whether knowledge of the sampling frame, and control over who takes part, are important for a study, and if so aim to use direct-contact methods rather than posting adverts in open, public online spaces

Response rates and dropout

- Take care to ensure participation invitations maintain a professional appearance, clearly stating researcher affiliation and highlighting the value of the research
- Including the URL link to the survey, towards the end of the participation request, is typically good practice
- Carefully consider how the different sampling options available may impact upon response rates and sample size (e.g. there is evidence that emailed requests produce higher response rates than adverts placed on web pages, but the latter can produce very large sample sizes due to high exposure)
- Sending participation reminders, including re-posting newsgroup requests, is good practice and can help increase response rates, but care should be taken to avoid over-zealous 'spamming'
- Be aware that sampling from online panels can offer the highest response rates, but carefully consider the possible impact of self-selection bias which is associated with this method
- Remain mindful that choices made regarding implementation technologies may impact upon response and dropout rates; as a general guiding principle, using the lowest tech and most widely available solutions possible is best practice
- Keep surveys to an appropriate length (which may vary depending on the particular research context and target sample) in order to maximise response and reduce dropout
- Provide clear information on expected completion times, to help minimise dropout rates

(Continued)

Table 6.6 (Continued)

Maximising data validity

- Remain mindful that over-lengthy procedures might lead participants to submit poorly considered, rushed (or even completely random, invalid) responses
- Be aware that different presentation formats and design choices might impact upon data validity (e.g. due to measurement error)
- Use procedures which help maximise the ability to detect multiple submissions from the same person where this is important to the research design and data validity

Maximising reliability

- Careful piloting of a web-based survey across different platforms (and especially a range of browsers) is crucial to identifying any reliability issues and making suitable modifications

Ethical issues

- Use procedures and techniques which help maximise participants' engagement with consent (e.g. using checkbox questions) and debrief information
- Take care to devise effective withdrawal procedures, for example placing an 'exit' button on each page to discourage participants from exiting by closing their browser
- As a basic principle, only collect personally identifying information (e.g. email addresses, demographic information) where this is essential to the study
- Allow participants to skip individual survey items without providing a response, unless there is a good argument for forced responses
- Carefully check how survey response data are stored, considering how this impacts upon data security and confidentiality, as well as legal (data protection) issues

---

Online Survey Software Packages

For many researchers, being able to implement successfully the various design choices and good-practice principles as outlined in the previous section will involve locating suitable software solutions. Robust, reliable, flexible systems are what is required, which can accommodate and support new principles and guidelines as they emerge. Some principles may be harder to find technical solutions for than others. The challenge of being able to debrief reliably participants who close their browser and exit early has already been noted. Another challenge is participant tracking to avoid or detect multiple submissions, due to the lack of a direct one-to-one mapping between individuals, and devices which access the survey (i.e. computers and browsers). Thus solutions which rely on cookies to track browsers are not foolproof (someone could re-enter using a different browser, or delete cookies and start again).

A large number of online survey software packages are now available. Here we consider how to find out about the various options, and how a researcher might go about choosing between them. At the low end are packages that offer free solutions with limited functionality, and at the high end are complete systems to be installed on the customer's own server which offer an array of sophisticated functions, including integration with other tools and resources (e.g. databases). As expected, the latter tend to be expensive, though open-source options do also exist (e.g. LimeSurvey) for the more experienced, computer-literate user. Many of the more advanced packages also offer a free basic or trial version and then a multi-tiered pricing system depending on the level of functionality and features required (e.g. SurveyMonkey). A good place to start browsing the available options is one of the several resources which list and provide information and/or reviews of individual packages; a particularly useful resource is found on the WebSM. org website (follow the *Software* or *Browse software* links; there were 332 packages included in this searchable database on 7 January 2014). The WebSM database incorporates a useful search function which utilises the basic feature information included alongside each listed package (e.g. price range, languages supported, free trial availability, server hosting options). For any search this will return a number of packages which can then be further explored by visiting their webpages (URLs are provided). Since the number and range of packages, as well as their particular individual features, are constantly changing, it is important to check these details by visiting the homepage of the relevant software package. Researchers may be pleasantly surprised to find additional options and functions now available, or alternatively they may find a package has become defunct, or changed its pricing structure and subscription options. Certainly some of the more enduring packages (such as SurveyMonkey, which first appeared in 1999) continue to undergo constant development and upgrades to their functionality and performance. Even regularly updated database collections such as the WebSM catalogue will struggle to keep up to date with the latest developments and features. For example, the databases we checked at the time of writing still listed SurveyMonkey and Zoomerang as separate packages, although they merged in 2012 as a result of SurveyMonkey acquiring Zoomerang. Another useful catalogue to consult is GESIS (http://www.gesis.org/en/services/study-planning/online-surveys/ [accessed April 2015]).

Despite the very useful feature-searchable databases described above, choosing from among the many online survey software options available today can still be a daunting prospect. Reviews which offer more detailed evaluations of particular packages do exist, and can be helpful, but many of these are now rather dated (e.g. Crawford, 2002). Even more recent reviews (e.g. Carter-Pokras et al., 2006; Hewson, 2012b; Kaczmirek, 2008) quickly become out of date in their details, given the pace of development of IMR survey software packages. Identifying some of the key basic features which are likely to be important for the target group of interest can be a good starting point, as different user groups will have different basic requirements (e.g. Crawford, 2002). Considering some of the important basic features required by academic social and behavioural researchers – our key focus here – the seven features as set out in Table 6.7 would seem appropriate (adapted from Hewson, 2012b; see also Crawford, 2002; Kaczmirek, 2008). Thus, for the moderately computer-literate (but non-expert) user wishing to implement an online survey, a package which is not overly expensive, will not die out and disappear quickly, provides server hosting as inclusive, is relatively easy to use (i.e. incorporates a user-friendly graphical interface for design and management), and which can support basic ethics and presentation format requirements, seems to be a basic requirement. Of course, in some cases not all these features will be applicable, such as when a large research budget is available which can accommodate a bespoke implementation managed by an expert IT team, but here we are assuming a more modest project managed by an individual or small research team with limited funds available. Two important general requirements of an online survey software solution are *flexibility* and *robustness*. In agreement with Crawford (2002) we consider these features to be of crucial importance: flexibility allows a range of design options and choices to be implemented, and enables workaround solutions to incorporate design elements which were not initially anticipated and explicitly built in as features by the software designers (e.g. in response to new emerging IMR good-practice design principles, derived from ongoing testing and research in this area); robustness of a system is needed for reliability, and validity, of web-based survey data.

Table 6.7 **Set of key basic requirements for online survey software packages, for social and behavioural researchers**

1. Low cost (<£400 pa)
2. Longevity, endurance, regular updates
3. Minimal technical/computing skills and equipment
4. Good range of question and response formats
5. Support consent and debrief procedures (customisable text, multi-pages) and data security
6. Control over collected data
7. Flexibility and robustness

Source: Adapted from Hewson (2012b)

We now consider a popular package which we feel fits the criteria as set out in Table 6.7, and will meet the needs of many academic researchers working on a modest budget, wishing to implement relatively straightforward survey designs.

SurveyMonkey – An Illustration

Gordon (2002) presents an evaluation of the popular package SurveyMonkey, reaching very positive conclusions, though this review is by now very dated. SurveyMonkey has undergone extensive developments since 2002, now offering a hierarchy of subscription options incorporating some quite advanced functions at the top end. Given its popularity, competitive pricing, range and flexibility of features, robustness, and endurance and development over the last 10 years or so, this package fulfils the criteria outlined in Table 6.7 very well. It has a large client base including some very respected research organisations (e.g. the UK government's Office of National Statistics [ONS]). Here we present a more detailed look at this package, focusing on an implementation from our own research, to consider what it has to offer. We also draw upon findings from evaluation research conducted by Hewson (2012b) who also tested implementations in SurveyMonkey.

SurveyMonkey's homepage is accessed at surveymonkey.com. Here, you will find information about the subscription options available, along with pricing information, and tips, illustrative survey examples and information about other services offered. For example, SurveyMonkey provides access to a participant panel, which it claims is representative of the US population, for a reasonable fee per response (starting from $1). It also provides an option to sign up to take part in surveys. A free basic subscription is available, but very limited, only allowing 10 questions per survey (and up to 100 responses per survey). This is unlikely to be useful for anything but the most basic pilot work. A basic account costs £199 per year (slightly more if paid monthly) and offers a good range of features for basic surveys, including unlimited questions and responses, multi-language support, page and question logic, randomisation of answer choices, progress bar indicator, collection and analysis features, and 24-hour email support.[5] For an extra £100 per year (£299 in total) the Gold option offers all the basic features, plus the following additional features which we feel are of particular interest to social and behavioural researchers: random assignment of participants to conditions (enabling experimental designs), question randomisation, question and answer piping, redirect to a specific URL on completion, SPSS integration (allowing easy import of data as an SPSS data file). Both basic and Gold subscriptions implement stringent data security procedures and conform to standardised accessibility standards (SurveyMonkey reports compliance with the Section 508 US Federal Law Act that outlines standards to make online information and services accessible to users with disabilities). Considering the range of available features SurveyMonkey offers, and the requirements of social and behavioural researchers as outlined earlier, we would recommend the Gold package as the most suitable and good-value option. There is a rather more expensive (£799 per year) option, but this seems to offer little additional functionality to justify this additional cost, for the needs of the current user group, including just two additional features: phone support; and 'white label surveys', which means that the 'SurveyMonkey' branding can be removed from within survey pages and also in the survey page URL (yet any knowledgeable respondent could easily recognise the substitute 'research.net' URL as a rebranded SurveyMonkey survey).

Upon signing up for a free account, you will initially be presented with a screen as shown in Figure 6.3.

---

[5]These details were correct at the time of writing, but no doubt will have changed somewhat by the time this book is in print.

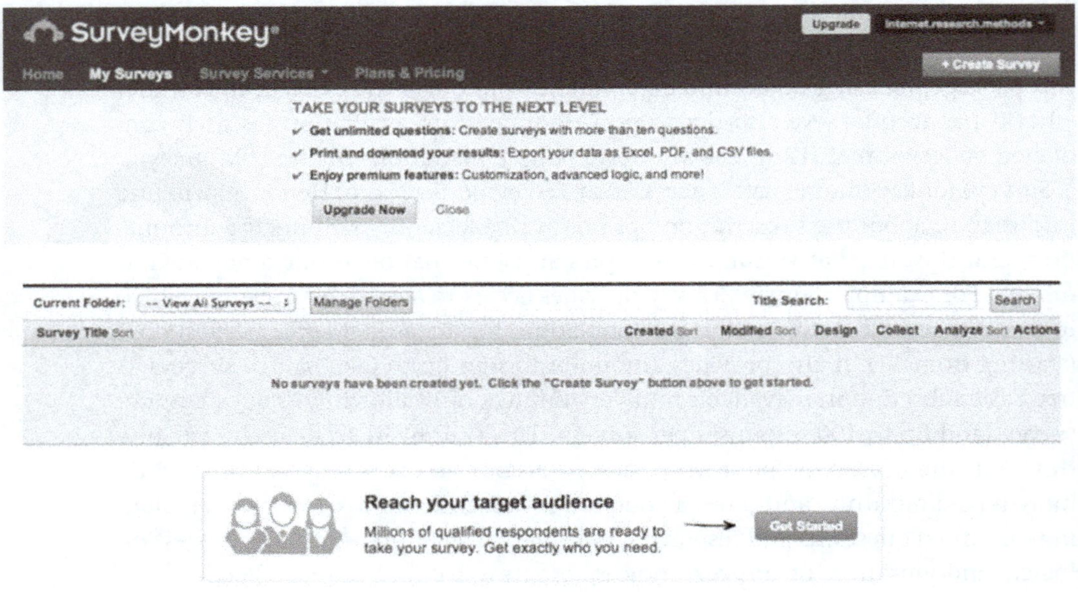

Figure 6.3 Screenshot of the SurveyMonkey page displayed after signing up for a free account

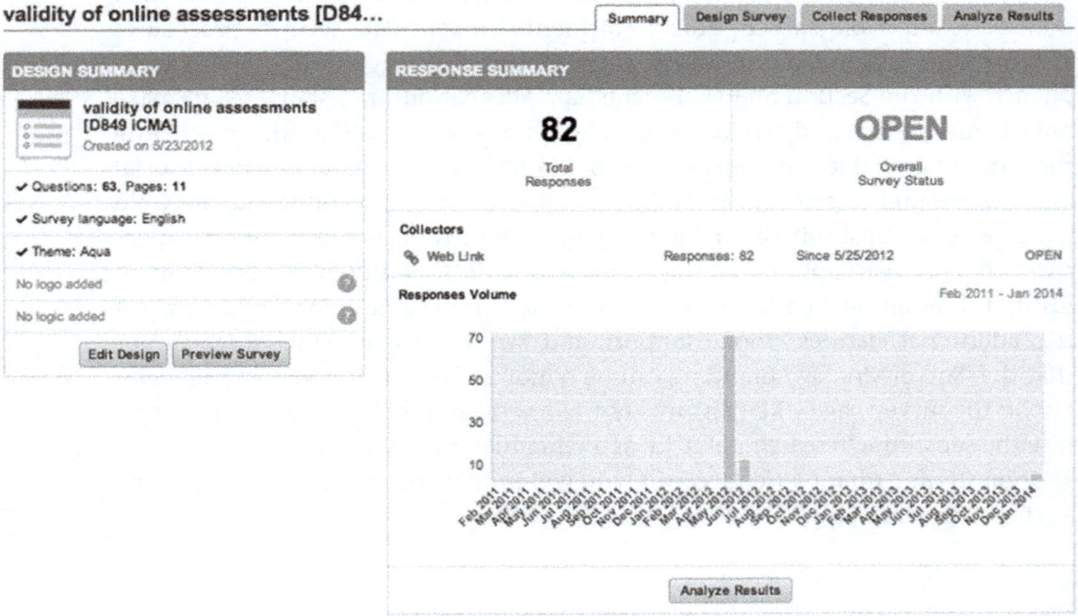

Figure 6.4 Screenshot of the SurveyMonkey 'Summary' page which shows the overview information for a created survey (Gold account)

From here – or the equivalent page for a paid account option – you can start to create a survey, using an existing template or starting from scratch. Figure 6.4 shows the overview information for a study which presents student respondents (registered on a university course) with a psychometric scale designed to measure computer-related attitudes (as used by Hewson & Charlton, 2005) and some additional questions about online assessment methods.

The page in Figure 6.4 shows how many responses have been received (82) and during which months; it also provides information on the number of questions and pages in the survey. This survey is shown as being currently open. Clicking on the 'Design Survey' tab, to the right of the selected 'Summary' tab, opens up a main page which allows the user to make edits to the survey pages and questions and how these are displayed. Figure 6.5 shows a section of the informed consent page from the computer attitudes survey.

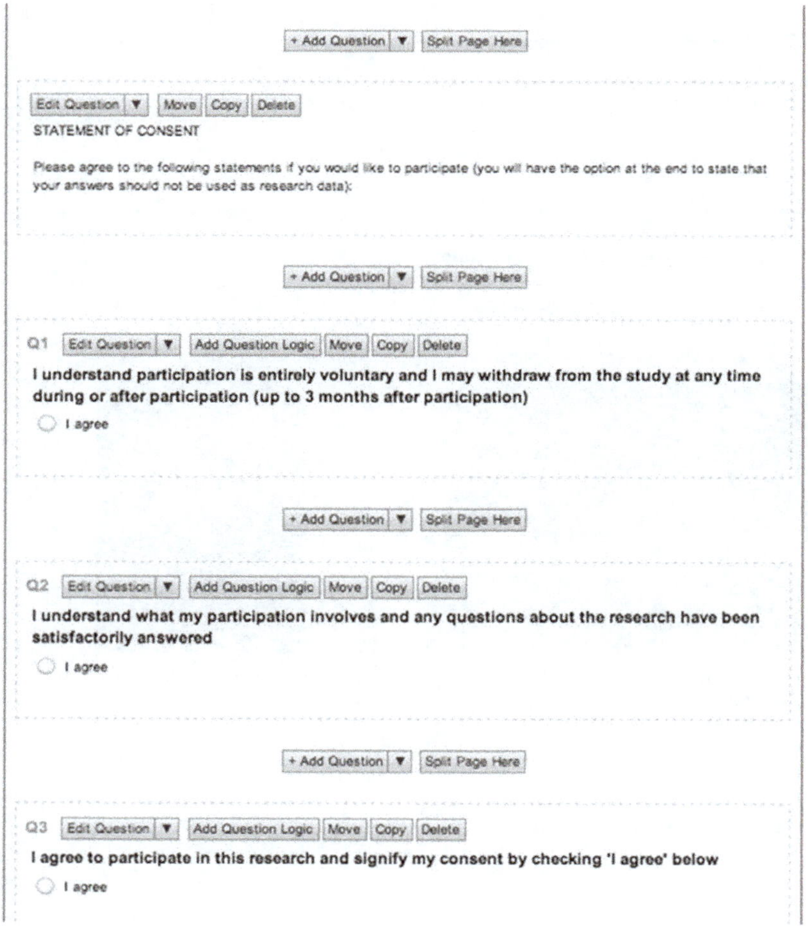

Figure 6.5 Screenshot of the computer attitudes study 'Design Survey' page which shows a section of the informed consent page

(a)

Random Assignment Type

| Choose Type ▼ |
| Image Variable |
| Text Variable |
| Question Variable |

(b) After selecting 'Image Variable'

Random Assignment Type

Image Variable ▼

Name: This is for your use only. Your respondents will not see this name.
Image Random Assignment

Image Variables

Upload two or more images, add descriptive text and set the percentage of your respondents to see each.
- **Upload an Image from your computer**
  Choose File No file chosen   Add
- **Enter the URL to an image online**

Image Random Assignment – Oscar Wilde   ✕   Image Random Assignment – Hangzou   ✕

Respondents: 50 %   **Respondents:** 50 %
Description   Description
Oscar Wilde   Hangzou

☐ Change Question Size & Placement (optional)
To change the default size and placement of this question, click the checkbox above.

Cancel   Save & Close

(c) After selecting, uploading and naming two images

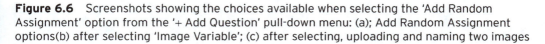

Random Assignment Type

Image Variable ▼

Name: This is for your use only. Your respondents will not see this name.

Image Random Assignment

Image Variables

Upload two or more images, add descriptive text and set the percentage of your respondents to see each.

● **Upload an Image from your computer**

  Choose file No file chosen   Add

○ **Enter the URL to an image online**

☐ Change Question Size & Placement (optional)
To change the default size and placement of this question, click the checkbox above.

Figure 6.6 Screenshots showing the choices available when selecting the 'Add Random Assignment' option from the '+ Add Question' pull-down menu: (a); Add Random Assignment options(b) after selecting 'Image Variable'; (c) after selecting, uploading and naming two images

As shown, it is easy to create page breaks and add new questions using pull-down menu options (which also offer randomisation functions). Other options are readily available, including copy, move, delete, for questions. Question logic allows you to specify a survey page to jump to depending on the answer provided to the specified question. Question text, type, answer options, and size and placement can also be edited from this page ('Edit Question'). When adding new questions ('+ Add Question') random assignment can be employed, so that respondents are presented with either of several stimulus options, or 'conditions'. While not used in the computer attitudes study described here, this feature could be of use in experimental designs, such as those which present different vignettes, images, and so on, which participants are asked to answer questions about. Figure 6.6 displays the series of screens providing selection options to specify the parameters for this function to be implemented.

As seen in Figure 6.6(b), several images can be uploaded, descriptive text added, and the percentage of respondents to see each image specified. As can be seen in Figure 6.6(b), the number of respondents to be 'randomly' presented with each of the image choices (i.e. randomly assigned to each image condition) has been selected as 50% by default, and these figures can be changed but cannot be omitted in order to allow true randomisation (true randomisation would rarely lead to equal percentages of participants receiving each choice).

After selecting the turquoise 'Save & Close' box, the 'Design Survey' screen is displayed again, now with the new images added beneath question 3 (see Figure 6.7(a)). From the 'Design Survey' page, clicking on the 'Preview Survey' box displays the survey as it will appear to participants (in preview rather than design mode). Figure 6.7(b) shows the displayed bottom section of the survey page in this mode, and testing the random assignment function by re-loading the survey in preview mode several times does indeed display either the 'Oscar Wilde' or 'Hangzou' image, with what appears to be random occurrence.

The computer attitudes study example does not require the use of images, randomisation or more advanced survey features such as question piping or question logic. However, these functions (e.g. as demonstrated here) are easy to work out how to implement. Forcing participants to respond in order to proceed (useful for

(a) 'Design Survey' mode

(b) 'Preview' mode

STATEMENT OF CONSENT

Please agree to the following statements if you would like to participate (you will have the option at the end to state that your answers should not be used as research data):

I understand participation is entirely voluntary and I may withdraw from the study at any time during or after participation (up to 3 months after participation)
○ I agree

I understand what my participation involves and any questions about the research have been satisfactorily answered
○ I agree

I agree to participate in this research and signify my consent by checking 'I agree' below
○ I agree

Hangzou

Next

Figure 6.7 Screenshots showing the new random assignment images included beneath Q3: (a) 'Design Survey' mode; (b) 'Preview' mode

consent pages, but not advisable elsewhere) is also easy to implement by simply selecting a checkbox while editing the question.

Having set up a survey design, and thoroughly tested it within the SurveyMonkey 'Preview' mode and made any required edits, the next step is to make the survey live in order to test it 'in the field' so to speak. This allows testing across different browsers, testing the effects of having JavaScript turned off, deleting cookies and attempting to re-enter (it may be unlikely that participants will attempt such actions but it is good to have an idea of any limitations and potential issues that could arise), and so on. The SurveyMonkey Collector function manages dissemination of the survey; from the 'My Surveys' page (which is where you land when first logging on to a SurveyMonkey account) this is accessed by clicking on the title of the relevant survey, to reach the 'Survey Summary' page, and then clicking on the 'Collect Responses' tab on the right. Selecting the turquoise '+ Add Collector' button on the right takes you to the page shown in Figure 6.8(a). From here several options are available, allowing dissemination by creating a web link (which can be partially customised) to distribute manually, by specifying a list of email addresses and a message including the survey URL to be sent to these (a specific delivery date can be set), embedding a survey in a webpage or creating a pop-up (to appear when a page is visited) which contains either an invitation or the survey itself, and disseminating via Facebook (by embedding the survey, or specifying a URL link).

The SurveyMonkey Collector functions feature quite an impressive, and potentially very useful, range of options. Some of these are generic across the different collection methods. For example, Figure 6.8(b) shows the page displayed after selecting 'Web Link' as the collector type to be used. On the left hand navigation menu a 'Change Settings' link is visible. Figure 6.8(c) shows a selection of the options available upon clicking on this link, which as can be seen include whether

(a) Collector Type Selection screen

validity of online assessments [D849 iCMA]

| Summary | Design Survey | Collect Responses | Analyze Results |

« Cancel   Next Step »

Select the method you would like to use to collect responses. We refer to the method that you use to collect responses as a "collector". While most people use only a single collector, you may want to use multiple collectors if you are sending your survey to different groups of people. Each collector can have its own unique settings and restrictions, and can be closed and opened independently. For more information about collectors, visit the help center.

How Would You Like to Collect Responses?

⦿ **Web Link**
Create a Web Link to send via email or post to your web site.

◌ **Email**
Create custom email invitations and track who responds in your list.

◌ **Website**
Embed your survey on your website or display your survey in a popup window.

◌ **Share on Facebook**
Post your survey to your Facebook Wall or Friends, or embed on your Page.

Enter a Name for this Collector:

Name: New Link   (max 100 characters)

« Cancel   Next Step »

(b) Web Link Collector screen

validity of online assessments [D849 iCMA]

| Summary | Design Survey | Collect Responses | Analyze Results |

Edit Web Link

Change Settings

Change Restrictions

Manual Data Entry

Close Collector Now

Edit Web Link   STATUS: OPEN

Weblink Collector

Buy a Targeted Audience: Need a specific group of people to take your survey? We can help. Learn more »

🐦 **Your Survey Web Link**

Collector Name: **New Link** Edit

Copy, paste and email the web link below to your audience.

https://www.surveymonkey.com/s/XQ77KRZ   Customize

Copy and paste the HTML code below to add your Web Link to any webpage:

<a href="https://www.surveymonkey.com/s/XQ77KRZ">Click here to take survey</a>

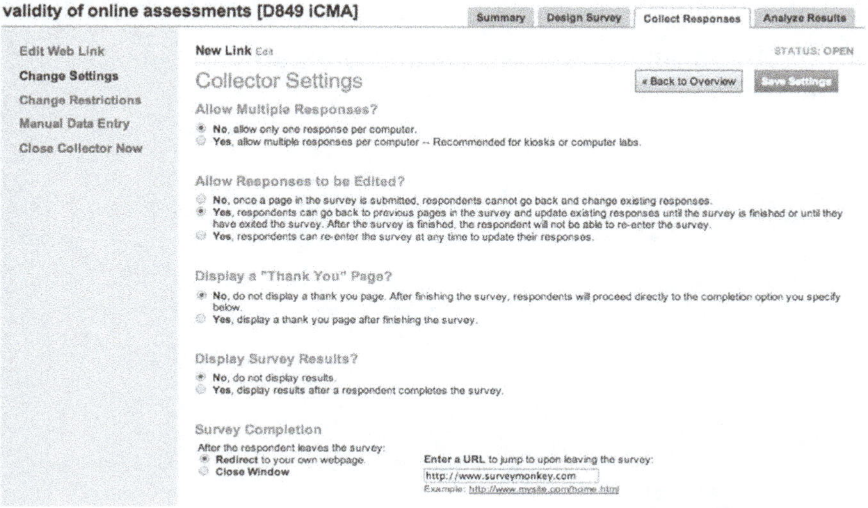

Figure 6.8 Screenshots showing the Collector Management screens: (a) Collector Type Selection screen; (b) Web Link Collector screen; (c) Collector Settings options screen

to allow multiple responses from the same 'computer', whether to allow respondents to revisit previous survey pages and edit their responses, and whether they can exit and re-enter the survey to complete it at a later time. Pages to be displayed upon completion are also set here (in most cases a suitable debrief page will be appropriate). Also (not shown here) is the option to display a customised 'disqualification page', and whether to use SSL encryption and store IP address information (the latter option indicating that entirely anonymised surveys are possible).

Other more generic options include setting up password-restricted access and setting a cut-off date/time and maximum response count (available under the 'Change Restrictions' tab). Options tailored to particular collection methods are also available; for example, the email list option allows tracking who has responded or not (of those invited), and identifies any bounced email addresses. The ability to set up multiple 'collectors' means that unique links can be set up (e.g. for different groups of respondents), or even with some time and effort a unique link for each individual respondent, which, if kept track of in a separate database, will allow the linking of individuals to response sets. Tips on how to achieve this, as well as many other searchable questions and answers, are available via the SurveyMonkey help page.

Looking back at the screens in Figure 6.8, an 'Analyze Results' tab can be seen to the right of the collector tab. Since many social and behavioural researchers will have access to, and be most familiar and comfortable with using, their own chosen dedicated data analysis software packages (e.g. SPSS, R), analysis functions tend to be of less importance to this user group. The ability to import data easily into their chosen dedicated package will often be most useful, however. SurveyMonkey

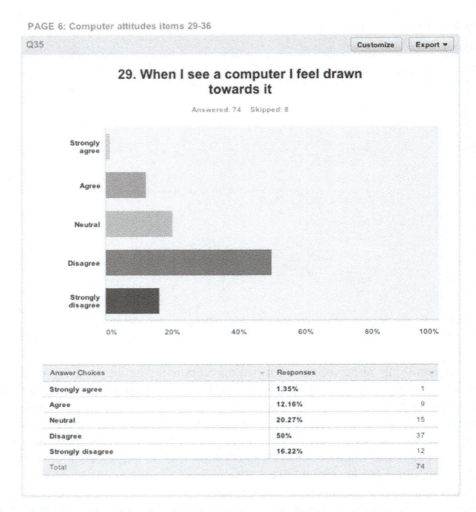

Figure 6.9 Screenshot showing a bar chart (generated by default) summarising responses to an item in the computer attitudes study

makes importing collected data sets directly into SPSS very easy for Gold-level subscription accounts, and with a little more effort (involving exporting data in a specified file format which can be imported into SPSS, or other third-party software packages) this can also be achieved using basic and free accounts. For Gold accounts, the left hand 'EXPORTS' menu tab (from the 'Analyze Results' page) opens various options which can be chosen; selecting '+ New Export' and then 'All responses data' allows an SPSS format file to be downloaded (other options are XLS, XLS+ and PDF). This file is downloaded in zip format to a local computer, and can then be accessed and opened to produce a 'result.sav' file. Assuming SPSS is installed on the local computer, this file can be opened and, all going according to plan, the user should then have the complete data set displayed neatly as an SPSS data file (in the authors' experience this has always worked very smoothly).

Other options available via the 'Analyze Results' tab include a variety of formats for summarising and presenting collected survey data. Figure 6.9 shows one such example summary output for a response item in the computer attitudes study example (under 'Question Summaries'). Such functions may be useful for gaining a quick snapshot summary of data as they are being collected, but these functions are limited to fairly basic descriptive statistics options (compared with what an advanced, specialist package such as SPSS can achieve). The interested reader is left to explore the further analysis functions available here.

The above illustrative example has demonstrated some of the key functionalities offered by a well-respected, widely used online survey software package. Further features and options are available, but space precludes discussing them in detail here, but they can be explored by trial and error and consulting the helpful available FAQs and tutorials also offered (access these via the 'Help Center', by clicking on the drop-down menu alongside your account username). Previous reviews have identified SurveyMonkey as a robust, effective solution for the typical academic social and behavioural researcher (e.g. working at a university) (Gordon, 2002; Hewson, 2012b). Since these conclusions were reached, SurveyMonkey has continued to undergo development, including adding new features and improving existing procedures – though it should be noted that there seems to have been a recent move towards supporting more corporate applications and interests, including marketing and consumer research (based on the first author's perusal of the regular email updates that SurveyMonkey sends to subscribers). This is to be expected with commercial packages, where corporate customers offer the greatest financial returns, and so are likely to drive the development and direction of such packages.

To conclude this section, we now report the outcome of a pre-testing phase (conducted February 2014) using a live version of the computer attitudes survey discussed here, as good practice dictates should be carried out before launching any IMR survey for use with actual participants (see Table 6.6 above, *Maximising reliability*). Referring to the principles of good practice presented in Table 6.6, and the essential and desirable features outlined in Table 6.7, we tested for reliability of procedures and adherence to ethics principles in the computer attitudes study implementation using SurveyMonkey. Hewson (2012b) carried out an earlier very similar evaluation using a simple survey design (very similar to the computer attitudes study demonstrated here) and an experimental design which used images and random assignment to conditions. Hewson (2012b) identified issues with (a) the reliability of the 'Exit Survey' button (with some browsers); (b) text boxes not resizing appropriately when changing browser size; (c) multiple responses being possible by using different browsers or prohibiting/deleting cookies; (d) the ability to revisit previous pages using the browser back button; (e) no method for presenting debrief information if browser is closed to exit early, (f) limited possibilities for gathering meta-information (e.g. response times) and (g) some limitations in presentation options (font characteristics, and page positioning, particularly when placing multiple images). We consider each of these issues in our updated tests using the example presented here.

The computer attitudes study was tested on a Macbook Pro laptop, connected to the Internet by broadband, by pasting the dedicated SurveyMonkey URL link into each of three different browsers: Chrome (version 32), Safari (version 7.0.1) and Firefox (version 26). Of course, testing on a PC and range of relevant browsers would also be appropriate, but for illustrative purposes here we just report the Mac tests. In all browsers the survey displayed well and looked the same (colour, layout, font, etc.). Proceeding through the survey pages was very straightforward, and the consent checkbox forced-response items worked correctly, preventing the respondent from moving on to participate unless these statements had been verified. Advanced skip logic and question piping functions were not used in this example (though in previous tests we have found all of these to function correctly).

The first issue encountered was with both the reliability and flexibility of the 'Exit Survey' button. This is an option which can be specified (appearing by default at the top right of each page) by visiting 'Survey Options' from the 'Design Survey' page. To specify what happens if the 'Exit Survey' button is clicked, 'Change Settings' needs to be visited from the 'Collect Responses' page; here only two options are available: to close the browser window, or redirect to a specified URL. The reliability problem we encountered was that the 'Exit Survey' button seemed simply to have no effect when the 'Close Browser' option had been selected. Checking the SurveyMonkey help pages identified this to be a known issue, which occurred if the survey URL had been pasted directly into a web browser, or a link accessed within an email message, as opposed to having been embedded within a webpage. This reliability issue could thus cause problems for many studies. However, it is worth bearing in mind that since ethics principles dictate that in most cases participants exiting early should be presented with debrief information, the 'Close Browser' setting will not be appropriate for many studies. The flexibility issue we encountered relates to this point; there seemed to be no straightforward way to specify (during survey design) that participants who selected the 'Exit Survey' button should be taken to the 'Survey Debrief' page, which in the computer attitudes study was simply the last page of the survey. The only way to present debrief information reliably to both those participants completing and exiting early seemed to be to use the URL-redirect option to specify a webpage which contained the debrief statement. Doing this within SurveyMonkey by setting up a new one-page survey and referring to this is perhaps a rather cumbersome workaround, but does avoid requiring access to an external web server on which to house the debrief webpage.

Unfortunately, there seems to be no solution, presently, which allows respondents who close their browser mid-study to be presented with debrief information (in SurveyMonkey or any other package we have tested), so taking other pre-emptive measures, such as urging participants to use the 'Exit Survey' button should they wish to withdraw, or asking for an email address to which a debrief statement can then be sent, is advisable. The process for controlling how many times participants could participate was not foolproof; re-entry after completing the survey once was possible by using a different browser (on the same or a different computer) and also if a browser was set to not accept cookies, or installed cookies were subsequently deleted. It is unlikely that many participants would take any of these steps in order to gain re-entry and submit another set of responses (though bear in mind the earlier point about incentives perhaps providing a motivation to do so). Collecting IP addresses, time and date of submission, and possibly other personal information such as demographics, could be argued to be a useful strategy for detecting multiple submission attempts. Also, if a user has cookies blocked in his or her browser settings, then exit and re-entry at the appropriate point to complete the survey will not work; rather the user will enter back at the start.

Regarding the presentation and display options, no major problems were noted with the display upon resizing the web browser, though any free text response boxes will not reduce from the set size, which means they will be only partially displayed if the browser is made very small. It is advisable to set the default text box size bearing this in mind, and considering use on smaller laptop or tablet screens. The respondent is able to expand text boxes manually as desired during survey completion. The flexibility in controlling font characteristics, for the designer, was considered; the 'Create Custom Theme' function (under 'Edit Survey' on the 'Design Survey' page) allows some customisation of presentation parameters, but is quite limited. For example, the survey font (Arial, or one of seven other options) can be set as a global parameter, as can the background colour. To achieve a greater degree of flexibility, HTML code can be included in appropriate places (e.g. alongside descriptive text) when editing the 'Design Survey' page. This requires enabling HTML mode as a global parameter, which is done under preferences in 'My Account'.

The ability to revisit previous pages using the browser back button was tested, after specifying that participants should not be allowed to go back and change previous responses ('Collect Responses' page, 'Change Settings'). While tests showed that revisiting earlier pages was indeed possible (though the 'prev' button within the survey page was no longer present, thus not suggesting to participants that it was intended they should do so), altering the original saved answers was not possible. Still, this could of course be problematic for the validity of memory experiments, where trusting participants to follow instructions not to visit earlier pages would seem a very high-risk strategy. In such contexts, this software package is likely not suitable, though of course future developments may resolve this issue, as the developers continue to monitor and respond to customer feedback.

Finally, the ability to collect meta-information was investigated, having been identified as a limitation by Hewson (2012b). SurveyMonkey records the time and date that the survey was started, last modified and the total time taken. This limited but useful information can help to gauge whether the respondent completed in one go, skimmed through the survey without sufficient time to provide properly considered answers, and so on. Obtaining more detailed response time and pattern information would require the ability to access and analyse server logs.

<> SEVEN </>

<> WHAT CAN GO WRONG? </>

INTRODUCTION

Although we maintain in Chapter 4 that the Internet provides an effective and economical means for accessing a vast and diverse number of potential participants, IMR shares with many other modes certain methodological problems relating to, for example, the participant's willingness to participate and the nature of interactions with the researcher.[1] However, even here IMR has some crucial advantages, particularly in the way certain effects can be controlled for (such as the influence of biosocial attributes), thereby allowing for both reduction of the influence of these effects and giving a handle on isolating the role of these factors. A primary feature of IMR which contributes to the control of experimental artefacts is that Internet access can be anonymous. Research may be conducted from computer accounts which can also be assigned names suggesting at least gender and nationality, perhaps race as well. There are no necessary voice or appearance effects, just the image that is conveyed through communications associated with the study – it is thus possible to manipulate the portrayed gender, race and nationality effects in order either to reduce the role of these attributes or deliberately to convey some specific attribute, depending on the nature of the research question.

This chapter outlines methods for addressing some of the issues raised in previous chapters. We also outline specific pitfalls that can emerge and suggest solutions,

---

[1] In this chapter we focus on IMR using primary research means – studies of various sorts that rely on the Internet for access to participants and/or the traces they produce (as in unobtrusive research). Chapter 2 discussed methodological issues with secondary research (as distinguished in Chapter 1) in which the Internet is used as a point of access to information codifying primary research. The primary methodological risks discussed in Chapter 2 were: too much trust in a particular Internet resource; and habituation to the idea that Internet resources are the only ones worth checking.

preventative and, where possible, post hoc. However, awareness of the potential for things to go wrong is the first step in preventing mishaps. The sorts of issues that are at stake are, among others, data loss (via corruption or transmission failures based on the technology), participant dropout rates and hacker vandalism. We suggest solutions that entail in the main maximal researcher control of materials and in fact all electronic communications associated with research. Some of these issues have arisen in our own work, others are discussed in the literature (e.g. Joinson et al., 2007; Reips, 2002a). While the theme of the chapter is the space of things that can go wrong in Internet-administered studies, the focus is on how to anticipate problems and how to recover from them when they have been unanticipated.

The main areas we address are matters associated with equipment, methodology, netiquette, data scraping, hackers and data protection. Many of the issues discussed here emerge only within certain categories of research projects: those in which the researcher requires a special computing artefact that collects data from participants. However, studies requiring interviews over the Internet also raise issues of data protection, and observational studies of individuals interacting in online communities are limited by the affordances provided in those virtual worlds. Nonetheless, the focus here is skewed towards issues associated with using devices for IMR whose primary function is more than interpersonal communication. Issues that arise from the participant's perspective are independent of whether the researcher has developed the software that facilitates participation or used something available in the market. From the researcher's side, there is more control available when using bespoke software, but there are also more considerations to attend to in ensuring that the research may proceed as intended.

EQUIPMENT

There is often a basic trade-off between having Internet-mediated studies that make it possible to test what one is interested in and having the facilities for participating in those studies generally available among potential participants. The more facilities required, the fewer participants will be available with access to comparable equipment. Increasingly, the concept of the 'Internet of things' is gaining currency (examples were offered in earlier chapters); a simple version of this is the availability of web camera data, and a more complex version is in the availability of arrival departure data on the web for train stations, buses and airports, just a step away from sensors in the home or biomedical sensors that people might voluntarily attach to themselves for health monitoring purposes. As a rule of thumb, the more specialised the equipment requirements, the less broad based the participant pool. Equally, the more complex the materials used in a study, the more difficult it can be to set up the study and control the data collection. Items of equipment (hardware or software) are always at risk of fault, in themselves and the links among items. This section discusses some tools and techniques, pointing out where some of the problems mentioned can be addressed and where additional problems may reside.

As pointed out throughout this book, it is not essential that an Internet study be fully interactive. Indeed, we also discuss below the sorts of unobtrusive research studies that can be conducted using data scraping methods, which are not interactive at all. However, for the purposes of this section, it is convenient to suppose that the researcher prefers to construct a study that makes the most of interactive text and graphics, with accessibility running through common modes of access to the Internet – web browsers like Mozilla, Firefox, Chrome or Internet Explorer, or chat rooms and discussion forums. Such interactive settings are equally available to surveys, interviews, participant observation, experiments, and so on. Considerations addressed here also apply if the researcher has implemented a study using advanced programming languages – dynamic HTML pages, and Java and JavaScript coding, for example. However, some risks are open even to the researcher who is using existing third-party software (e.g. to construct experiments or surveys) rather than programming from scratch. For example, it is incumbent on the researcher to view an experiment or web-based survey (in a preview mode, without recording data) on as many browser platforms as possible, including older versions of platforms. This is because, despite claims to the contrary, portable code does not always behave as expected in other platforms.

The last thing most researchers want to do is become web programmers, and the demands of becoming proficient are actually quite substantial, with many details to attend to (the first edition of this book provided a primer on web programming in JavaScript, but the emergence of third-party software makes this now less necessary). Some of these are very simple, such as maintaining proper security over the files, perhaps by issuing passwords to intended users, and monitoring logs of access. Even though facilities like the Apache server which run under UNIX and are freely available provide security options, the researcher must still expend a great deal of energy implementing them, in the general case. Moreover, testing is extremely important, as it can easily happen that a study with HTML pages designed with one particular browser for the prototyping platform has a vastly different behaviour when viewed from an alternative browser (or even the same browser family, but executed from a distinct hardware architecture). At any rate, in some of our work and that of our students, this has been an occasional problem (McGowan, 1999). The most trivial version of the problem is for HTML pages to view in vastly different font sizes on various platforms. It is not safe to assume that HTML5, for example, or whatever the most recent version is, will work on all of the browsers that are popularly used, and not even will all popular settings within different versions of a single browser. For any browser, Firefox, for example, individuals use different release versions depending on when they commenced using the browser and how often they upgrade their browser. Further, individuals may elect to enable or disable the functionality that one's study might depend on (automatic spelling checking, video display or JavaScript interpretation, for example). One can imagine this fact ruining a study if the original design depended on all of a text being visible at once, yet some participants (without even knowing which) are able to see only one small sector of the intended viewing field. Those who develop their own bespoke web experiment system may use techniques from Internet programming in order to test what browser a research participant uses to access a survey or experiment. For example, JavaScript makes available an object-oriented resource for testing this (see http://www.javascriptkit.com/javatutors/navigator.shtml [accessed April 2015]). From the information about browsers and their versions, it is possible to reason about the availability of HTML5 support. Version 10 of Chrome is reported to have the greatest level of support, and Internet Explorer version 8 the least, of those browsers tested in 2011, for example.[2] Online resources are available to allow one to determine if one's own browser is HTML5 compatible (http://html5test.com/ [accessed April 2015]). Such facilities make use of the same system tools that a researcher would need to use in order to test the level of technology available to a participant.

Other browser-related points are also important to attend to. Default settings and HTML are important to avoid. One should not rely on default settings in constructing HTML but should set colours and relative font sizes as explicitly as possible. To see the importance of this, consider a study in which colour is important, and in which various colours have been placed against a default background. If participants' web browsers have different default settings, they will essentially be presented with unintended materials, materials that perhaps lack the intended effect of colour contrasts. This can be an issue even if colour contrasts are not the topic of research. Texts presented on the webpage can become impossible to read when set against an ill-chosen background colour.[3] Therefore, it is important that the researcher designing webpages fill in appropriate values for defaults wherever possible.[4] We emphasise that it is advisable to test the presentation of materials and interaction with the materials thoroughly in these respects before the study

---

[2]See http://html5tutorial.net/general/which-browsers-support-html5.html (accessed April 2015).

[3]The issue of Internet use by vision-impaired individuals arises here. Some users in this population do have speech synthesis facilities. The methodologically relevant point here is to encourage HTML encoding that maximizes use of meta-tags identifying materials so that visually impaired participants can know what they are not seeing, and to include questioning about whether a participant relies on such facilitating access software in any study for which it is a critical issue. See also http://www.hobo-web.co.uk/design-website-for-blind/ (accessed April 2015) for tips on making webpages accessible to vision-impaired individuals.

[4]For some studies in which only one browser may offer the requisite behaviour for the stimulus materials, it may be necessary simply to restrict participation to individuals with the appropriate browser. Of course, this applies to equipment generally.

takes place. Testing is important whether the research is constructed in custom-developed software or using the tools designed for research purposes and supplied by commercial software providers.

Additionally, for an advanced Java application to work correctly, whether 'home-grown' or licensed by the researcher, it is necessary for the participant's browser to be set to Java-enabled mode. This applies whether the researcher deploys a bespoke system or one available 'off the shelf'. The very nature of Java is that it is not permitted to change the setting for the user; thus, certain partici-pants will be eliminated by the equipment if they do not happen to be using a Java-enabled browser (many of these will not experience much of the study at all, therefore it is necessary to provide mechanisms that supply informative texts to those participants explaining why their experiment is not proceeding). Similarly, assumptions may be made in one of two directions about 'cookies'. Some packages allow the possibility of login session tracking which prevents multiple responses from the same computer, but which still preserves a kind of anonymity for the user through a mechanism known as 'cookies', which share information between the client and server. Many potential participants from the general public are aware of the notion because they will have encountered Internet-based services that do not work for them unless their browsers are set to enable the passing of cookies. On the other hand, many are also unaware of the underlying reason why their interactions with sites that are functional to others are without function for themselves. Not every server which depends on cookies explains this reason for failed interactions. Thus, a system may demand cookie passing in order to function, but without an actual need on the part of the researcher to track user sessions, and with the result that some potential participants may be denied access (due to incompatible browser configurations). In the other direction, a researcher may intend to monitor session interactions with cookies in order to address the multiple participation problem (see Reips, 2002b), yet these researchers face the risk that recalcitrant participants may simply clear cookies after participation, thus effectively setting the stage to present as a new session, and new participant. Studies that rely on certain software 'plugins' are also problematic when partici-pants lack the necessary plugin at the start of interaction. In a worst-case scenario, the need for the plugin becomes relevant only partway through the study, but the participant's home machine lacks sufficient disk space (or has some similar con-straint) to download the software, thus nullifying the participant's contribution altogether. Through testing the software from the perspective of participants on a number of platforms, a researcher may discover what prerequisites a participant will have to have installed at the outset. It is best in conducting such testing to use 'clean' installations of browsers, with only default settings. If testing is conducted using systems that have had many facilities added, it is more difficult to discover which of these are required to be added by participants before their participation commences. However, good software packages will declare their dependencies on other packages. Still this does not avert the need for testing.

Researchers who are depending on accurate reaction-time data should also be aware of the foibles of measuring such data remotely. That is, network lags during busy times of the day may artificially inflate the amount of time participants require for particular events within the study. However, measuring those events not on the server but on the participant's home machine (using an applet) is sensitive to various hardware facts about the home machine. Essentially, it becomes a requirement to have a part of the research study server software responsible to identify what sort of software and hardware each participant is using. This is one way to cope with some of the problems both with browser versions and with applet-calculated timings. In any case, the accuracy of timings remains a current topic of research in itself (see Keller, Gunasekharan, Mayo & Corley, 2009; Reimers & Stewart, 2007). Forgetting the complexity of determining accurate timing information to arbitrary levels of precision on a participant's machine (a 'client' in the argot of Internet computer services) because of the range of issues there, not least of which is in the fact that computer processor time is shared among processes even on a single-user machine, timing precision on the server side is also open to confounding measures. Therefore, it is necessary to study carefully the degree of precision admitted by a system, through client and server assumptions, before relying on reaction-time data in IMR experiments conducted in this way. The level of precision available may be sufficient for the intended analysis. Alongside the need for caution at the time of designing experiments is the need to scrutinise the data recorded in light of known limits to available precision as part of the general process of log analysis that a researcher should engage in to assess patterns of contact with the server, abandonment of experiments or surveys, and perhaps paradata (such as mouse clicks, areas of pointing, etc.) that might be recorded, depending on the software adopted. Some log analysis tools are available specifically for web-based experiment methods (e.g. Reips & Steiger, 2004), and log file analysis is itself a research area in the methodology of IMR (see Berker, 2002; Tobin & Vogel, 2009).

More mundane issues enter the picture for researchers intending to embark on longitudinal studies given a certain degree of flux that currently exists in Internet usage patterns. In particular, many Internet users, most notably the population of university undergraduates and students generally, often have annually changing usernames and passwords. Also, participants who participate from 'free' accounts on providers like Yahoo or Google sometimes maintain several accounts (sometimes corresponding to distinct outward-facing personae) and wish to engage in Internet activities seamlessly through all of those accounts. The possibility of maintaining multiple online identities is fostered by some browser settings that remember user IDs and passwords for the user on various host sites, thereby reducing the cognitive load of managing multiple accounts, but is obstructed when browsers are updated or settings are cleared for other reasons. Thus, users with many online personae may lose track of the one used for any particular purpose. This suggests the value of running a study on a server that hosts user accounts for studies requiring longitudinal data (for these purposes, this means any study lasting more than a year, or involving sampling of the same participants for more than one year). This follows, because then the user simply needs to remember an agreed account and password on the server hosting the study. In such cases, where participants register with an email address it is further possible to generate renewed passwords for participants who forget them. Of course, when participants forget their passwords, and their user ID information has changed, it is non-trivial to match the participant to the correct account and password while still maintaining overall integrity of the participant's data. Where the study allows the participant to be anonymous as far as the researcher is concerned, this may well mean that the corresponding data are effectively lost, since follow-up is rendered impossible. It becomes necessary to monitor a larger amount of personal information about the participant in those cases, in order to verify continuity of the same participant under a new home user ID. Worse, though, is if the longitudinal participant obtains a new account, and for whatever reason ceases to check an old account; then it becomes impossible to email participants successfully to remind them of appointments for updated participation. This said, longitudinal studies are difficult for conventional research paradigms as well.

Recently, researchers have begun developing general purpose systems intended to accommodate many of the issues raised in this section. That is, as discussed in Chapter 6, there are a number of software systems that can be downloaded from the Internet or used remotely.[5] For example, the online psychology laboratory, an extensive suite of studies, is freely available at http://opl.apa.org/ (accessed April 2015) and intended for psychology instructors to get students to participate in classic experimental designs. The site is configured to record participant data for registered users and has facilities for monitoring reaction times. The main drawback of the system is that it presumes PC or Mac environments, and for users to contribute new studies it is necessary that they be developed using certain Authorware scripting tools. McGraw and Tew (1997) were critical of the Internet Psychology Laboratory (formerly hosted by the University of Illinois)[6] on the basis of the fact that it did not make use of Shockwave, a freely downloadable but limited platform technology that enables multimedia studies, but used Java instead. While their arguments about the fleetingness of many programming languages in the history of computing systems cannot be dismissed, due consideration is

---

[5]Note that many studies currently exist on the Web via online study clearing houses, as noted in earlier chapters, and one can easily stumble upon them. We suspect that for many purposes, these studies are not controlled enough for participant access. Note as well that not all of the studies generated by such software are intended for Internet participation; some are designed for downloading over the Internet and execution on local hosts.

[6]The URL (http://kahuna.psych.uiuc.edu/ipl2) is no longer valid, although still cited (e.g. http://christophercurrie.sys-con.com/ [accessed February 2015]).

not given to the fact that many programs that work and for which hardware and compilers exist have never been transported to other systems – it is not the case that all applications that people find useful are re-implemented in each new high-level programming language that comes along.[7] Given that Java has been given an international standard, there is no reason to think that Java programs will drift into uselessness any time soon, especially since many browsers are designed to interpret Java programs in particular. Nonetheless, the McGraw and Tew (1997) system does facilitate fairly extensive multimedia-reliant research; it is intended to be freely available; and it is designed around the premise that IMR creates access to unfathomable numbers of participants. See also McGraw et al. (2000).

Reips and his colleagues have developed an extensive suite of tools and research programs in validating methods, tools and features for use in IMR experiments (see http://iscience.deusto.es/archive/ulf/Lab/WebExpPsyLab.html [accessed February 2015]). The main limit to systems that provide remote services to experimenters is that they constrain the ease of access that remote experimenters have to the overall system and its data files. Other limits are a natural consequence of this. For example, paradata – records of idle cursor hovering and flicking – are not recorded by most such systems and therefore are not available to researchers to study. Nonetheless, experimental paradata is likely to be among the richest sources of information made possible to record by this kind of web data collection. This is not particularly enhanced with services offered by commercial providers. However, the capacity for such systems to be extended in an open-source mode is where their value lies for experimenters with access to competent software developers. Drupal (Drupal.org [accessed April 2014]) is an example of an open-source content management system that many researchers may wish to explore.

In sum, the technology for running advanced multimedia studies interactively over the Internet is still under development. While a great number of products exist for purchase or for free, a number of them come with inherent limitations in excessive demands on the technological prowess of the researcher or the participant (or both), limitations on potential for customisation, or with constraints on the level of equipment a study (or participant) must have easy access to in order to become involved (Buckley & Vogel, 2003; Graham, 2006; Guennouni, 2000; Keller, Corley, Corley, Konieczny, & Todirascu, 1998; Kenny, 1998; McGowan, 1999; Timothy, 2000). Nonetheless, not every study requires sounds, graphics or animations. A great many can be facilitated by modest ftp transfers or email communication, particularly if the research is based on questionnaires or interviews. These techniques create more responsibility for the researcher in maintaining control over the data (e.g. ensuring in experiments that distinct conditions are

---

[7]Worries about some of these programs were fundamental to the Y2K hysteria, and it remains possible to sustain oneself by maintaining programs written in unfashionable languages like COBOL and FORTRAN.

inaccessible to participants who should not be able to download them, and with methods of verifying this control). Nor are they immune to difficulties. In an ftp setting the researcher must decide whether to allow both upload and download of files. Few systems administrators who control researchers' computing facilities allow anonymous uploading, and certainly researchers would be at risk of losing important data in a setting in which participants are allowed to log in and anonymously deposit data, possibly destructively, on top of previously uploaded files. A more secure alternative requires the researcher to obtain individual accounts with permissions to write files for each participant. However, in times of increased monitoring of network security, many network systems administrators are also reluctant to grant such privileges to outside users.

In recent years new facilities for file hosting have emerged. These afford varying levels of security and corresponding risks. For example, as an alternative to ftp hosting, one might take advantage of Google Documents (docs.google.com [accessed April 2015]) or Dropbox (dropbox.com [accessed April 2015]). This allows research participants to have direct access to files to the extent of being able to collaborate in the construction of a document or spreadsheet or the like. Risks are obvious in the capacity for documents to be destroyed altogether. With a group of participants who are trusted, this might be a viable facility that avoids the need to provide access to a local server, compromising security for other users. However, potential participants who are not particularly trusting may be extremely reluctant to register with Google or other providers of such hosting arrangements. An intermediate kind of provision comes from popular web services like the blog-hosting arrangements of WordPress (wordpress.com [accessed September 2014]). This facility also supports group conversation. Here, limited, coarse-grained access analytics can be provided, and surveys hosted. Participants may prefer the possibility of 'registering' with such a service that does not check the validity of registry and email addresses.

Generally, the ftp setting is best suited to participants downloading materials and responding to them in some form of email reply. This abets cross-checking of access logs and email time stamps (though accuracy cannot be guaranteed in the latter case), as well as information about the remote host that forms part of the logs in both, and which can be used for authentication. It is also possible to have users upload their reply with ftp, but security-minded administrators for the computer networks used by researchers are often reluctant to allow uploads of files by external users via ftp. Just as interactive models of research can be sensitive to network lag time, so too can ftp. User connections can time out after seriously long delays. This tends to have an impact on large file transfers (as in multimedia interactions which can involve enormous amounts of data movement), but there are also issues with having users transfer a large number of small files: it becomes very easy for a remote user to overlook one or more. While it is possible to create tar files (or the equivalent) that bundle things together, this can make the single data transfer too large, in some cases; worse, more explicit instructions are required for participants who are not familiar with how to unbundle the files. In very few words, the researcher is best advised to keep technical requirements at the minimum acceptable to the research question. We have noticed in our collaborations that ordinary email communications with colleagues in certain geopolitical regions need to be as 'light' as possible for reasons of local economy.[8] In such situations, fully interactive multimedia is not an option and therefore excludes most potential participants. However, provided the researcher adopts a sensible sampling technique, appropriate to the research domain (inclusive of appropriately screening respondents), the Internet can provide a very cheap mode of access to appropriately equipped participants in research. Appeal to ftp may seem somewhat archaic; however, this is consistent with an overarching methodological principle of keeping the technology involved as simple as possible in order to ensure that it is maximally accessible.

METHODOLOGY

Because of the ease of access to participants in IMR, it is somehow equally easy to make silly methodological mistakes, some more or less devastating than others. One of the issues discussed at length in Chapter 4 is identifying the appropriate sampling strategy. It may be desirable to send an email that invites replies to express interest in participating to a large number of web forums, Internet lists, chat rooms, etc., where these are selected more or less on the basis of size of accessed community and focal point of the community interest. However, at the extreme of such participation solicitation, it is important to ensure that all the announcements are correct in all details, and that the full study is sorted out: once one has made one wide-fan solicitation, it is methodologically suspect to make a second call for a minor variant of the study (as subsequent participants will not experience the same conditions as earlier participants). Of course, this is no different than in research situations away from the Internet. However, the relative ease of hitting the 'Send' button on an incomplete message or providing undesirable access to materials and conditions, in comparison with more traditional methods for spoiling one's participant pool, is as mind-boggling as the extreme scale of the pool of potential participants afforded by the Internet. It has never been so easy to quickly invalidate the participation of so many participants. It may in the near future be possible to apply outgoing email filters in order to mitigate the risks of sending unintended emails. The topic of outgoing email filtering (ensuring

---

[8]Additionally, there can be difficulties that emerge due to the impoverished nature of ASCII character encoding for languages that make extensive use of diacritics. Character-set encoding incompatibilities can also cause technical problems in transfer of materials. Appel and Mullen (2000) also offer reflections on this issue.

that outgoing emails are actually intended for the indicated recipients, potentially with implicit offence triggers highlighted for the sender prior to final release) is the inverse of spam email detection (cf. O'Brien & Vogel, 2003), and is an application in automatic text classification that one of us has begun investigating. This issue is paramount in constructing studies to be administered via the Internet. The ease of sending out access to materials prematurely is perhaps the locus of the greatest amount that can go wrong in IMR.

Many other methodological issues are the same in the case of IMR as in other modes of research. All of the traditional issues must be sorted out before actually soliciting any participants, and that may create certain timetabling issues: Internet traffic is far greater during the academic year than outside it; and Internet traffic troughs during holiday periods widely celebrated internationally. Any study with a critical amount of time between conditions should be sensitive to both global fluctuations and constancies in the availability of participants. This simply means that there are more methodological issues to consider, and that the traditional ones (including the correct way of soliciting and screening participants for the task at hand) need to be sorted out early on.

At least one other methodological issue is more or less unique to studies administered via the Internet, and is particularly important to studies involving participants collaborating such as in collaborative dialogue research (e.g. Healey, 1995). The basic issue at stake is the potential difference between synchronous and asynchronous communication made possible by the Internet (as discussed at length in Chapter 3, when considering interview and observation methods). There, and previously here, we have emphasised the advantages offered by asynchronous communication, notably (say, in comparison with a questionnaire administered by telephone) that the participant can respond at greater leisure (Hewson et al., 1996). For those studies in which the completion timescale allows, that can be an advantage in obtaining more thoughtful, accurate and perhaps cooperative responses. However, the Internet also offers access to approximately synchronous and fully synchronous communications. Email is again an example of the former category, and IRC, chat rooms, multi-user dungeons (MUDs), MUDs object-oriented (MOOs), virtual worlds more generally, etc. (see earlier chapters), are an example of the latter. Whether at adjacent machines in the same laboratory, or accessing machines from opposite sides of the globe, it is possible to use email in a nearly synchronous fashion. The methodological upshot of this is that it can become important to a study to know the geographical location of the participants. Traditional collaboration studies involve participants situated locally, and the issue of time zone differences does not arise. However, it is a potentially important fact to know whether one's participants are participating in the wee hours of the morning or during what ought to have been lunch time, by their local watch. A corollary is that it can be difficult to timetable specific joint cooperation for nearly synchronous events between participants who have never met; it is far from impossible, but it remains an additional methodological issue for the researcher to resolve (see also discussion of online interview and focus group methods, in Chapter 3). The issue is that potential fatigue of participants usually does not have to be monitored in (nearly) synchronous tasks locally executed, but it almost certainly does have to be monitored in the case of IMR because of the vast geographical distances that may be involved. While videoconferencing and telephone interviews are accompanied by the same constraints, videoconferencing is as new as IMR (and in many cases actually is administered via Internet), and both videoconferencing and telephone interviews are outpaced in scale of potential participation by the possibilities enabled by asynchronous email exchange.

A host of methodological issues that would not arise in other settings need to be resolved for Internet administration of a study, but this need not be problematic, depending on the research question. One that has been discussed is how researcher and participant user accounts are named – anonymously or not, with gendered names, or not, etc. For some research questions, it may be anticipated that responses will be partly conditioned by qualities attributable to the researcher on the basis of the researcher's own account name. Another issue is in informing participants that all of their communications will be recorded (but rendered anonymous in reporting situations). Just as it becomes relevant to many linguistic judgement tasks to know facts about an individual's handedness (Schutze, 1996), when studies are administered via the Internet and involve rapid production of texts by the participants (perhaps in a communicative setting, e.g. an online synchronous interview), then it becomes relevant to have a preliminary screening that allows balancing for typing prowess – it may matter for some studies that some participants are touch-typists and others not – and handedness.[9] Further, depending on how remote reaction-time studies are arranged, it may also be necessary to determine facts of participants' hardware setup, in conjunction with the experimental interface (e.g. the location of 'Y' and 'N' keys on a keyboard, which might not be a Qwerty keyboard, in relation to whether a participant is left- or right-handed, and how those keys are interpreted as responses within the study).

A similar factor to control for (or at least to obtain questionnaire data about) is whether the participant has free email access from home (or workplace) and whether emails sent from the workplace are monitored. It is sometimes important to know whether the respondent is participating from home or workplace as well (as discussed in Chapter 5 in the context of ethical issues). The issue at stake is the degree of leisure and freedom that the participant feels. However, the appropriate range of questioning is obviously delicate, as some respondents-from-work might easily be put off, suspecting the study itself as a form of management monitoring. On the other hand, in many work settings daytime diversions are encouraged. In any case, it is valuable to know the actual constraints the participant is operating under.

---

[9]In multimedia settings, this can be avoided by using speech-to-speech communications, much like a telephone; however, the resulting implications for level of equipment possessed by both researcher and participant become prohibitive.

Knowing that the participant pays for email separate from Internet access can provide an independent explanation for brevity of reply in some cases. Equally, free Internet access can inspire a different length of participation in studies not based on email, but still relying on Internet interactions. Thus, we advocate including questions that solicit information on that range of issues in any pre-study exercise that screens participants. A connected issue is that it is important to offer participants opportunities to withdraw from the study (as discussed in some detail in Chapter 5). The methodological and ethical issues relevant here are guarantees of anonymity of even partial participation, and whether partial data are to be analysed at all, or wholly deleted.

Finally, authenticity issues may need consideration in some studies; there is unprecedented capacity for individuals to misrepresent themselves and their personal attributes in Internet interactions, to the extent of adopting alternative personae for their Internet interactions from their 'real-life' interactions. Certainly, aggressive behaviours can be manifest in Internet communications in ways that are not apparent in other forms of social interaction (such as 'trolling'). These features of communicative styles online are an important topic of current research and must be taken into account in any study that hopes to generalise from Internet-mediated communication styles to communication in general (Berzsenyi, 1999; Herring, 1996; Kiesler, Siegel, & McGuire, 1984; Rossetti, 1998).

NETIQUETTE

Recruiting participants is a part of the research phase that interacts with 'netiquette'. This is particularly relevant to Usenet newsgroups (UseNews) and email mailing lists, which have developed a certain canon of acceptable behaviours, some of which Internet researchers can easily unwittingly infringe. One of the basic rules is that postings (to either) should 'be relevant'. This in particular can run counter to the needs of many studies in which one explicitly does not want to post invitations to participate in a study on a particular topic to a group or list devoted to discussion of that topic (of course, this is not always the case). Note that it is possible to select target locations within any mode of Internet access (lists, newsgroups, etc.) at random, provided one has an enumeration of them to select from randomly (or to select on the basis of discussion content). However, as pointed out in Chapter 4, it is important to keep in mind that not all locations yield access to the same numbers (or types) of potential participants. Thus, if one is balancing invitations across locations defined by contrasting topics of discussion, one is not necessarily balancing invitations across even population sizes. This can be controlled for somewhat by monitoring the degree of activity in the relevant locations.

An invitation to participate in a research study is nearly always completely irrelevant to the main intended discussion, and in this case one is hopeful for the generosity of moderators (in cases where moderation exists) to allow the post-ing. In many cases, by approaching moderators directly initially, this particular constraint can be overcome. However, it is crucial not to be deemed as posting profiteering 'spam'. One thing to pay particular attention to is that there are also net-vigilantes who do not directly moderate lists, but who have an apparently syntactic definition of what constitutes 'spam'. Hewson and Vogel (1994), for example, found their invitations cancelled when they were posted to more than 20 newsgroups at a time, regardless of whether there was a semantically uniting relationship among the groups or a purely scientific non-commercial motive to the advertisement: posting to more than 20 newsgroups at a time is what cer-tain net-vigilantes deem to be unacceptable, and can result in having to re-post in smaller numbers. Therefore, it is important never to exceed that threshold.[10] While it is tempting to suggest the alternative response, to post to each individu-ally, this also violates the netiquette of 'cross-posting': in order to save bandwidth it is desirable to have one copy of the text around rather than multiple copies, one in each group. There is a difference in how many times an individual participant will see the notice (this is a salient difference between newsgroups and mailing lists, in fact; for mailing lists even cross-posting to multiple lists entails that a multiple subscribed individual will run across the advertisement in each setting, while an invitation cross-posted to newsgroups will be seen by a reader only in the first group the reader is subscribed to where it is encountered). In the early days of the Internet, bandwidth referred to network and memory capacity; these days it applies mainly to the capacity of humans to wade through content.

One final point is that participation invitations posted to mailing lists and newsgroups should be formulated in text-only format so that they can be read on any news or mail reader; in particular, they should not be posted as attach-ments nor include attachments. It has become quite easy for PC users to send computer viruses to other users without even realising that their own computers were infected. Sending viruses will alienate a great many participants, and if they focus on a virus itself, particularly because of the fairly random contact made between researcher and participant, a researcher could easily find the advertise-ment circulating the globe with cautions to avoid reading messages about the study as it is 'false and contains simply a virus'.[11]

Of course, as discussed in Chapter 5, and elsewhere in this book, postings in mailing lists, newsgroups, social and professional networks, or other online community websites, may themselves be the topic of research (see Hofmann,

---

[10]Our experience was that rational discussion was of no use. It was utterly irrelevant that we were not sending chain letters or seeking profits; simply exceeding the 20 address rule caused us considerable wastage of time.

[11]This stands in spite of the point made in Chapter 2 that most virus warnings have been bogus. The effect of association with a bogus, yet globally circulated virus warning is immeasurable.

2002; Vogel & Janssen, 2009; Vogel & Mamani Sanchez, 2012). Confounding factors may arise depending on how the ethical issue of consent is handled in these contexts. If one concludes that, despite the fact that the data are visible to anyone with Internet access, one must disclose to participants that the content of the discussion forum of whatever sort is being monitored for research purposes, then one risks uncertainty regarding whether behaviour in the group will adapt significantly in response to being observed. An alternative is to allow the publication of the research to act as a debriefing after the fact, informing individuals that they have been studied. A rule of thumb that some feel comfortable[12] with is the conclusion that if communication on the forum is restricted to a group such that one must be a member in order to see the communication, then monitoring without additional explicit consent is unethical (note that not all mailing lists are such that communications are visible only to members; many mailservers make public archives of interactions). Moreover, even if the data are visible to the public, they may be restricted to ethically behaving data scraping 'robots' (see more on this below).

The researcher using attachments in soliciting participants can fairly quickly become a pariah. The best way to avoid the problem is to refrain from using attachments altogether and to stick to text-based messaging. At least two less invasive alternative methods exist for obtaining participants. One is to use the experiment clearing house approach mentioned earlier. In this method, the researcher designs a study to be located in a place in which a number of other studies are hosted. These tend to become familiar to the community of psychology teachers who will have their students participate in studies that are created on the Web, and thus have a more or less cyclical flow of participants coursing through them. In addition to the educational community, one might also have interested lay parties seeking out such things to participate in, just like avid crossword solvers. However, these latter participants come with self-selection characteristics that may not be desirable for a study depending on a wide sample of the population. The student population may also be skewed for some purposes. Another possibility is to take advantage of free webpage hosting and the mechanics of Internet search engines. Some Internet companies earn their living by obtaining high 'hit rates' for webpages. The adaptation of their essential trick is to place an innocuous webpage (possibly containing content otherwise unrelated to the study) on a separate site from the study, but with a host of tagwords attached to the page. The choice of tagwords can be tailored to the sort of subject interests relevant to the group from which one is hoping to obtain participants. For example, in a study about attitudes towards immigration, one could encode many of the words associated with the topic into the link page. Thus, the link page, along with the link to the study,

---

[12]It is difficult to predict on many questions of ethics who will feel what way in any particular scenario.

has a greater chance of being identified during a random potential participant's search of the Internet for information about the topic.

Equally, one can load an HTML keyword field with a completely random set of tags, or one can employ only very frequently searched tags if one wants to obtain the widest pool possible. By using such a method that makes it likely for potential participants to discover the possibility of participating, one can attract participants without cluttering their favourite newsgroup or their mailbox with postings that solicit their participation. A related technique is to place pointers to the study on chat pages that are devoted to particular domains. Chat pages are often dynamic HTML pages that accept small texts from users and leave them posted for subsequent readers. They are unlike newsgroups in that postings do not expire nearly as rapidly (and this can have its own annoyances once a study has ended, so this last form of participant gathering should be approached cautiously). In fact, in virtually any of the currently available forums for individuals to communicate synchronously or asynchronously over the Internet, it is possible to advertise for participants in a study. The suitability of each method depends on the factors discussed above: the longevity of the notice, the suitability of the participant pool accessed, the size of the pool. The differences are that in different settings it can be more or less complicated to advertise, as follows from attending to the issues raised here.

UNOBTRUSIVE DATA COLLECTION METHODS

Unobtrusive research methods also entail risks. In an unobtrusive study one may be hoping to extract and amass information from existing databases or other relatively structured resources, or one may be using the Internet as an open data source which is crawled using a 'spider' program, a program that traverses Internet links collecting and indexing data connected by those links. It is necessary to make such spider programs, as well as programs that target specific sites, comply with robots.txt directives declared by site owners. These directives indicate what files or directories on a site, perhaps all completely visible to a human to monitor manually, that a host manager permits to be processed automatically by programs like spiders that index the Internet. A researcher trying to scrape data from the Internet in this fashion is faced with the monumental task of sifting away structure from unstructured material, and also patent garbage from genuine data. The risks of being confounded by junk are great; so too is the risk of data counts being confounded by multiple copies of the same content residing at many locations. Thus, it is possibly safest to constrain such research methods to structured sources. Where this is not an obvious effective strategy (web indexing for search engines is an activity in which one cannot effectively confine search to structured sources), one must have a strategy for at least filtering spam and applying other sorts of automatic text classification (such as language guessing) in order to weed away content that amounts to data to virtually no one. In the field of corpus linguistics,

Kilgarriff and Grefenstette (2003) note a number of risks in using summaries of responses to phrasal queries made to search engines as a source of data, not least that the summary statistics of 'hits' are misleading due to, for example, the effects of duplicate content existing on the Web via mirror sites. Mere duplication of content across multiple websites does not constitute bona fide distinct uses that should inform calculations of relative frequencies of expressions. Linguists might be interested in the relative frequency of expressions in natural language, at the same time that sociologists might be interested in knowing how widely the senti-ment expressed by a sentiment is shared, and mirrored content distorts the data for both sorts of research questions (on the other hand, others argue for the merits of the Web as a data source where data are otherwise scarce; see Keller, Lapata, & Ourioupina, 2002). Clearly, in linguistic research that depends on the Web as a corpus, it is necessary to be able to correctly filter irrelevant content. These issues are also relevant in other disciplines (e.g. behavioural economics) where Internet-based mentions of concepts (e.g. 'scarce') may serve as proxies for market senti-ment indications (e.g. attitudes towards commodities markets).

It was noted above that some forms of Internet-based data collection amount to harvesting data (generally, in the form of text, image or sound files) from publicly visible locations. This is a form of data collection that at present requires access to competent programmers, but is significantly less involved than the competence required to host one's own experiment server and exploit all of its data logging facilities, or adapt its open-source code to one's own needs. In fact, any number of open-source data scrapers are readily available online, open for tuning to one's own purposes. The general idea is to seed a program with a URL or list of URLs in order to have the program engage in some sort of search (typically, breadth-first) of links visible from the initial link, reading the content available at links. Any reasonable such system will have a 'redundancy check' incorporated in order to avoid infinite looping through link cycles. A 'netiquette' element arises here, in that it is customary to check any directory that is searched in this fashion for the presence of a robots.txt file, as discussed above. The convention is that such a file is used in order to signal to a data scraper whether that directory is intended for scrutiny by 'robotic' data scraping programs. A directory that is freely available to public viewing may not be intended for scraping. The content of the robot.txt file is used to indicate whether the data are open or not. The convention is that the robot.txt file should be respected and that in the absence of directives in a robot.txt file, the content is available for scraping. Another convention that sometimes is put into use is to present one or more layers of 'captcha' interfaces in which humans are presented with typically distorted combinations of letters and numbers as an image file, such that a human can read and retype the content as a sort of password, but limiting robotic access by virtue of the fact that programs are not likely to be able to read the image, randomly generated for each access. Of course, such programs may have access to optical character recognition used to automate the reading process, and this is the reason that the images are typically distorted. Clearly what can go wrong in robot-aided web data collection includes the possibility that a data set ends up incomplete because the information collection required is not possible to collect ethically.[13]

However, this is not the extent of the risk of unobtrusive data scraping methods. A persistent problem with the Web is that it has no real editor. While crowdsourcing is increasingly popular as a method of achieving consensus-oriented data validation, and by its very nature contains a kind of peer review, it also by its nature does not necessarily include expert validation or completeness of review. Further, it is not particularly mindful of redundancy and, rather, appears to celebrate redundancy through activities that amount to content 'going viral'. For example, if a study in linguistics wishes to consider whether some sample of language is statistically anomalous by comparing the word n-grams[14] in the text with distributions expected for the language at large as estimated by texts that are visible on the Internet, then the study must attend to the fact that a corpus constructed by scraping the Internet is at high risk of having duplicate content, simply because the same content was re-posted thousands of times. This risk is independent of inadvertently sampling from mirror sites that provide complete copies of resources such as Wikipedia. While the presence of virally replicated content potentially, at least, indicates a separate ratification of the content by each person who repeats the act of posting it, mirrored content does not. Repeated content therefore presents a clear challenge to conducting research on language change, for example, as well as a host of other research topics. It is not just in linguistics that research questions, at first glance, seem readily possible to address because of the scale of data visible via the Internet. In political science, too, attempts to assess public sentiment may also be susceptible to the same risk of conclusions confounded by repeated content, unless care is taken to control the links that are searched by robotic programs for content. Further, where the task actually is to access public opinion, this kind of method of assessing opinion without actually asking questions of people must contend with the fact that data scraping will give access at most to positive expression of opinion (which may itself be positive or negative), but will leave inaccessible the opinions that a direct question to a conscious participant, if asked, would have elicited.

HACKERS

It is an odd thing about the Internet that one can easily have a substantial number of people actively looking for studies to participate in. One can equally have a substantial number of people searching the Web looking for ways to test their

---

[13]See Thelwall and Stuart (2006) for a general discussion of the ethics of scraping.

[14]These n-grams are sequences of tokens (words, for example) of length n; *n-gram* is a term of art in computational linguistics.

skills in cracking into systems and having an impact on them. In connection with IMR some of these individuals will appear in the guise of participants, and some of them will simply be attempting to break into the site, with little interest in the study that is running. Password cracking programs abound freely on the Net, and a typical exercise for novice hackers is to attempt to obtain illicit access to a system by breaking into accounts. There are standard safeguards against this practice, and they come with varying degrees of hassle for the researcher. The first issue is with user account names for participants allowed system privileges on the researcher's host system, if this is permitted in order to support collaborative activity in a controlled environment or to support upload of files via ftp, or whatever other reason. Additional to the possibility that the research project entails providing participants with accounts on the researcher's host network is the scenario in which the researcher's project is mediated by a software tool that hosts user accounts (for a longitudinal study, for example) without those participants having user privileges in the rest of the researcher's institutional computer network. In general, a hacker requires both a user ID and a password to gain access. Therefore, one can protect oneself to some extent by not positing a very predictable set of user IDs (such as MyExperiment1, MyExperiment2, ...). However, once a potential intruder identifies an actual user ID for the account it becomes possible to test out arbitrarily many possible passwords, simply by running scripts that generate and test passwords (of course, many systems administrators configure systems so that any particular user account is denied access after three or so failed attempts, and system logs will typically reveal the pattern of automated attempt; however, systems administrators typically have much else to do that precludes daily inspection of system access logs).

Consequently, it is very important that a sensible strategy for generating passwords be identified. Systems administrators are the best source of tips on this, but in short the passwords should not be words or names found in dictionaries for any human language; they should contain combinations of upper case and lower case letters, as well as numeric characters.[15] The effects of random hackers intent on breaking into accounts can usually be forestalled that way. However, if they do gain access, then it is important to identify this and close the leak as soon as possible. Again, systems administrators have standard ways of monitoring this – generally this involves monitoring access logs to verify that access is made to the systems from known remote hosts, and to verify that data files do not suddenly disappear or radically change in properties (such as size). System backups may provide partial recovery from the effects of hackers. On the other hand, access

---

[15]Reporting this here does not compromise the efficacy of the strategy: the password cracking programs have to check all possible combinations of case and numerics. Typical systems administrators monitor and prevent repeated login attempts that continue for extended periods. Of course, occasionally monitoring slips, and the researcher should be as aware of the illicit login monitoring facilities at the home site as the file backup frequency.

log monitoring is often undertaken when a security breach is suspected, rather than systematically monitored, and security breaches can go undetected for long periods of time.

Researchers should ensure, whether through an online study clearing house facility or on the researcher's own hosting site, that all materials associated with the study and data obtained from it are located in places that are not permitted to external readers without clearance. That is, webpages are usually accessed through a specific URL (e.g. http://psych.hanover.edu/research/exponnet.html – a list of such links [accessed April 2015]); however, unless permissions are set appropriately, it is also possible for anyone at all to view files listed at higher points in the directory structure. For example, some time ago, the link http://darkwing.uoregon.edu/~prsnlty/surveySBO existed (January 2012), but at the time of writing (September 2014), anyone in the world with a web browser can examine the URL related to the one just mentioned (http://darkwing.uoregon.edu/~prsnlty/ [accessed April 2015]) to find the content in Figure 7.1.

Name	Last modified	Size Description
Parent Directory		–
ADSTUDY/	15-Jul-2009 08:51	–
SAUCIER/	17-May-2005 17:25	–
SBO/	23-Jul-2006 09:27	–
TODOWN/	25-Feb-2009 11:06	–
food/	21-Jun-2007 21:59	–
mcvs/	04-Nov-2007 15:25	–
surveySBO/	12-Feb-2007 00:57	–
wyoming/	12-Oct-2008 00:20	–

Apache/2.0.63 (Unix) Server at darkwing.uoregon.edu Port 80

Figure 7.1 Index of /~prsnlty

In the case of access via a web browser, this effect is avoided by placing an index. html file in each directory (and controlling permissions on files and directories). With such a file in place, its contents will be viewed and processed by the client browser, but the accompanying information about directory structure, file names, file sizes, date of update, etc., will not. Of course, the extent to which this level of protection is important depends entirely on the intended security of the files which are potentially made visible if these security measures are not implemented.

In this particular example, the files available are not alternative conditions (such as are typically used in experimental designs) in a study. Certainly, in most circumstances involving separate conditions in a study, one does not want the alternative conditions to be visible to participants. Thus, multiple site entrance techniques (Reips, 2002b) should be carefully deployed with genuinely different URLs and not merely different directories within a fixed URL prefix. Moreover, ethical considerations are relevant here. One does not want to make prior participant data (experimental data nor any personal data that participants have given consent to record) freely visible to new participants, or to anyone for that matter, in most cases. The extent to which visibility of files to random hackers can result in data loss or other disruptions of a study is less clear, but caution (certainly regarding confidentially) suggests that most materials and directory structures and file naming schemes should be quite invisible to everyone.

The other primary issue associated with hacking behaviour is the activity of participants who are keen to discover things about the study prematurely or who are simply bent on derailing the results. Ways that an individual might do this include multiple participation and attempting to examine other conditions. We have just discussed how file permissions should be set to prevent the possibility of participants consciously wandering into other experimental conditions. However, as indicated above, it is also important to give semantically unrelated names (and not minimal alphabetic variants) to directories for various conditions, or to files for distinct conditions within the same directory. The reason for this is that even without a hacker mentality, a participant could easily wander via typographical error or free association from the provided URL into a URL for a distinct condition. Similarly, an individual might attempt to participate in a study (say, a survey) more than once. Protections against this hinge on monitoring the domain address from which a user accesses the study. This, of course, is not a completely ideal method since there can be more than one user for an individual machine, and more than one user may participate in any given study. The technique of Keller et al. (1998) to identify whether participants are bogus can be applied here. These authors used the technique of demanding participants supply email addresses (which can, but does not necessarily, incorporate the domain address of the host to which they connect from; for example, a user may have an account on one machine, but handle all email from a remote host, for instance via a Yahoo.com account). At the end of the study a 'thank you' email is sent to the participant, and if it bounces back there is a fair chance that the participant is bogus (or at least entered a bogus email address, for whatever reason). The technique can equally be used to monitor for multiple participation. However, it is only viable if the participants have not been guaranteed anonymity. When a single domain address (or closely related one) turns up in the log files for more than one user, it can be verified whether the same or different email address was associated with each login. Of course, it is possible for a hacker to have more than one email address, but the possibility of a hacker having a sufficient number of distinct addresses to derail the study diminishes rapidly. Consider the problems faced by the online auction industry as an example of the reality of the problem in non-research domains: Dobrzynski (2000) reports on the monitoring practices of eBay, the Internet auction agency, to prevent individuals with multiple addresses (or actual cartels) from bidding up their own offerings; the company's algorithm for discovering cartels is proprietary, but one may speculate that it involves a social network analysis of bidding behaviours to detect sets of individuals who are commonly reacting to each other's bids and commonly acting as sellers without frequently winning auctions. A difficult problem in this monitoring process is that users can have more than one login, and can enter the system from more than one host. Thus, eBay's monitoring procedures do not provide a guaranteed safeguard against individuals with multiple addresses bidding up their own offerings. Guarantee of single participation in IMR remains a topic of research.

It is a good idea to rely on software that provides assurance of reliable performance under adverse conditions (whether second-hand software or researcher-produced interactive webpages). Here a significant issue is the standard use of cut and paste from word processing packages. It is easy to overlook having highlighted enormous amounts of text (and as easy to highlight the same intentionally) and with the click of a key dump the entire chunk into a text box in some form or other. A participant in a study may do this unintentionally, or a hacker may try the same thing in order to 'inject' nefarious code into a system in order to gain access to the host computer network in the background. Now this is not necessarily problematic; however, if the pasted text includes various control codes (such as explicit HTML encoding), many systems can suffer consequent data loss. The reason is that field delimiters in the underlying database are suddenly used within one field. The result is a software confusion about where the field boundaries are, and corruption of data from that point on. Similarly, if an encoded URL is included in a text box, perhaps in an online communication task, one can suddenly find that another participant has clicked on the URL and finds the browser launched to some site external to the study.[16] The way to guard against these problems is to test software rigorously with unintended inputs (such as null inputs, garbage inputs, random HTML, large files, etc.) in advance. On the one hand, the issues here are those that should be addressed by programmers who provide software tools for Internet experimentation (whether or not those programmers are also the researchers intending to use the software), but on the other hand, it is the responsibility of the researcher to make sure that the system actually does behave as intended when presented with garbage inputs, verifying that the systems used actually do function as advertised.

IMR makes it easy to bring a study online very quickly and with commensurate responsibility to avoid doing so too soon, before appropriate testing and piloting. One must reflect on the ramifications of pressing the equivalent of the

---

[16]In some studies it is important to know whether participants have consulted external data sources. Additionally, it is a common bug in nascent Internet experiment management systems for transfer to external hosts to freeze the server, effectively crashing it. It is certainly a common enough bug that one should try out during pilots using a system.

'Send' button, at every instance. The results of acting too quickly can be disastrous. There is a direct relationship between pre-study testing of materials and procedures in IMR and diminished risk of all sorts at study time.

LEGAL CONSIDERATIONS

Internet research methods create additional legal risks, compared with more traditional data collection methods. Some elements of risk are no different – namely, those associated with data protection regarding personal information that may be recorded by participants. A researcher can easily become a data controller in the legal terms of data protection legislation, on the basis of information stored in relation to participants. This is true of researchers who do not avail of Internet accessibility. A new risk for IMR is the potential to compromise data security inadvertently by making information visible on the Internet, in the way that one occasionally learns that private companies unintentionally leave private data of individuals exposed on the Internet. Still, this is not a risk that arrives because a project is run via the Internet, merely because the researcher has Internet-accessible data. A researcher who conducts research offline may also compile a data set containing personal data about identifiable individuals and locate the data in places that are electronically accessible via the Internet. It is rather more likely that data collected via IMR will be located with visibility to others on the Internet, either directly as in some of the scenarios discussed above, or through hacking. Care must be taken to ensure that participant data are behind security 'firewalls' and on computer systems not linked to the Internet.

Other risks appear to arise uniquely through research conducted using IMR methods. For example, a data scraping exercise may unwittingly acquire private data on individuals that have been unintentionally left unexposed by other researchers. It may also collect material that is illegal in relation to other statutes about data prohibited to produce or retain (a spider program may locate and download child pornography, for example, and in many jurisdictions statutes prohibit download or retention of such data). In some cases, data may come into the possession of a researcher who is otherwise abiding by good netiquette in scraping data but which nonetheless leaves the researcher in violation of copyright law or other forms of intellectual property protection. To some extent it is possible to rely on filters that are outside the control of the researcher, effectively the national Internet censorship policy, or the filters that are created by Internet service providers. The liability of Internet service providers has recently been tested in some jurisdictions with respect, for example, to content deemed defamatory that is hosted by their service. Liability appears to increase commensurate with moderatorship activity – the more a provider takes on the role of an editor, the greater the liability for defamatory content assumed; in merely indexing and even caching content search engines do not appear to become liable for defamation. However, one of the key issues that emerges in law with respect to the Internet is the jurisdiction that applies in any instance. This is because many of the issues discussed here are handled differently in different jurisdictions, but it is not settled whose jurisdiction matters – that of the participant, the researcher or the actual data (which could be virtually anywhere as services move increasingly to 'cloud computing'). This is a space that is extremely fluid as both legislation and judicial tests of legislation force the evolution of Internet law (see Edwards & Waelde, 2009; Reed, 2004).

Although complicated and fluid, the issues cannot be ignored. Returning to the notion of equipment, many systems for managing (for example) surveys via the Internet involve cloud-based systems. Even for a 'home-grown' system, a researcher has a choice between developing it so that it operates on a specific real machine with local disk space under the researcher's control behind a firewall, or on a virtual machine provided as a 'cloud instance' on a host machine that is under the physical control of a cloud services provider (such as Amazon) and specifically not behind a firewall controlled by the researcher. The popular and powerful Qualtrics system provides a cloud-based offering. At issue here is that the data stored 'in the cloud' are not in a device that may be physically secured by the researcher. This has implications for the provisions of data protection legislation, which require that data controllers provide guarantees of data integrity and data security. Where individuals may be identified in a data set and where that data are to contain sensitive personal information,[17] then it may not be compliant with the researcher's institutional policies to use public cloud computing facilities to store that data, even if the cloud services provider is compliant with international standards (e.g. ISO/IEC 27001).[18] Of course it is possible to use cloud-based systems and comply with relevant data protection law, but the specific issues germane to the study must be addressed in order to guarantee that personal data are not compromised. Moreover, not every study requires personal data, and researchers should resist the temptation to collect more personal data about individuals than is really necessary. However, while retention of personal data about individuals may be well motivated within the context of some research projects and therefore collected explicitly, this is not the sole manner in which personal data associated with individuals may accrue in Internet research.

The use of cookies allows websites generally to track a lot of information about preferences and behaviours of users; thus, they can be argued to contain personal

---

[17]In the 'Cloud Computing Policy and Guidelines' of Trinity College Dublin, The University of Dublin, at the time of writing, such data may be deemed 'confidential' and 'critical': 'Information relating to the mental and physical health of individuals.... Biometric identification data.' See http://www.tcd.ie/about/policies/cloud-policy.php (accessed February 2015).

[18]See http://www.iso.org/iso/home/standards/management-standards/iso27001.htm (accessed February 2015).

data and therefore fall under data protection laws. Data protection varies considerably (within Europe and between Europe and the United States, for example). Some websites are constructed so that they do not function unless users give permissions for cookies to be stored on their computers (personal experience with travel booking online is such that it is impossible unless cookies are permitted to the booking site in question). However, these cookies in principle can yield a lot of information, particularly to Internet service companies whose services are such that a majority of online activity can happen through them, since they own popular search engines, video entertainment, and so on. Users benefit from a highly personalised experience. However, this is at the loss of some privacy.[19] We mentioned the use of cookies in Chapter 6, noting the principal use in detecting whether participants have engaged more than once in an IMR activity. Our recommendation is to avoid requiring cookies where at all possible.

Participants may, depending on the nature of a study, have other alternative means of being identifiable in a data set amassed through IMR. Apart from simply providing personal details, answers to some combinations of questions can create a situation in which the respondent is uniquely identifiable. It is incumbent on the researcher to attend to these possibilities in developing research instruments and seeking ethical clearance for research studies. The aspect of this particular to IMR is the potential discoverability of the data sets by individuals outside the research through either accident (e.g. lost memory sticks) or system hacking. Therefore, in all cases, researchers are strongly advised to encrypt and password-protect data files (and where data are to be stored in the cloud, it is in the researcher's interest to encrypt the data before uploading them to the cloud, rather than relying solely on encryption facilities supplied by the cloud storage provider) that are not explicitly approved for open data repositories.

SUMMARY

In this chapter we have examined six main categories of problems that can arise for studies conducted over the Internet. The first of them related to *equipment* available for conducting such studies. We pointed out that the more complex the equipment required, the more limited the pool of potential participants becomes, and the more difficult it is for a non-specialist in programming issues to construct the study. We also provided pointers to a range of studies available on the Internet that currently actively gather data and provide examples of the range of things possible. Our discussion of the range of facilities currently

---

[19]See Angwin, J., & McGinty, T. (2010). What they know: Sites feed personal details to new tracking industry. *Wall Street Journal*. http://online.wsj.com/news/articles/SB100014240527 48703977004575393173432219064 (accessed May 2014).

or soon to be available to researchers interested in presenting studies on the Internet but disinterested in becoming expert programmers hopefully provides guidelines to researchers intending to use the Internet. *Methodological* issues particular to the Internet as well as those common in other areas but exacerbated (or ameliorated) by Internet research were also outlined. The primary issue there is to proceed cautiously and carefully before implementing a study over the Internet, resisting the unprecedented speed of access to participants that it offers. Additionally we suggested guidelines for attracting participants, without violating *netiquette*. Alternative methods that harvest data from the Internet for primary analysis (*scraping*) also create risks while avoiding issues of interactive studies. All sorts of studies are potentially compromised by *hackers*. *Data protection* creates risks of litigation for ethical and legal reasons; data protection is therefore a major consideration for IMR. These risks can only be mitigated (and we have suggested how) but not eliminated. We have provided pointers on how to avoid problems that arise from attracting recalcitrant participants and outright hackers. Researchers wishing to keep abreast of ongoing discussion of risks and risk-mitigating tactics for IMR are advised to follow the outputs of a consortium of researchers involved in the European COST Action IS1004, WebDataNet[20] (Steinmetz et al., 2012; Steinmetz, et al., 2014).

---

[20]http://www.webdatanet.eu (accessed April 2014).

<> AFTERWORD </>

FINAL REFLECTIONS

In this second edition of *Internet Research Methods* we have made extensive revisions and additions in order to reflect the extent of developments in the field since publication of the first edition, just over a decade ago. Given the range, scope and interdisciplinary reach of IMR methods today, it would be practically impossible for any researcher to keep abreast of all the developments, applications and studies carried out. Inevitably, this book has a bias towards our own disciplines and areas of research; however, we have tried to include a good selection of examples and illustrations from outside this range. One of the most notable developments over the last decade or so has been the expanding range and prevalence of unobtrusive methods which harvest data from online archives, published documents and behavioural traces; these approaches have been facilitated by emerging Web 2.0 technologies and services, and the increasing permeation of the Internet into people's daily lives. They have provoked intensified debates and controversies regarding what is acceptable ethical practice in IMR, particularly relating to the public–private domain distinction online, as discussed in the newly added Chapter 5 in this edition. A central tenet of Chapter 5 is that there are no clear-cut answers to the questions that emerge, and that ethical decisions and choices need to be made within the context of any particular research study, taking into account a range of relevant factors. Further, ethics guidelines for IMR need to be flexible in order to be able to adapt to evolving online contexts and technologies. Obtrusive methods have also developed and expanded since publication of the first edition. Most notably, web-based survey methods have proliferated, facilitated by effective software solutions becoming readily available to allow researchers without extensive programming skills to implement robust, reliable, sophisticated systems (as discussed in detail in Chapter 6).

We continue to argue that there are compelling benefits of IMR, one of these being the ready access to a vast, diverse pool of potential participants. In this edition we have offered a broad range of illustrations and examples which demonstrate the benefits afforded by IMR, including facilitating access to extremely large sample sizes, time- and cost-effectively, as well as specialist, traditionally hard-to-reach populations. The time and cost efficiency of an IMR study, compared with offline methods, may play an important role in facilitating research at smaller institutions where resources might be more limited. Another important message from this book is that IMR methods, across a broad range of domains, perspectives and methodological orientations, have now been demonstrated to be able to generate valid, reliable, trustworthy data, comparable with those data generated using offline methods. The illustrations presented throughout this edition show this to be the case, and particularly the 'validation studies' which have set out to test directly the integrity of IMR methods, in comparison with more traditional offline implementations. Studies have now even indicated that IMR samples may sometimes allow levels of generalisability comparable with what is possible using offline 'gold standard' probability samples, though, as noted, there are still some significant limitations in obtaining probability samples in IMR.

So what does the future hold for IMR? There is no doubt that IMR methods are flourishing, and evolving, and the diverse range of illustrative examples discussed throughout this book evidences this. As technologies, solutions, strategies and discoveries continue to emerge, we predict the following likely developments. As the penetration of the Internet into individuals' daily lives continues and expands, IMR researchers will gain access to an even broader, more vast pool of potential research participants. Many countries are likely to reach close to saturation levels for Internet access in the near future, and expansion in terms of international reach looks set to continue; for example, the initiative 'one laptop per child' aims to facilitate access to the Internet for children in some of the world's poorest countries (see http://one.laptop.org/ [accessed April 2015]). Opportunities for observing and monitoring individuals through their online activity traces and interactions will expand, due to ongoing socio-technical developments, and this will lead to further developments and innovations in unobtrusive IMR methods. The ways in which people connect to and use the Internet are evolving, and it is likely that more and more people will gain mobile access, which will extend opportunities for a range of obtrusive and unobtrusive innovative IMR methods, such as *in situ* studies, and those recording (as well as delivering) multimedia and geolocation information (as discussed in Chapter 3). The expanding 'Internet of things' will also open further opportunities for gathering data in IMR, mainly in unobtrusive ways. This may create extended scope for obtaining very large-scale 'big data' sets. Ethics principles and guidelines for IMR will become more established, and widely available, with a broader range of discipline-related professional bodies publishing these, as well as funding agencies and RECs/IRBs. However, new ethical challenges and dilemmas are also likely to emerge, as novel

IMR techniques and opportunities present themselves. In obtrusive research, technological developments will expand possibilities for methods which more closely mimic offline proximal interaction, such as interviews using audio and video, due to the enhanced reliability and quality of these applications. Also, more complex, sophisticated experiments and other interactive methods will be facilitated by technological developments, such as reaction-time experiments which require very precise timings. Of course, the way for IMR to evolve, as we stated in the first edition of this book, is for researchers to implement procedures, identify problems and seek solutions. We hope that the updated guidelines and discussion in this second edition will help inspire interested readers to engage in these activities, and so contribute to the ongoing development of IMR methods.

<> REFERENCES </>

AbuAlRub, R. F. (2006). Replication and examination of research data on job stress and coworker social support with Internet and traditional samples. *Journal of Nursing Scholarship, 38*(2), 200–204.

Acquisti, A., & Gross, R. (2006). Imagined communities: Awareness, information sharing and privacy on the Facebook. In G. Danezis & P. Golle (Eds.), *Privacy enhancing technologies. Lecture notes in computer science*, Vol. 4258 (pp. 36–58). Heidelberg: Springer.

Adler, C. L., & Zarchin, Y. R. (2002). The 'Virtual Focus Group': Using the Internet to reach pregnant women on home bed rest. *Journal of Obstetric, Gynecologic, & Neonatal Nursing, 31*(4), 418–427.

Ahmad, K., Cheng, D., & Almas, Y. (2006). Multilingual sentiment analysis of financial news streams. In *Proceedings of the 1st International Conference on Grid in Finance*, Palermo. http://pos.sissa.it/archive/conferences/026/001/GRID2006_001.pdf (Accessed October 2014).

Ahmed, A. M., & Hammarstedt, M. (2008). Discrimination in the rental housing market: A field experiment on the Internet. *Journal of Urban Economics, 64*(2), 362–372.

Aho, A. L., Paavilainen, E., & Kaunonen, M. (2012). Mothers' experiences of peer support via an internet discussion forum after the death of a child. *Scandinavian Journal of Caring Sciences, 26,* 417–426.

Al-Sa'Di, R. A., & Haman, J. M. (2005). 'Synchronous online chat' English: Computer-mediated communication. *World Englishes, 24*(4), 409–424.

Alvarez, R. M., Sherman, R. P., & VanBeselaere, C. (2003). Subject acquisition for web-based surveys. *Political Analysis, 11*(1), 23–43.

Anderson, G., Kaldo-Sandstrom, V., Strom, L., & Stromgren, T. (2003). Internet administration of the Hospital Anxiety and Depression Scale in a sample of tinnitus patients. *Journal of Psychosomatic Research, 55*(3), 259–262.

Andrews, D., Nonnecke, B., & Preece, J. (2003). Conducting research on the internet: Online survey design, development and implementation. *International Journal of Human–Computer Interaction, 16*(2), 185–210.

Appel, M. C., & Mullen, T. (2000). Pedagogical considerations for web-based tandem language exchange. *Computers and Education, 34*(3–4), 291–308.

Arnett, J. (2008). The neglected 95%: Why American psychology needs to become less American. *American Psychologist, 63*(7), 602–614.

Bagnoli, A. (2009). Beyond the standard interview: The use of graphic elicitation and arts-based methods. *Qualitative Research, 9*(5), 547–570.

Bainbridge, W. S. (2007). The scientific research potential of virtual worlds. *Science, 317*(5837), 472–476.

Balch, C. V. (2010). *Internet survey methodology*. Cambridge: Cambridge Scholars Publishing.

Baltar, F., & Brunet, I. (2012). Social research 2.0: Virtual snowball sampling method using Facebook. *Internet Research, 22*(1), 57–74.

Barak, A., & Miron, O. (2005). Writing characteristics of suicidal people on the Internet: A psychological investigation of emerging social environments. *Suicide and Life-threatening Behavior, 35*(5), 507–524.

Barbeite, F. G., & Weiss, E. M. (2004). Computer self-efficacy and anxiety scales for an Internet sample: Testing measurement equivalence of existing measures and development of new scales. *Computers in Human Behavior, 20*(1), 1–5.

Barchard, K. A., & Williams, J. (2008). Practical advice for conducting ethical online experiments and questionnaires for United States psychologists. *Behavior Research Methods, 40* (4), 1111–1128.

Bargh, J. A., McKenna, K. Y. A., & Fitzsimons, G. M. (2002). Can you see the real me? Activation and expression of the 'True Self' on the Internet. *Journal of Social Issues, 58*(1), 33–48.

Barratt, M. J. (2012). The efficacy of interviewing young drug users through online chat. *Drug and Alcohol Review, 31*(4), 566–572.

Batinic, B. (1997). How to make an Internet based survey. In W. Bandilla & F. Faulbaum (Eds.), *SoftStat'97: Advances in Statistical Software 6* (pp. 125–132). Stuttgart: Lucius and Lucius.

Batinic, B., Reips, U.-D., & Bosnjak, M. (2002). *Online social sciences*. Seattle: Hogrefe and Huber.

Baym, N. (2000). *Tune in, log on: Soaps, fandom, and online community*. Thousand Oaks, CA: Sage.

Becker, B., & Mark, G. (2002). Social conventions in computer mediated communication: A comparison of three online shared virtual environments. In R. Schroeder (Ed.), *The social life of avatars* (pp. 19–39). London: Springer: London. http://dx.doi.org/10.1007/978-1-4471-0277-9_2 (accessed October 2014).

Berker, T. (2002). World Wide Web use at a German university – Computers, sex, and imported names. Results of a logfile analysis. In B. Batinic, U.-D. Reips, & M. Bosnjak (Eds.), *Online social sciences* (pp. 364–381). Seattle: Hogrefe & Huber.

Berzsenyi, C. A. (1999). Chat theory: Renovating rhetorical education in electronic composition classrooms. In *The Penn State Conference on Rhetoric and Composition Rhetorical Education in America*, 4–7 July 1999. web.archive.org/web/20011225233631/ http://www.wb.psu.edu/faculty/berzsenyi/cbpres.html

Best, S. J., Krueger, B., Hubbard, C., & Smith, A. (2001). An assessment of the generalizability of Internet surveys. *Social Science Computer Review, 19*, 131–145.

Bigelsen, J., & Schupak, C. (2011). Compulsive fantasy: Proposed evidence of an under-reported syndrome through a systematic study of 90 self-identified non-normative fantasizers. *Consciousness and Cognition, 20*, 1634–1648.

Birnbaum, M. H. (1999). Testing critical properties of decision-making on the Internet. *Psychological Science, 10*(5), 399–407.

Birnbaum, M. H. (Ed.) (2000). *Psychological experiments on the Internet.* San Diego, CA: Academic Press.

Birnbaum, M. H. (2001). A web-based program of research and decision making. In U.-D. Reips & M. Bosnjak (Eds.), *Dimensions of Internet science.* Lengerich: Pabst.

Birnbaum, M. H. (2004). Human research and data collection via the Internet. *Annual Review of Psychology, 55*, 803–832.

Björk, P., & Kauppinen-Räisänen, H. (2012). A netnographic examination of travellers' online discussions of risks. *Tourism Management Perspectives, 2*, 65–71.

Bogaert, A. F. (1996). Volunteer bias in human sexuality research: Evidence for both sexuality and personality differences in males. *Archives of Sexual Behavior, 25*(2), 125–140.

Bordia, P. (1996). Studying verbal interaction on the Internet: The case of rumour transmission research. *Behavior Research Methods, Instruments, & Computers, 28*, 149–151.

Bowen, A., Williams, M., & Horvath, K. (2004). Using the Internet to recruit rural MSM for HIV risk assessment: Sampling issues. *AIDS and Behavior, 8*(3), 311–319.

Bowker, N., & Tuffin, K. (2004). Using the online medium for discursive research about people with disabilities. *Social Science Computer Review, 22*(2), 228–241.

Bowling, A. (2005). Mode of questionnaire administration can have serious effects on data quality. *Journal of Public Health, 27*(3), 281–291.

BPS (2007). Report of the working party on conducting research on the Internet: Guidelines for ethical practice in psychological research online. *British Psychological Society.* REP62/06.2007.

BPS (2011). Code of human research ethics. *British Psychological Society.* INF.180/04.2011. http://www.bps.org.uk/sites/default/files/documents/code_of_human_research_ethics. pdf (accessed April 2015).

BPS (2013). Report of the working party on conducting research on the Internet: Ethics guidelines for internet-mediated research. *British Psychological Society.* INF206/1.2013. http://www.bps.org.uk/system/files/Public%20files/inf206-guidelines-for-internet-mediated-research.pdf (accessed April 2015).

Bradley, N. (1999). Sampling from Internet discussion groups. https://web.archive.org/web/20080325075336/http://users.wmin.ac.uk/~bradlen/papers/sam05.html (accessed August 2015).

Brady, E., & Guerin, S. (2010) 'Not the romantic, all happy, coochy coo experience': A qualitative analysis of interactions on an Irish parenting web site. *Family Relations, 59*, 14–27.

Brenner, V. (2002). Generalizability issues in Internet-based survey research. In B. Batinic, U.-D. Reips, & M. Bosnjak, *Online social sciences.* Seattle: Hogrefe and Huber.

Brock, R. L., Barry, R. A., Lawrence, E., Dey, J., & Rolffs, J. (2012). Internet administration of paper-and-pencil questionnaires used in couple research: Assessing psychometric equivalence. *Assessment, 19*(2), 226–242.

Brotsky, S. R., & Giles, D. (2007). Inside the 'pro-ana' community: A covert online participant observation. *Eating Disorders, 15*(2), 93–109.

Browndyke, J. N., Santa Maria, M. P., Pinkston, J., & Gouvier, W. (1998). A survey of general head injury and prevention knowledge between professionals and non-professionals. Presented at *The 17th Annual National Academy of Neuropsychology National Conference.* http://www.neuropsychologycentral.com/vita/posters/nan97_MHI_misconceptions_poster_handout.pdf (accessed November 2012).

Brownlow, C., & O'Dell, L. (2002). Ethical issues for qualitative research in on-line communities. *Disability & Society, 17*(6), 685–694.

Bryman, A. (2012). *Social research methods* (4th ed.). Oxford: Oxford University Press.

Buchanan, E. (2002). Internet research ethics and institutional review board policy: New challenges, new opportunities. *Advances in Library Organization and Management, 19*, 85–100.

Buchanan, T., & Reips, U.-D. (2001). Technological biases in online research: Personality and demographic correlates of Macintosh and JavaScript use. Poster presented at *Psychology and the Internet: A European Perspective*. Farnborough, 8 November 2001.

Buchanan, T., & Smith, J. L. (1999a). Using the Internet for psychological research: Personality testing on the World-Wide Web. *British Journal of Psychology, 90*, 125–144.

Buchanan, T., & Smith, J. L. (1999b). Research on the Internet: Validation of a World-Wide Web mediated personality scale. *Behavior Research Methods, Instruments, & Computers, 31*(4), 565–571.

Buckley, M. (2004). Cross-disciplinary research into improving Internet-based research methodology applied to the interpretation of natural language. Masters in Computational Linguistics, Trinity College Dublin.

Buckley, M., & Vogel, C. (2003). Improving Internet based research methods: A Web laboratory. In P. Isaias & N. Karmakar (Eds.), *Proceedings of the IADIS International Conference WWW/Internet 2003* (pp. 467–476).

Buckley, P., & Clark, D. (2009). *The rough guide to the Internet*. London: Dorling Kindersley.

Caro, F. G., Ho, T., McFadden, D., Gottlieb, A. S., Yee, C., Chan, T., & Winter, J. (2012). Using the Internet to administer more realistic vignette experiments. *Social Science Computer Review, 30*(2), 184–201.

Carter-Pokras, O., McClellan, L., & Zambrana, E. (2006). Surveying free and low-cost survey software. *Journal of the National Medical Association, 98*(6), 881–886.

Chang, L., & Krosnick, J. A. (2009). National surveys via RDD telephone interviewing versus the Internet: Comparing sample representativeness and response quality. *Public Opinion Quarterly, 73*(4), 641–678.

Chen, P., & Hinton, S. M. (1999). Realtime interviewing using the World Wide Web. *Sociological Research Online, 4*(3). http://eprints.unimelb.edu.au/archive/00000210/01/realtime.pdf.

Cho, H., & LaRose, R. (1999). Privacy issues in Internet surveys. *Social Science Computer Review, 17*(4), 421–434.

Clarke, J., & van Amerom, G. (2008). A comparison of blogs by depressed men and women. *Issues in Mental Health Nursing, 29*(3), 243–264.

Coomber, R. (1997a). Using the Internet for survey research. *Sociological Research Online, 2*(2). http://www.socresonline.org.uk/2/2/coomber.htm (accessed October 2014).

Coomber, R. (1997b). Dangerous drug adulteration – An international survey of drug dealers using the Internet and World Wide Web (www). *International Journal of Drug Policy, 8*(2), 71–81.

Corley, M., & Scheepers, C. (2002). Syntactic priming in English sentence production: Categorical and latency evidence from an Internet-based study. *Psychonomic Bulletin Review, 9*(1), 126–131.

Couper, M. P. (2000). Web surveys: A review of issues and approaches. *Public Opinion Quarterly, 64*(4), 464–494.

Couper, M. P. (2005). Technology trends in survey data collection. *Social Science Computer Review, 23*(4), 486–501.

Couper, M. P. (2008). *Designing effective web surveys*. New York: Cambridge University Press.

Couper, M. P., Tourangeau, R., Conrad, F. G., & Crawford, S. (2004). What they see is what we get: Response options for web surveys. *Social Science Computer Review, 24*(2), 227–245.

Coye, R. W. (1985). Characteristics of participants and non-participants in experimental research. *Psychological Reports, 56*(1), 19–25.

Crawford, S. (2002). Evaluation of web survey data collection systems. *Field Methods, 14*(3), 307–321.

Cullen, D. (2011). Facebook concerns: Ireland, Germany and USA investigate. *Data Protection Law & Policy, 8*(11), 14–16.

Dahlen, M. (1998). Controlling the uncontrollable: Toward the perfect web sample. Paper presented at the *ESOMAR Worldwide Internet Seminar and Exhibition*. 28–30 January 1998, Paris.

Davidson, J. (2006). Probability (random) sampling. In V. Jupp (Ed.), *The Sage dictionary of social research methods*. London: Sage.

Davis, M., Bolding, G., Hart, G., Sherr, L., & Elford, J. (2004). Reflecting on the experience of interviewing online: Perspectives from the Internet and HIV study in London. *AIDS CARE, 16*(8), 944–952.

Davis, R. N. (1999). Web-based administration of a personality questionnaire: Comparison with traditional methods. *Behavior Research Methods, Instruments and Computers, 31*(4), 572–577.

de Pedraza, P., Tijdens, K., de Bustillo, R., & Steinmetz, S. (2010). A Spanish continuous volunteer web survey: Sample bias, weighting and efficiency. *Revista Espanola de Investigaciones Sociologicas, 33*(131), 109–130.

Dillman, D. A. (1991). The design and administration of e-mail surveys. *Annual Review of Sociology, 17*, 225–249.

Dillman, D. A. (2007). *Mail and Internet surveys: The tailored design method – 2007 update with new Internet, visual, and mixed-mode guide*. Hoboken, NJ: Wiley.

Dillman, D. A., & Bowker, D. K. (2001). The web questionnaire challenge to survey methodologists. In U.-D. Reips and M. Bosnjak (Eds.), *Dimensions of Internet science*. Lengerich: Pabst.

Dillman, D. A., Smyth, J. D., & Christian, L. M. (2009). *Internet, mail, and mixed-mode surveys: The tailored design method*. Hoboken, NJ: Wiley.

DiNucci, D. (1999). Fragmented future. *Print, 53*(4), 32. http://darcyd.com/fragmented_future.pdf (accessed October 2014).

Dobrzynski, J. H. (2000). Cyberauctions try to stop shill bidding: Ebay watches for players who form rings to artificially raise prices. *International Herald Tribune*, 3–4 June, 11.

Dollinger, S. J., & Frederick, T. (1993). Volunteer bias and the five-factor model. *Journal of Psychology, 127*(1), 29–36.

Dommeyer, C. J., & Moriarty, E. (1999). Comparing two forms of an email survey: Embedded vs. attached. *Journal of the Market Research Society, 42*(1), 39–50.

Double, R. (1985). The case against the case against belief. *Mind*, 375, 420–430.

Dutton, W. H., & Blank, G. (2011). Next generation users: The Internet in Britain: Oxford Internet Survey 2011 Report. University of Oxford. http://oxis.oii.ox.ac.uk/reports (accessed October 2014).

Dutton, W. H., Blank, G., & Groselj, D. (2013). *Cultures of the Internet: The Internet in Britain*. Oxford Internet Survey 2013 Report. University of Oxford. http://oxis.oii.ox.ac.uk/reports (accessed October 2014).

Edgington, E. S. (1966). Statistical inference and nonrandom samples. *Psychological Bulletin, 66*(6), 485–487.

Edwards, L., & Waelde, C. (Eds.) (2009). *Law and the Internet* (3rd ed.). Oxford: Hart.

Eichstaedt, J. (2002). Measuring differences in preactivation on the Internet: The content category superiority effect. *Experimental Psychology, 49*(4), 283–291.

Epstein, J., Klinkenberg, W. D., Wiley, L., & McKinley, L. (2001). Insuring sample equivalence across Internet and paper-and-pencil assessments. *Computers in Human Behavior, 17*, 339–346.

Fielding, N., Lee, R. M., & Blank, G. (Eds.) (2008). *The Sage handbook of online research methods*. London: Sage.

Fielding, N., & Macintyre, M. (2006). Access grid nodes in field research. *Sociological Research Online, 11*(2). http://www.socresonline.org.uk/11/2/fielding.html (accessed April 2104).

Fouladi, R. T., McCarthy, C. J., & Moller, N. (2002). Paper-and-pencil or online? Evaluating mode effects on measures of emotional functioning and attachment. *Assessment, 9*(2), 204–215.

Fox, J., Murray, C., & Warm, A. (2003). Conducting research using web-based questionnaires: Practical, methodological, and ethical considerations. *Social Research Methodology, 6*(2), 167–180.

Fox, N., Ward, K., & O'Rourke, A. (2005). Pro-anorexia, weight-loss drugs and the internet: An 'anti-recovery' explanatory model of anorexia. *Sociology of Health & Illness, 27*(7), 944–971.

Fox, R., Crask, M. R., & Kim, J. (1988). Mail survey response rates: A meta-analysis of selected techniques for inducing response. *Public Opinion Quarterly, 52*(4), 467–491.

Frankel, M. S., & Siang, S. (1999). Ethical and legal aspects of human subjects research in cyberspace: A report of a workshop. *American Association for the Advancement of Science.* https://nationalethicscenter.org/resources/187/download/ethical_legal.pdf (accessed April 2015).

Frick, A., Bächtiger, M.-T., & Reips, U.-D. (2001). Financial incentives, personal information and dropout in online studies. In U.-D. Reips & M. Bosnjak (Eds.), *Dimensions of Internet science*. Lengerich: Pabst.

Fricker, R. D. Jr. (2008). Sampling methods for web and email surveys. In N. Fielding, R. M. Lee, & G. Blank (Eds.), *The Sage handbook of online research methods*. London: Sage.

Frohlich, D. O., & Zmyslinski-Seelig, A. (2012). The presence of social support messages on YouTube videos about inflammatory bowel disease and ostomies. *Health Communication, 27*(5), 421–428.

Fuchs, M. (2009). Gender-of-interviewer effects in a video-enhanced web survey. *Social Psychology, 40*(1), 37–42.

Fullwood, C., Sheehan, N., & Nicholls, W. (2009). Blog function revisited: A content analysis of MySpace blogs. *CyberPsychology & Behavior, 12*(6), 685–689.

Gaiser, T. (1997). Conducting online focus groups: A methodological discussion. *Social Science Computer Review, 15*(2), 135–144.

Gaiser, T. (2008). Online focus groups. In N. Fielding, R.M. Lee, & G. Blank (Eds.), *The Sage handbook of online research methods*. London: Sage.

Givaty, G., van Vaan, H. A. H. C., Christou, C., & Bulthoff, H. H. (1998). Tele-experiments – Experiments on spatial cognition using VRML-based multimedia. In S.N. Spencer (Ed.), *Proceedings of the Annual Symposium on the Virtual Reality Modeling Language, VRML, January 1998*. New York, United States: ACM. (pp. 101–105).

Gjoka, M., Kurant, M., Butts, C. T., & Markopoulou, A. (2010). Walking in Facebook: A case study of unbiased sampling of OSNs. In *INFOCOM, 2010 Proceedings. IEEE* (pp. 1–9).

Gordon, A. (2002). SurveyMonkey.com – Web-based survey and evaluation system. *Internet and Higher Education, 5,* 83–87.

Göritz, A. S. (2007). Using online panels in psychological research. In A. Joinson, K. McKenna, U. Reips, & T. Postmes (Eds.), *Oxford handbook of internet psychology.* Oxford: Oxford University Press.

Göritz, A. S., & Birnbaum, M. H. (2005). Generic HTML form processor: A versatile PHP script to save Web-collected data into a MySQL database. *Behavior Research Methods, Instruments & Computers, 37*(4), 703–710.

Göritz, A. S., & Schumacher, J. (2000). The WWW as a research medium: An illustrative survey on paranormal belief. *Perceptual & Motor Skills, 90,* 1195–1206.

Göritz, A. S., Reinhold, N., & Batinic, B. (2002). Online panels. In B., Batinic, U.-D., Reips, and M. Bosnjak, (Eds.), *Online social sciences* (pp. 27–47). Seattle: Hogrefe and Huber.

Gosling, S. D., & Johnson, J. A. (Eds.) (2010). *Advanced methods for conducting online behavioral research.* New York: American Psychological Association.

Gosling, S. D., Vazire, S., Srivastava, S., & John, O. P. (2004). Should we trust web-based studies? A comparative analysis of six preconceptions about Internet questionnaires. *American Psychologist, 59*(2), 93–104.

Gosling, S.D., Sandy, C.J., John, O.P., & Potter, J. (2010). Wired but not WEIRD: The promise of the Internet in reaching more diverse samples. *Behavioral and Brain Sciences, 33,* 94–95.

Goyder, J. C. (1982). Further evidence on factors affecting response rates to mailed questionnaires. *American Sociological Review, 47*(4), 550–553.

Graham, Y. (2006). Services for experimentation in the human sciences: An online experimentation tool. Master's thesis, Computational Linguistics Group, Trinity College Dublin.

Grandcolas, U., Rettie, R., & Marusenko, K. (2003). Web survey bias: Sample or mode effect? *Journal of Marketing Management, 19*(5), 541–561.

Groves, R. M., Fowler, F. J. Jr., Couper, M. P., Lepkowski, J. M., Singer, E., & Tourangeau, R. (2013). *Survey methodology.* Hoboken, NJ: Wiley.

Guennouni, M. (2000). Extension of a web-based environment for cognitive science experiments. Department of Computer Science, Trinity College Dublin. Final Project Dissertation.

GVU (1997). Graphics Visualisation and Usability Center 7th WWW user survey. https://web.archive.org/web/20140407021851/http://www.cc.gatech.edu/gvu/user_surveys/survey-1997-04/ (accessed August 2015). Georgia Tech Research Corporation, Atlanta, GA.

GVU (1998). Graphics Visualisation and Usability Center 10th WWW user survey. www.cc.gatech.edu/gvu/user_surveys/survey-1998-10/ (accessed November 2012). Georgia Tech Research Corporation, Atlanta, GA.

Halavais, A. (2006). Scholarly blogging: Moving toward the visible college. In A. Bruns & J. Jacobs (Eds.), *Uses of blogs.* New York: Peter Lang.

Hanna, P. (2012). Using internet technologies (such as Skype) as a research medium: A research note. *Qualitative Research, 12*(2), 239–242.

Healey, P. (1995). Communication as a special case of misunderstanding: Semantic coordination in dialogue. PhD thesis. Centre for Cognitive Science, University of Edinburgh.

Healey, P. G. T., Vogel, C., & Eshghi, A. (2007). Group dialects in an online community. In R. Artstein & L. Vieu (Eds.), *Decalog 2007: Proceedings of the 11th Workshop on the Semantics and Pragmatics of Dialogue.* Trento, Italy, 30 May–1 June 2007. (pp. 141–147).

Heberlein, T. A., & Baumgartner, R. (1978). Factors affecting response rates to mailed questionnaires: A quantitative analysis of the published literature. *American Sociological Review, 43*(4), 447–462.

Heeren, T., Edwards, E. M., Dennis, J. M., Rodkin, S., Hingson, R. W., & Rosenbloom, D. L. (2008). A comparison of results from an alcohol survey of a prerecruited Internet panel and the National Epidemiologic Survey on alcohol and related conditions. *Alcoholism: Clinical and Experimental Research, 32*(2), 222–229.

Heinz, B., Gu, L., Inuzuka, A., & Zender, R. (2002). Under the rainbow flag: Webbing global gay identities. *International Journal of Sexuality and Gender Studies, 7*(2–3), 107–124.

Henrich, J., Heine, S. J., & Norenzayan, A. (2010). The weirdest people in the world? *Behavioral and Brain Sciences, 33,* 61–135.

Herrero, J., & Meneses, J. (2006). Short web-based versions of the perceived stress (PSS) and Center for Epidemiological Studies-Depression (CESD) Scales: A comparison to pencil and paper responses among Internet users. *Computers in Human Behavior, 22,* 830–846.

Herring, S. (1996). Posting in a different voice: Gender and ethics in computer-mediated communication. In C. Ess, (Ed.), *Philosophical perspectives in computer mediated communication.* Albany, NY: State University of New York Press.

Herring, S. C. (2010). Web content analysis: Expanding the paradigm. In J. Hunsiger, L. Klastrup, & M. Allen (Eds.), *The international handbook of internet research.* Dordrecht: Springer.

Herring, S. C., Johnson, D. A., & DiBenedetto, T. (1998). Participation in electronic discourse in a 'feminist' field. In J. Coates (Ed.), *Language and gender: A reader.* Oxford: Blackwell.

Herring, S. C., Scheidt, L. A., Bonus, S., & Wright, E. (2005). Weblogs as a bridging genre. *Information, Technology & People, 18*(2), 142–171.

Hesse-Biber, S., & Griffin, A. J. (2013). Internet-mediated technologies and mixed methods research: Problems and prospects. *Journal of Mixed Methods Research, 7*(1), 43–61.

Hessler, R. M., Downing, J., Beltz, C., Pelliccio, A., Powell, M., & Vale, W. (2003). Qualitative research on adolescent risk using email: A methodological assessment. *Qualitative Sociology, 26*(1), 111–124.

Hewson, C. (2003). Conducting psychological research on the Internet. *The Psychologist, 16*(6), 290–292.

Hewson, C. (2007). Gathering data on the Internet: Qualitative approaches and possibilities for mixed methods research. In A. Joinson, K. McKenna, U. Reips, & T. Postmes (Eds.), *Oxford handbook of internet psychology.* Oxford: Oxford University Press.

Hewson, C. (2008). Internet-mediated research as an emergent method and its potential role in facilitating mixed methods research. In S. N. Hesse-Biber & P. Leavy (Eds.), *Handbook of emergent methods.* New York: Guilford Press.

Hewson, C. (2012a). Can online course-based assessment methods be fair and equitable? Relationships between students' preferences and performance within online and offline assessments. *Journal of Computer Assisted Learning, 28*(5), 488–498.

Hewson, C. (2012b). Recommendations for implementing online surveys and simple experiments in social and behavioural research: A review and evaluation of existing online survey software packages. Poster presented at the *General Online Research Conference*, March 2012, Mannheim, Germany. http://conftool.gor.de/conftool12/index.php?page=browseSessions&presentations=show

Hewson, C. (2014a). Qualitative approaches in Internet research: Opportunities, issues, possibilities. In P. Leavy (Ed.), *The Oxford handbook of qualitative research methods* (Oxford library of psychology series). New York: Oxford University Press.

Hewson, C. (2014b). Conducting research on the Internet: Updates in a Web 2.0 era. *The Psychologist, 27*, 946–951.

Hewson, C. (2015). Ethics issues in digital methods research. In C. Hine & H. Snee (Eds.), *Digital methods as mainstream methodology: Inspirational digital/social research*. Basingstoke: Palgrave.

Hewson, C., & Charlton, J. P. (2005). Measuring health beliefs on the Internet: A comparison of paper and Internet administrations of the Multidimensional Health Locus of Control Scale. *Behavior Research Methods, Instruments & Computers, 37*(4), 691–702.

Hewson, C., & Laurent, D. (2008). Research design and tools for Internet research. In N. Fielding, R.M. Lee, & G. Blank (Eds.), *The Sage handbook of online research methods*. London: Sage.

Hewson, C., Charlton, J., & Brosnan, M. (2007). Comparing online and offline administration of multiple choice question assessments to psychology undergraduates: Do assessment modality or computer attitudes influence performance? *Psychology Learning and Teaching, 6*(1), 37–46.

Hewson, C. M. (1994). Empirical evidence regarding the folk psychological concept of belief. In *Proceedings of the Sixteenth Annual Conference of the Cognitive Science Society*, Atlanta, GA. (pp. 403–408).

Hewson, C. M., & Vogel, C. M. (1994). Psychological evidence for assumptions of path-based inheritance reasoning. In *Proceedings of the Sixteenth Annual Conference of the Cognitive Science Society*, Atlanta, GA. (pp. 409–414).

Hewson, C. M., Laurent, D., & Vogel, C. M. (1996). Proper methodologies for psychological and sociological studies conducted via the internet. *Behavior Research Methods, Instruments, & Computers, 32*, 186–191.

Hewson, C. M., Yule, P., Laurent, D., & Vogel, C. M. (2003). *Internet research methods: A guide for the social and behavioural sciences*. London: Sage.

Hine, C. (2000). *Virtual ethnography*. London: Sage.

Hine, C. (2008). Virtual ethnography: Modes, varieties, affordances. In N. Fielding, R. Lee, & G. Blank (Eds.), *The handbook of online research methods*. London: Sage.

Hirshfield, S., Chiasson, M. A., Wagmiller, R. L., Remien, R. H., Humberstone, M., Scheinmann, R., & Grov, C. (2010). Sexual dysfunction in an internet sample of US men who have sex with men. *Journal of Sexual Medicine, 7*, 3104–3114.

Hofmann, J. (2002). 'Let a Thousand Proposals Bloom' – Mailing lists as research sources. In B. Batinic, U.-D. Reips, & M. Bosnjak (Eds.), *Online social sciences* (pp. 309–331). Seattle: Hogrefe & Huber.

Hogan, B. (2008). Analysing social networks via the internet. In N. Fielding, R. Lee, & G. Blank (Eds.), *The handbook of online research methods*. London: Sage.

Horton, J. J., Rand, D. G., & Zeckhause, R. J. (2011). The online laboratory: Conducting experiments in a real labor market. *Experimental Economics, 14*, 399–425.

Horvath, K. J., Iantaffi, A., Grey, J. A., & Waiter, B. (2012). Hackers: Militants or merry pranksters? A content analysis of defaced web pages. *Health Communication, 27*(5), 457–466.

Hou, H.-T., Chang, K. E., & Sung, Y. T. (2010). What kinds of knowledge do teachers share on blogs? A quantitative content analysis of teachers' knowledge sharing on blogs. *British Journal of Educational Technology, 41*, 963–967.

Hudson, J. M., & Bruckman, A. (2004). Go away: Participant objections to being studied and the ethics of chatroom research. *Information Society, 20*(2), 127–139.

Huffaker, D. A., & Calvert, S. L. (2005). Gender, identity, and language use in teenage blogs. *Journal of Computer-Mediated Communication, 10*(2).

Im, E.-O., & Chee, W. (2004). Issues in an Internet survey among midlife Asian women. *Health Care for Women International, 25*(2), 150–164.

James, N., & Busher, H. (2006). Credibility, authenticity and voice: Dilemmas in online interviewing. *Qualitative Research, 6*(3), 403–420.

Jankowski, N.W., & van Selm, M. (2005). Epilogue: Methodological concerns and innovations in internet research. In C. Hine (Ed.), *Virtual methods: Issues in social research on the Internet.* Oxford: Berg.

Janssen, J., & Vogel, C. (2008). Politics makes the Swedish :-) and the Italians :-(. *Workshop on Sentiment Analysis: Emotion, Metaphor, Ontology & Terminology.* The 6th Language Resources and Evaluation Conference LREC 2008 (pp. 53–61).

Janta, H., Lugosi, P., & Brown, L. (2012). Coping with loneliness: A netnographic study of doctoral students. *Journal of Further and Higher Education, 38*(4), 553–571.

Jensen, C., Potts, C., & Jensen, C. (2005). Privacy practices of Internet users: Self-reports versus observed behavior. *International Journal of Human-Computer Studies, 63*(1–2), 203–227.

Joinson, A., & Paine, C. B. (2007). Self-disclosure, privacy and the Internet. In A. Joinson, K. McKenna, U. Reips, & T. Postmes (Eds.), *Oxford handbook of internet psychology.* Oxford: Oxford University Press.

Joinson, A., McKenna, K., Postmes, T., & Reips, U.-D. (2007). *The Oxford handbook of internet psychology.* Oxford: Oxford University Press.

Joinson, A. N. (1999). Social desirability, anonymity and Internet-based questionnaires. *Behavior Research Methods, Instruments & Computers, 31,* 433–438.

Joinson, A. N. (2001). Knowing me, knowing you: Reciprocal self-disclosure in Internet-based surveys. *Cyberpsychology and Behavior, 4*(5), 587–591.

Joinson, A. N. (2005). Internet behaviour and the design of virtual methods. In C. Hine (Ed.), *Virtual methods: Issues in social research on the Internet.* Oxford: Berg.

Jones, P., Bunce, G., Evans, J., Gibbs, H., & Hein, J. R. (2008). Exploring space and place with walking interviews. *Journal of Research Practice, 4*(2), Article-D2.

Jowett, A., Peel, E., & Shaw, R. (2011). Online interviewing in psychology: Reflections on the process. *Qualitative Research in Psychology, 8,* 354–369.

Kaczmirek, L. (2008). Internet survey software tools. In N. Fielding, R. Lee, & G. Blank (Eds.), *The handbook of online research methods.* London: Sage.

Kalton, G., & Schuman, H. (1982). The effect of the question on survey responses: A review. *Journal of the Royal Statistical Society, 145*(1), 42–73.

Kanuk, L., & Berenson, C. (1975). Mail surveys and response rates: A literature review. *Journal of Marketing Research, 12,* 440–453.

Kaye, B. K., & Johnson, T. J. (1999). Research methodology: Taming the cyber frontier. *Social Science Computer Review, 17*(3), 323–337.

Keller, F., Corley, M., Corley, S., Konieczny, L., & Todirascu, A. (1998). Webexp: A Java toolbox for web-based psychological experiments. Technical Report HCRC/TR-99, University of Edinburgh.

Keller, F., Lapata, M., & Ourioupina, O. (2002). Using the web to overcome data sparseness. *Proceedings of the Conference on Empirical Methods in Natural Language Processing (EMNLP),* Association for Computational Linguistics, Philadelphia, July 2002 (pp. 230–237).

Keller, F., Gunasekharan, S., Mayo, N., & Corley, M. (2009). Timing accuracy of web experiments: A case study using the WebExp software package. *Behavior Research Methods, 41*(1), 1–12.

Keller, H. E., & Lee, S. (2003). Ethical issues surrounding human participants research using the Internet. *Ethics and Behavior, 13*(3), 211–219.

Kendall, L. (2002). *Hanging out in the virtual pub: Masculinities and relationships online.* Los Angeles: University of California Press.

Kenny, A. J. (2005). Interaction in cyberspace: An online focus group. *Journal of Advanced Nursing, 49*(4), 414–422.

Kenny, S. (1998). A generic automatic experiment creation and presentation tool. Department of Computer Science, Trinity College Dublin. Final Project.

Kiesler, S., & Sproull, L. (1986). Response effects in the electronic survey. *Public Opinion Quarterly, 50,* 402–413.

Kiesler, S., Siegel, J., & McGuire, T. W. (1984). Social psychological aspects of computer-mediated communication. *American Psychologist, 39*(10), 1123–1134.

Kilgarriff, A., & Grefenstette, G. (2003). Introduction to the special issue on the web as a corpus. *Computational Linguistics, 29*(3), 333–347.

King, S. A. (1996). Researching internet communities: Proposed ethical guidelines for the reporting of results. *Information Society, 12*(2), 119–128.

Knoll, M. A., Uther, M., & Costall, A. (2011). Using the Internet for speech research: An evaluative study examining affect in speech. *Behaviour & Information Technology, 30*(6), 845–851.

Kosinski, M., Bayliss, M. S., Bjorner, J. B., Ware, J. E. Jr., Garber, W. H., Batenhorst, A., Cady, R., Dahlöf, C. G. H., Dowson, A., & Tepper, S. (2003). A six-item short-form survey for measuring headache impact: The HIT-6™. *Quality of Life Research, 12*(8), 963–974.

Kozinets, R. V. (2002). The field behind the screen: Using netnography for marketing research in online communities. *Journal of Marketing Research, 39*(1), 61–72.

Krantz, J. H., & Williams, J. E. (2010). Using graphics, photographs, and dynamic media. In S.D. Gosling & J.A. Johnson (Eds.), *Advanced methods for conducting online behavioral research.* New York: American Psychological Association.

Krantz, J. H., Ballard, J., & Scher, J. (1997). Comparing the results of laboratory and World-Wide Web samples of the determinants of female attractiveness. *Behavior Research Methods, Instruments, & Computers, 29,* 264–269.

Kraut, R., Olson, J., Banaji, M., Bruckman, A., Cohen, J., & Cooper, M. (2004). Psychological research online: Report of Board of Scientific Affairs' Advisory Group on the Conduct of Research on the Internet. *American Psychologist, 59*(4), 1–13.

Laugwitz, B. (2001). A web experiment on colour harmony principles applied to computer user interface design. In U.-D. Reips and M. Bosnjak (Eds.), *Dimensions of Internet science.* Lengerich: Pabst.

Lee, R. M., Fielding, N., & Blank, G. (2008). The Internet as a research medium: An editorial introduction. In N. Fielding, R. M. Lee, & G. Blank (Eds.), *The Sage handbook of online research methods.* London: Sage.

Lenzner, T., Kaczmirek, L., & Lenzner, A. (2010). Cognitive burden of survey questions and response times: A psycholinguistic experiment. *Applied Cognitive Psychology, 24*(7), 1003–1020.

Lipinski, T. (2008). Emerging legal issues in the collection and dissemination of Internet-sourced research data: Part I, basic tort law issues and negligence. *International Journal of Internet Research Ethics, 1*(1).

Liu, B. (2010). *Web data mining: Exploring hyperlinks, contents and usage data.* Berlin: Springer.

Locey, M. L., Safin, V., & Rachlin, H. (2013). Social discounting and the prisoner's dilemma game. *Journal of the Experimental Analysis of Behavior, 99*(1), 85–97.

Lockett, A., & Blackman, I. (2004). Conducting market research using the Internet: The case of Xenon Laboratories. *Journal of Business & Industrial Marketing, 19*(3), 178–187.

Madge, C., & O'Connor, H. (2002). On-line with e-mums: Exploring the Internet as a medium for research. *Area, 34*(1), 92–102.

Maher, P. (ed.) (2011). Tom Waits on Tom Waits: Interviews and Encounters. Chicago, IL USA: Chicago Review Press.

Malhotra, N., & Krosnick, J. A. (2007). The effect of survey mode and sampling on inferences about political attitudes and behavior: Comparing the 2000 and 2004 ANES to Internet surveys with non-probability samples. *Political Analysis, 15*(3), 286–323.

Marcus, B., & Schütz, A. (2005). Who are the people reluctant to participate in research? Personality correlates of four different types of nonresponse as inferred from self- and observer ratings. *Journal of Personality, 73*(4), 959–984.

Marcus, M. A., Westra, H. A., Eastwood, J. D., & Barnes, K. L. (2012). What are young adults saying about mental health? An analysis of internet blogs. *Journal of Medical Internet Research, 14*(1). http://www.ncbi.nlm.nih.gov/pmc/articles/PMC3374526 (accessed October 2014).

Markham, A. (1998). *Life online: Researching real experience in virtual space.* Walnut Creek, CA: AltaMira.

Markham, A., & Buchanan, E. (2012). Ethical decision-making and internet research. Recommendations from the AoIR ethics working committee (version 2). http://www.aoir.org/reports/ethics2.pdf (accessed April 2015).

Martin, C. L. (1994). The impact of topic interest on mail survey response behaviour. *Journal of the Market Research Society, 36*(4), 327–337.

Martin, S. P., & Robinson, J. P. (2007). The income digital divide: Trends and predictions for levels of Internet use. *Social Problems, 54*(1), 1–22.

Mathy, R. M., Schillace, M., Coleman, S. M., & Berquist, B. E. (2002). Methodological rigor with Internet samples: New ways to reach underrepresented populations. *Cyberpsychology & Behavior, 5*(3), 253–266.

McCreanor, T., Lyons, A., Griffin, C., Goodwin, I., Moewaka Barnes, H., & Hutton, F. (2013). Youth drinking cultures, social networking and alcohol marketing: Implications for public health. *Critical Public Health, 23*(1), 110–120.

McDermott, E., & Roen, K. (2012). Youth on the virtual edge. *Qualitative Health Research, 22*(4), 560–570.

McGowan, C. (1999). Extension of a web based environment for cognitive science experiments, with testing for metaphor. Department of Computer Science, Trinity College Dublin. Final Project Dissertation.

McGraw, K., & Tew, M. (1997). Psychology experiments on the Internet: Use of shockwave technology. https://web.archive.org/web/20040215223811/http://home.olemiss.edu/~pymc graw/fipse.htm (accessed September 2015).

McGraw, K. O., Tew, M. D., & Williams, J. E. (2000). The integrity of web-delivered experiments: Can you trust the data? *Psychological Science, 11*(6), 502–506.

McNemar, Q. (1946). Opinion-attitude methodology. *Psychological Bulletin, 43*, 289–374.

Mehta, R., & Sivadas, E. (1995). Comparing response rates and response content in mail versus electronic mail surveys. *Journal of the Market Research Society, 37*(4), 428–439.

Meyerson, P., & Tryon, W. W. (2003). Validating Internet research: A test of the psychometric equivalence of Internet and in-person samples. *Behavior Research Methods, Instruments, & Computers, 35*(4), 614–620.

Michalek, E. E., & Szabo, A. (1998). Guidelines for Internet research: An update. *European Psychologist, 3*(1), 70–75.

Miller, P. G., Johnston, J., Dunn, M., Fry, C. L., & Degenhardt, L. (2010). Comparing probability and non-probability sampling methods in ecstasy research: Implications for the Internet as a research tool. *Substance Use & Misuse, 45,* 437–450.

Mook, D. G. (1983). In defense of external invalidity. *American Psychologist, 38,* 379–387.

Moreno, M. A., Jelenchick, L. A., Egan, K. G., Cox, E., Young, H., Gannon, K. E., & Becker, T. (2011). Feeling bad on Facebook: Depression disclosures by college students on a social networking site. *Depression and Anxiety, 28*(6), 447–455.

Morokoff, P. J. (1986). Volunteer bias in the psychophysiological study of female sexuality. *Journal of Sexuality Research, 22,* 35–51.

Murphy, P. R., Daley, J., & Dalenberg, D. R. (1991). Exploring the effects of postcard prenotification on industrial firms' response to mail surveys. *Journal of the Market Research Society, 33*(4), 335–345.

Murray, C. D., & Sixsmith, J. (1998). E-mail: A qualitative research medium for interviewing? *International Journal of Social Research Methodology: Theory & Practice, 1*(2), 103–121.

Musch, J., & Reips, U.-D. (2000). A brief history of web experimenting. In M. H. Birnbaum (Ed.), *Psychological experiments on the Internet.* San Diego, CA: Academic Press.

Nosek, B. A., Banaji, M. R., & Greenwald, A. G. (2002). E-research: Ethics, security, design and control in psychological research on the Internet. *Journal of Social Issues, 58*(1), 161–176.

Nückles, M., & Bromme, R. (2002). Internet expert's planning of explanations for laypersons: A web experimental approach in the Internet domain. *Experimental Psychology, 49*(4), 292–304.

O'Brien, C., & Vogel, C. (2003). Spam filters: Bayes vs. chi-Squared; letters vs. words. In M. Alesky et al. (Eds.), *Proceedings of the International Symposium on Information and Communication Technologies* (pp. 298–303). Trinity College Dublin 2003.

O'Connor, H., & Madge, C. (2001). Cyber-mothers: Online synchronous interviewing using conferencing software. *Sociological Research Online, 5*(4). http://www.socresonline.org.uk/5/4/o'connor.html

O'Connor, H., Madge, C., Shaw, R., & Wellens, J. (2008). Internet-based interviewing. In N. Fielding, R.M. Lee, & G. Blank (Eds.), *The Sage handbook of online research methods.* London: Sage.

Ó Dochartaigh, N. (2012). *Internet research skills* (3rd ed.). London: Sage.

O'Floinn, M., & Ormerod, D. (2011). Social networking sites, RIPA and criminal investigations. *Criminal Law Review, 10,* 766–789.

O'Reilly, T. (2005). What is Web 2.0? http://oreilly.com/web2/archive/what-is-web-20.html (accessed October 2014).

Orgad, S. (2006). The cultural dimensions of online communication: A study of breast cancer patients' internet spaces. *New Media & Society, 8*(6), 877–899.

Panyametheekul, S., & Herring, S. C. (2003). Gender and turn allocation in a Thai chat room. *Journal of Computer Mediated Communication, 9*(1).

Paolacci, G., Chandler, J., & Ipeirotis, P. G. (2010). Running experiments on Amazon Mechanical Turk. *Judgment and Decision Making, 5*(5), 411–419.

Papacharissi, Z. (2009). The virtual geographies of social networks: A comparative analysis of Facebook, LinkedIn and ASmallWorld. *New Media & Society, 11*(1–2), 199–220.

Pealer, L., & Weiler, R. M. (2003). Guidelines for designing a web-delivered college health risk behavior survey: Lessons learned from the University of Florida Health Behavior Survey. *Health Promotion Practice, 4*(2), 171–179.

Penkoff, D. W., Colman, R. W., & Katzman, S. L. (1996). From paper-and-pencil to screen-and-keyboard: Toward a methodology for survey research on the Internet. Paper presented at *The Annual Conference of the International Communication Association*, May, Chicago.

Pettit, F. A. (1999). Exploring the use of the World Wide Web as a psychology data collection tool. *Computers in Human Behavior, 15*(1), 67–71.

Pincott, G., & Branthwaite, A. (2000). Nothing new under the sun? *International Journal of Market Research, 42*(2), 137–155.

Pitkow, J. E., & Recker, M. M. (1994). Results from the first World Wide Web user survey. www.cc.gatech.edu/gvu/user_surveys/survey-01-1994/survey-paper.html (accessed April 2015).

Pohl, F., Bender, M., & Lachmann, G. (2002). Hindsight bias around the world. *Experimental Psychology, 49*(4), 270–282.

Rademacher, J. D. M., & Lippke, S. (2007). Dynamic online surveys and experiments with the free open-source software dynQuest. *Behavior Research Methods, 39*(3), 415–426.

Rageh, A., Melewar, T. C., & Woodside, A. (2013). Using netnography research method to reveal the underlying dimensions of the customer/tourist experience. *Qualitative Market Research: An International Journal, 16*(2), 126–149.

Reece, M., Rosenberger, J. G., Schick, V., Herbenick, D., Dodge, B., & Novak, D. S. (2010). Characteristics of vibrator use by gay and bisexually identified men in the United States. *Journal of Sexual Medicine, 7*, 3467–3476.

Reed, C. (2004). *Internet law* (2nd ed.). Law in Context. Cambridge: Cambridge University Press.

Reimers, S., & Stewart, N. (2007). Adobe Flash as a medium for online experimentation: A test of reaction time measurement capabilities. *Behavior Research Methods, 39*(3), 365–370.

Reips, U.-D. (2000). The web experiment method: Advantages, disadvantages, and solutions. In M. H. Birnbaum (Ed.), *Psychological experiments on the Internet*. San Diego, CA: Academic Press.

Reips, U.-D. (2001). The Web Experimental Psychology Lab: Five years of data collection on the Internet. *Behavior Research Methods, Instruments, and Computers, 33*(2), 201–211.

Reips, U.-D. (2002a). Theory and techniques of conducting web experiments. In B. Batinic, U.-D. Reips, & Michael Bosnjak (Eds.), *Online social sciences* (pp. 229–250). Seattle: Hogrefe & Huber.

Reips, U.-D. (2002b). Standards for Internet-based experimenting. *Experimental Psychology, 49*(4), 243–256.

Reips, U.-D. (2007). The methodology of internet-based experiments. In A. Joinson, K. McKenna, U. Reips, & T. Postmes (Eds.), *Oxford handbook of internet psychology*. Oxford: Oxford University Press.

Reips, U.-D. (2010). Designing and formatting Internet-based research. In S.D. Gosling & J.A. Johnson (Eds.), *Advanced methods for conducting online behavioral research*. New York: American Psychological Association.

Reips, U.-D., & Buffardi, L. E. (2012). Studying migrants with the help of the Internet: Methods from psychology. *Journal of Ethnic and Migration Studies, 38*(9), 1405–1424.

Reips, U.-D., & Krantz, J. H. (2010). Conducting true experiments on the web. In S. D. Gosling & J. A. Johnson (Eds.), *Advanced methods for conducting online behavioral research*. New York: American Psychological Association.

Reips, U.-D., & Lengler, R. (2005). The web experiment list: A web service for the recruitment of participants and archiving of Internet-based experiments. *Behavior Research Methods, 37*(2), 287–292.

Reips, U.-D., & Musch, J. (2002). Special issue: Internet-based psychological experimenting. *Experimental Psychology, 49*(4), 241–242.

Reips, U.-D., & Neuhaus, C. (2002). WEXTOR: A web-based tool for generating and visualising experimental designs and procedures. *Behavior Research Methods Instruments & Computers, 34*(2), 234–240.

Reips, U.-D., & Steiger, S. (2004). Scientific LogAnalyzer: A web-based tool for analyses of server log files in psychological research. *Behavior Research Methods, Instruments & Computers, 36*(2) 304–311.

Riva, G., Teruzzi, T., & Anolli, L. (2003). The use of the Internet in psychological research: Comparison of online and offline questionnaires. *Cyberpsychology & Behavior, 6*(1), 73–80.

Rodino, M. (1997). Breaking out of binaries: Reconceptualizing gender and its relationship to language. *Journal of Computer-Mediated Communication, 3*(3). http://jcmc.indiana.edu/vol3/issue3/rodino.html (accessed January 2013).

Rollman, J. B., Krug, K., & Parente, F. (2000). The chat room phenomenon: Reciprocal communication in cyberspace. *CyberPsychology and Behavior, 3*(2), 161–166.

Ross, T. L., Castronova, E., & Wagner, G. G. (2012). Empirical research methods in virtual worlds. In C. N. Silva (Ed.), *Online research methods in urban and planning studies*. Hershey, PA: IGI Global.

Rossetti, P. (1998). Gender differences in e-mail communication. *The Internet TESL Journal, 4*(7). http://iteslj.org/Articles/RossettiGenderDif.html

Ruppertsberg, A. I., Givaty, G., Van Veen, H. A. H. C., & Bulthoff, H. (2001). Games as research tools for visual perception over the Internet. In U.-D. Reips & M. Bosnjak (Eds.), *Dimensions of Internet science*. Lengerich: Pabst.

Rushton, K. (2012). 'Facebook's share of UK social networking declines'. *Telegraph*. http://www.telegraph.co.uk/technology/facebook/9008525/Facebooks-share-of-UK-social-networking-declines.html (accessed January 2012).

Salmons, J. E. (2011). *Cases in online interview research*. London: Sage.

Sanders, T. (2005). Researching the online sex community. In C. Hine (Ed.), *Virtual methods: Issues in social research on the Internet*. Oxford: Berg.

Schneider, S. J., Kerwin, J., Frechtling, J., & Vivari, B. A. (2002). Characteristics of the discussion in online and face-to-face focus groups. *Social Science Computer Review, 20*(1), 31–42.

Schroeder, R., & Bailenson, J. (2008). Research uses of multi-user virtual environments. In N. Fielding, R. Lee, & G. Blank (Eds.), *The handbook of online research methods*. London: Sage.

Schulte-Mecklenbeck, M., & Neun, M. (2005). WebDiP: A tool for information search experiments on the World-Wide Web. *Behavior Research Methods, 37*(2), 293–300.

Schütz, A., & Machilek, F. (2003). Who owns a personal home page? A discussion of sampling problems and a strategy based on a search engine. *Swiss Journal of Psychology, 62*(2), 121–129.

Schutze, C. (1996). *The empirical base of linguistics: Grammaticality judgements and linguistic methodology*. Chicago: University of Chicago Press.

Schwarz, S., & Reips, U.-D. (2001). CGI versus JavaScript: A web experiment on the reversed hindsight bias. In U.-D. Reips & M. Bosnjak (Eds.), *Dimensions of Internet science*. Lengerich: Pabst.

Senior, C., & Smith, M. (1999). The Internet – A possible research tool. *The Psychologist, 12*(9), 442–445.

Senior, C., Phillips, M. L., Barnes, J., & David, A. S. (1999a). An investigation into the perception of dominance from schematic faces: A study using the World-Wide Web. *Behavior Research Methods, Instruments, and Computers, 31*, 341–346.

Senior, C., Barnes, J., Jenkins, R., Landau, S., Phillips, M. L., & David, A. S. (1999b). Attribution of social dominance and maleness to schematic faces. *Social Behaviour and Personality, 27*(4), 331–338.

Sheehan, K. B., & McMillan, S. J. (1999). Response variation in e-mail surveys: An exploration. *Journal of Advertising Research, 39*(4), 45–54.

Siah, C. Y. (2005). All that glitters is not gold: Examining the perils and obstacles in collecting data on the Internet. *International Negotiation, 10,* 115–130.

Slater, M., Sadagic, A., Usoh, M., & Schroeder, R. (2000). Small-group behavior in a virtual and real environment: A comparative study. *Presence: Teleoperators & Virtual Environments, 9*(1), 37–51.

Smart, R. (1966). Subject selection bias in psychological research. *Canadian Psychologist, 7,* 115–121.

Smith, C. B. (1997). Casting the Net: Surveying an Internet population. *Journal of Computer Mediated Communication, 3*(1).

Smith, M. A., & Leigh, B. (1997). Virtual subjects: Using the Internet as an alternative source of subjects and research environment. *Behavior Research Methods, Instruments, & Computers, 29*(4), 496–505.

Srivastava, S., John, O. P., Gosling, S. D., & Potter, J. (2003). Development of personality in early and middle adulthood: Set like plaster or persistent change? *Journal of Personality and Social Psychology, 84,* 1041–1053.

Stanton, J. M. (1998). An empirical assessment of data collection using the Internet. *Personnel Psychology, 51*(3), 709–725.

Steinmetz, S., Kaczmirek, L., de Pedraza, P., Reips, U.-D., Tijdens, K., Lozar Manfreda, K., Rowland, L., Serrano, F., Vidakovic, M., Vogel, C., Belchior, A., Berzelak, J., Biffignandi, S., Birgegard, A., Cachia, E., Callegaro, M., J Camilleri, P., Marco Campagnolo, G., Cantijoch, M., Cheikhrouhou, N., Constantin, D., Dar, R., David, S., de Leeuw, E., Doron, G., Fernandez-Macias, E., Ole Finnemann, N., Foulonneau, M., Fornara, N., Fuchs, M., Funke, F., Gibson, R., Grceva, S., Haraldsen, G., Jonsdottir, G., Kahanec, M., Kissau, K., Kolsrud, K., Lenzner, T., Lesnard, L., Margetts, H., Markov, Y., Milas, G., Mlacic, B., Mihaela Moga, L., Neculita, M., Irina Popescu, A., Ronkainen, S., Scherpenzeel, A., Selkala, A., Kalgraff Skjak, K., Slavec, A., Ernst Staehli, M., Thorsdottir, F., Toninelli, D., Vatrapu, R., Vehovar, V., Villacampa Gonzalez, A. & Winer, B., (2012) WebDataNet: A network on web-based data collection, methodological challenges, solutions and implementation. *International Journal of Internet Science, 7*(1): 79–89.

Steinmetz, S., Slavec, A., Tijdens, K., Reips, U.-D., de Pedraza, P., Popescu, A., Belchior, A., Birgegard, A., Bianchi, A., Ayalon, A., Selkala, A., Villacampa, A., Winer, B., Mlacic, B., Vogel, C., Gravem, D., Gayo Avello, D., Constantin, D., Toninelli, D., Troitino, D., Horvath, D., De Leeuw, E., Oren, E., Fernandez-Macias, E., Thorsdottir, F., Ortega, F., Frederik Funke,, Marco Campagnolo, G., Milas, G., Grünwald, C., Jonsdottir, G., Haraldsen, G., Doron, G., Margetts, H., Miklousic, I., Andreadis, I., Berzelak, J., Angelovska, J., Schrittwieser, K., Kissau, K., Lozar Manfreda, K., Kolsrud, K., Kalgraff Skjak, K., Tsagarakis, K., Kaczmirek, L., Lesnard, L., Mihaela Moga, L., Lopes Teixeira, L., Plate, M., Kozak, M., Fuchs, M., Callegaro, M., Cantijoch, M., Kahanec, M., Stopa, M., Ernst Staehli, M., Neculita, M., Ivanovic, M., Foulonneau, M., Cheikhrouhou, N., Fornara, N., Ole Finnemann, N., Zajc, N., Nyirå, N., Louca, P., Osse, P., Mavrikiou, P., Gibson, R., Vatrapu, R., Dar, R., Pinter, R., Martinez Torres, R., Douhou, S., Biffignandi, S., Grceva, S., David, S., Ronkainen, S., Csordas, T., Lenzner, T., Vesteinsdottir, V., Vehovar, V. &, Markov, Y. (2014) WEBDATANET: Innovation and Quality in Web-Based Data Collection, *International Journal of Internet Science, 9*(1): 64–71.

Stephenson, L. B., & Crete, J. (2010). Studying political behavior: A comparison of Internet and telephone surveys. *International Journal of Public Opinion Research, 23*(1), 24–55.

Stewart, K., & Williams, M. (2005). Researching online populations: The use of online focus groups for social research. *Qualitative Research, 5(4)*, 395–416.

Stich, S. (1983). *From folk psychology to cognitive science: The case against belief.* Cambridge, MA: Bradford Books, MIT Press.

Stones, A., & Perry, D. (1997). Survey questionnaire data on panic attacks gathered using the World-Wide Web. *Depression and Anxiety, 6*, 86–87.

Strassberg, D. S., & Holty, S. (2003). An experimental study of women's Internet personal ads. *Archives of Sexual Behavior, 32*(3), 253–260.

Strassberg, D. S., & Kristi, L. (1995). Volunteer bias in sexuality research. *Archives of Sexual Behaviour, 24*(4), 369–382.

Strickland, O. L., Moloney, M. F., Dietrich, A. S., Myerburg, J. D., Cotsonis, G. A., & Johnson, R. (2003). Measurement issues related to data collection on the World Wide Web. *Advances in Nursing Science, 26*(4), 246–256.

Subrahmanyam, K., Greenfield, P. M., & Tynes, B. (2004). Constructing sexuality and identity in an online teen chat room. *Journal of Applied Developmental Psychology, 25*(6), 651–666.

Sudman, S. (1980). Reducing response error in surveys. *The Statistician, 29*(4), 237–273.

Sue, V. M., & Ritter, L. A. (2012). *Conducting online surveys.* Thousand Oaks, CA: Sage.

Swoboda, W. J., Muhlberger, N., Weitkunat, R., & Schneeweib, S. (1997). Internet surveys by direct mailing. *Social Science Computer Review, 15*, 242–255.

Szabo, A., & Frenkl, M. D. (1996). Consideration of research on the Internet: Guidelines and implications for human movement studies. *Clinical Kinesiology, 50*(3), 58–65.

Szabo, A., Frenkl, R., & Caputo, A. (1996). Deprivation feelings, anxiety, and commitments in various forms of physical activity: A cross-sectional study on the Internet. *Psychologia, 39*, 223–230.

Tackett-Gibson, M. (2008). Constructions of risk and harm in online discussions of ketamine use. *Addiction Research & Theory, 16*(3), 245–257.

Taylor, S., & Lynn, P. (1998). The effect of a preliminary notification letter on response to a postal survey of young people. *Journal of the Market Research Society, 40*(2), 165–178.

Temple, E. C., & Brown, R. F. (2011). A comparison of Internet-based participant recruitment methods: Engaging the hidden population of cannabis users in research. *Journal of Research Practice, 7*(2), 1–20.

Thelwall, M., & Stuart, D. (2006). Web crawling ethics revisited: Cost, privacy, and denial of service. *Journal of the American Society for Information Science and Technology, 57*(13), 1771–1779.

Thelwall, M., Sud, P., & Vis, F. (2012). Commenting on YouTube videos: From Guatemalan rock to el big bang. *Journal of the American Society for Information Science and Technology, 63*(3), 616–629.

Thoreau, E. (2006). Ouch! An examination of the self-representation of disabled people on the Internet. *Journal of Computer-Mediated Communication, 11*(2), 442–468.

Thurlow, C., Lengel, L., & Tomic, A. (2004). *Computer mediated communication: Social interaction and the Internet.* London: Sage.

Timothy, B. (2000). Using a web-based tool for conducting cognitive science experiments. Department of Computer Science, Trinity College Dublin. Final Project Dissertation.

Tobin, J., & Vogel, C. (2009). A user-extensible and adaptable parser architecture. *Knowledge-Based Systems, 22*(7), 516–522.

Tonkin, E., Pfeiffer, H. D., & Tourte, G. (2012). Twitter, information sharing and the London riots? *Bulletin of the American Society for Information Science and Technology, 38*(2), 49–57.

Tourangeau, R. (2004). Survey research and societal change. *Annual Review of Psychology, 55,* 775–801.

Tourangeau, R., Couper, M. P., & Conrad, F. (2007). Color, labels, and interpretive heuristics for response scales. *Public Opinion Quarterly, 71*(1), 91–112.

Tse, A. C. B., Tse, K. C., Yin, C. H., Ting, C. B., Yi, K. W., Yee, K. P., & Hong, W. C. (1995). Comparing two methods of sending out questionnaires: Email versus mail. *Journal of the Market Research Society, 37*(4).

Tuten, T. L. (2010). Conducting online surveys. In S. D. Gosling & J. A. Johnson (Eds.), *Advanced methods for conducting online behavioral research.* New York: American Psychological Association.

Valliant, R., & Dever, J. (2011). Estimating propensity adjustments for volunteer web surveys. *Sociological Methods and Research, 40,* 105–137.

Vehovar, V., & Manfreda, K. L. (2008). Overview: Online surveys. In N. Fielding, R. M. Lee, & G. Blank (Eds.), *The Sage handbook of online research methods.* London: Sage.

Vicente, P., & Reips, E. (2010). Using questionnaire design to fight nonresponse bias in web surveys. *Social Science Computer Review, 28*(2), 251–267.

Vogel, C., & Janssen, J. (2009). Emoticonsciousness. In A. Esposito, A. Hussain, M. Marinaro, & R Martone (Eds.), *Multimodal signals: Cognitive and algorithmic issues. Lecture notes in computer science,* Vol. 5398 (pp. 271–287). Heidelberg: Springer.

Vogel, C. & Mamani Sanchez, L. (2012) Epistemic signals and emoticons affect kudos, in 2012 IEEE 3rd International Conference on Cognitive Infocommunications (CogInfoCom), pp.517–522, 2–5 Dec. 2012. http://dx.doi.org/10.1109/CogInfoCom.2012.6422036.

Wakeford, N., & Cohen, K. (2008). Fieldnotes in public: Using blogs for research. In N. Fielding, R. M. Lee, & G. Blank (Eds.), *The Sage handbook of online research methods.* London: Sage.

Waksberg, J. (1978). Sampling methods for random digit dialing. *Journal of the American Statistical Association, 73*(361), 40–46.

Wallston, K. A., & Wallston, B. S. (1981). Health locus of control scales. In H. M. Lefcourt (Ed.), *Research with the locus of control construct: Vol. 1. Assessment methods* (pp. 189–243). New York: Academic Press.

Ward, K. J. (1999). The cyber-ethnographic (re)construction of two feminist online communities. *Sociological Research Online, 4*(1). http://www.socresonline.org.uk/4/1/ward.html (accessed October 2014).

Weigold, A., Weigold, I. K., & Russell, E. J. (2013). Examination of the equivalence of self-report survey-based paper-and-pencil and internet data collection methods. *Psychological Methods, 18*(1), 53.

Welker, M. (2001). Email surveys: Non-response figures reflected. In U.-D. Reips and M. Bosnjak (Eds.), *Dimensions of Internet science.* Lengerich: Pabst.

Wesler, H. T., Smith, M., Fisher, D., & Gleave, E. (2008). Distilling digital traces: Computational social science approaches to studying the internet. In N. Fielding, R. Lee, & G. Blank (Eds.), *The handbook of online research methods.* London: Sage.

White, T. (2010). *Hadoop: The definitive guide* (2nd ed.). Beijing: O'Reilly.

Williams, M. (2003). Virtually criminal: Deviance and harm within online environments. PhD thesis. University of Wales Cardiff.

Williams, M. (2007). Avatar watching: Participant observation in graphical online environments. *Qualitative Research, 7*(1), 5–24.

Wilson, R. E., Gosling, S. D., & Graham, L. T. (2012). A review of Facebook research in the social sciences. *Perspectives on Psychological Science, 7*(3), 203–220.

Witmer, D. F., Colman, R. W., & Katzman, S. L. (1999). From paper-and-pencil to screen-and-keyboard. In S. Jones (Ed.), *Doing Internet Research*. London. Sage.

Yammarino, F. J., Skinner, S., & Childers, T. L. (1991). Understanding mail survey response behaviour. *Public Opinion Quarterly, 55*(4), 613–639.

Yan, T., Conrad, F. G., Tourangeau, R., & Couper, M. P. (2011). Should I stay or should I go: The effects of progress feedback, promised task duration, and length of questionnaire on completing web surveys. *International Journal of Public Opinion Research, 23*(2), 131–147.

Yeager, D. S., Krosnick, J. A., Chang, L., Javitz, H. S., Levendusky, M. S., Simpser, A. & Wang, R. (2011). Comparing the accuracy of RDD telephone surveys and Internet surveys conducted with probability and non-probability samples. *Public Opinion Quarterly, 75*(4), 709–747.

Yoo, J. H., & Kim, J. (2012). Obesity in the new media: A content analysis of obesity videos on YouTube. *Health Communication, 27*(1), 86–97.

Zakon, R. H. (2015). Hobbes' Internet timeline v.11. http://www.zakon.org/robert/internet/timeline (accessed April 2015).

Zhao, S., Grasmuck, S., & Martin, J. (2008). Identity construction on Facebook: Digital empowerment in anchored relationships. *Computers in Human Behavior, 24*(5), 1816–1836.

Zimmer, M. (2010). But the data is already public: On the ethics of research in Facebook. *Ethics & Information Technology, 12*(4), 313–325.

<> INDEX </>